THE LIFE

OF

VOLTAIRE

VOLUME II.

Voltaire
from a portrait by N. Largillière
belonging to The Rev. W. J. Dawson.

THE LIFE

OF

VOLTAIRE

BY

S. G. TALLENTYRE

(Evelyn Beatrice Hall)

'Je meurs en adorant Dieu, en aimant mes amis, en ne haïssant pas mes ennemis, et en détestant la superstition'

VOLTAIRE

IN TWO VOLUMES

VOLUME II.

BOOKS FOR LIBRARIES PRESS
FREEPORT, NEW YORK

First Published 1903
Reprinted 1972

Library of Congress Cataloging in Publication Data

Hall, Evelyn Beatrice, 1868-1919.
    The life of Voltaire.

    ([BCL/select bibliographies reprint series])
    Reprint of the 1903 ed.
    Bibliography: p.
    1. Voltaire, François Marie Arouet de, 1694-1778.
PQ2099.H3 1972   848'.5'09 [B]   72-2504
ISBN 0-8369-6867-0

PRINTED IN THE UNITED STATES OF AMERICA

CONTENTS

OF

THE SECOND VOLUME

ILLUSTRATIONS

TO VOLUME II

THE

LIFE OF VOLTAIRE

CHAPTER XXVII

THE ARRIVAL IN SWITZERLAND

RECEIVING no answer to his request to be allowed to travel, Voltaire prudently resolved to consider that silence gave consent. But he was still not a little nervous that if he took refuge in a foreign country Louis XV. might consider himself justified in seizing the pensions of his truant subject.

And then, where was he to go ? It seems most likely that if it had not been for that unromantic disorder called *mal de mer* he would have ended his days in Pennsylvania. He had still his *bizarre* liking for the Quakers ; and America was the country of the free. To be sure, *mal du pays* was a worse and a longer lived disorder with him than the other : and if he had tried Pennsylvania on one impulse, he would quickly have left it on another.

He looked back lovingly, too, on bold little England, 'where one asks of no one permission to think.' And on March 19, 1754, he asked M. Polier de Bottens, who had been a Calvinist minister at Lausanne, if he could assure him of as much freedom in Lausanne as in Britain. Meanwhile, there was no reason why, in the near future, that long-deferred and greatly discussed Plombières visit should not take place.

And, for the time, he was in Colmar. On January 12 of this year he had sent his Duchess of Saxe-Gotha twelve advance copies of those 'Annals of the Empire' written at her request, and just printed under Voltaire's own eye at Colmar by Schoepflin. In return, Madame had done her gracious best to reconcile him with Frederick. He was anxious to be reconciled. Frederick could influence France to receive back her prodigal, as could no one else. 'Brother Voltaire,' as he signed himself in his letters to her, also pleaded his cause once more with the Margravine of Bayreuth ; and then sent Frederick himself a copy of those 'Annals' as a tentative olive branch. Frederick accepted the book, and declined the peace overtures in a letter, dated March 16, 1754, which contained bitter allusion to the Maupertuis affair and showed that the kingly heart was still sore and that the kingly soul still angrily admired the great gifts of his Voltaire.

The famous suppers 'went to the devil' without him. But if the King missed his wit much, he dreaded it more ; and if Voltaire wanted the King's powerful friendship—he did not want the King's society. They were better apart. And, for the first time, both were wise enough to know it.

To this spring belongs a very active correspondence between Voltaire, the most voluble correspondent who ever put pen to paper, and Madame du Deffand. Blind, bored, and brilliant, the friend of Horace Walpole, a courtier at Sceaux, and the head of one of the most famous salons in Paris, Madame du Deffand had long

been a friend of Voltaire's, and had visited him in the
Bastille in 1726, just before his exile in England.

If she thought, as Frederick the Great wrote to
Darget on April 1 of this same year 1754, that Voltaire
was 'good to read and bad to know,' her cynic old soul
loved his wit if she feared it.   Perhaps she even loved
him—though mistrustingly.   Blindness had just fallen
upon her.   And ' the hermit of Colmar '—neither now
nor ever only *méchant*—wrote to her with the finest
sympathy and tact, cheering, amusing, rallying her.
' My eyes were a little wet when I read what had happened to yours. . . . If you are an annuitant, Madame,
take care of yourself, eat little, go to bed early, and live
to be a hundred, if only to enrage those who pay your
annuities.   For my part, it is the only pleasure I have
left.   I reflect, when I feel an indigestion coming on,
that two or three princes will gain by my death : and
I take courage out of pure malice and conspire against
them with rhubarb and sobriety.'

As Voltaire could have had nothing to gain by con-
tinually writing to amuse this blind old *mondaine*, it
may be conceded that he did it out of kindness ; and
that if he loved her cleverness, he also pitied her
misfortune.   The eighteenth century, which failed so
dismally in all other domestic relationships, perfectly
understood the art of friendship.

On the Easter Day of this 1754, Voltaire, having
first confessed to a Capuchin monk, received the Sacrament.   *Faire ses Pâques* declares the laxest Catholic
to be still a son of the Church.   What Voltaire's
motives were in this action, it is not easy to see.   It
is said that his anxious friends in Paris recommended
the action as an answer to the charges of unbelief
brought against him.   But a Voltaire must have known

well enough that such an answer as that would impose
on no one.   Besides, it was not like him to be governed
by the advice of fools—even if they happened to be
his friends.   The reasons he himself gave for the action
were that at Rome one must do as Rome does.   ' When
men are surrounded by barbarians . . . one must imi-
tate their contortions. . . . Some people are afraid to
touch spiders, others swallow them.'   ' If I had a
hundred thousand men, I know exactly what I should
do : but I have not, so I shall communicate at Easter,
and you can call me a hypocrite as much as you like.'

The hypocrisy was but ill acted.   Voltaire received the Sacrament with an irreverence painful to
believers and harmful to his own reputation.   To him
the thing was a jest—' the contortions of barbarians.'
He was quite mocking and gay.   When he got home,
he sent to the Capuchin convent a dozen of good wine
and a loin of veal.   I despise you too much to be ill-
natured to you !   If you believe in this mummery, you
are fools !   If you connive at it, unbelieving, you are
knaves !   Knaves or fools, I can laugh at you quite good-
humouredly.   If ever present conveyed a message, this
was the message conveyed by the dozen of wine and
the loin of veal.

To justify Voltaire for this act is not possible.   It
was at best a *méchanceté*.   It was the mocking, jesting
nature of the man getting the upper hand alike of his
prudence and of his consideration for others.   He was
himself a Deist, and a firmly convinced Deist.   To him
the religion of Rome was not merely a folly but the
stronghold of tyranny and of darkness.   The fact that
millions of faithful souls had found in her bosom consolation for the sorrows, and a key to the mysteries of
life and of death, did not soften him.

In Voltaire was lacking now and ever that 'crown of man's moral manhood,' reverence. To find in 'the last restraint of the powerful and the last hope of the wretched,' only subject for a laugh, was the greatest of his faults. If he had been a nobler nature, he would have seen the beauty and the virtue which lie even in the most degrading theologies : and respecting them, would have stayed his hand from the smashing blow, and for the sake of the virtue which sweetens corruption, have let corruption alone.

It has been done many times. 'No man can achieve great things for his country without some loss of the private virtues.' A reverent Voltaire—what a contradiction in terms !—to spare some goodness, must have spared much vice. To arouse eighteenth-century France, steeped to her painted lips in superstition, and the slavery which had debased her till she came to love it, the shrieks and the blasphemies of a Voltaire and a Rousseau were necessary. No calmer voice would have woke her from her narcotic sleep. 'Without Voltaire and Rousseau there would have been no Revolution.' No honest student of eighteenth-century France can doubt that that Revolution, though it crushed the innocent with the guilty and left behind it some of the worst fruits of anarchy, left behind it too a France which, with all its faults, is a thousand times better than the France it found.

By the middle of April the Plombières arrangements were well advanced. The d'Argental household was to be there ; and Madame Denis, more or less penitent and more or less forgiven, had asked to join the party. The waters would be good for a health—ruined, said her temperate uncle, by 'remedies and gourmandising.' Voltaire would come, with a couple

of servants at the most. He was anticipating the
change with pleasure when at the very last minute
Madame Denis wrote to tell him that Maupertuis was
at Plombières too. It was certainly not big enough
to hold both him and his enemy. The events of
the last months had taught even Voltaire some kind
of caution. He was absolutely *en partant* when
Madame Denis's letter came ; but on June 8, though
he left Colmar, it was to stop halfway between it and
Plombières, at the Abbey of Senones, as the guest of
Dom Calmet, who had himself been a visitor at Cirey.
Calmet had a splendid library. His visitor, who was
condemned, as he said, to work at a correct edition of
that ' General History, printed for my misfortune,'
made good use of it, during his three weeks' visit.
Absurd reports were noised abroad—which the Dom
did not contradict—that he had converted ' the most
pronounced Deist in Europe.' But, as the Deist
himself said, his business was with the library—not
with matins and vespers. Directly Maupertuis left
Plombières, Voltaire took leave of Calmet and his
monks, and on some day not earlier than July 2 left
for Plombières, where he found not only his dear
d'Argentals and Madame Denis, but her sister, Madame
de Fontaine, as well.

The little party passed here an agreeable fortnight or so. About July 22, Voltaire returned to
Colmar with Madame Denis, who from this time forth
managed, or mismanaged, his house for him till his
death. The ' Universal History ' greatly occupied him
after his holiday. But there was another subject
which was even more engrossing.

It was the idea of living in Switzerland. Since
March the plan of seeking ' an agreeable tomb

in the neighbourhood of Geneva,' or possibly near
Lausanne, had been growing—growing.   There were
many reasons why the little republic was a suitable
home for Voltaire.   In the first place, it *was* a republic.   It was quite close to France, though not in it ; and
though France might not like to have such a firebrand
as Voltaire burning in her midst, she would not object
to be lit by his light if it were burning near.

Then Switzerland was Protestant—and in Voltaire's
English experience of Protestantism he had found that
faith singularly tolerant and easy-going—in practice,
that is, not in principle.   By August he was negotiating
actively with M. de Brenles, a lawyer of Lausanne,
about ' a rather pretty property ' on the Lake of Geneva.
It was called Allamans ; and Voltaire was not a little
disappointed when his negotiations for buying it fell
through.   In October he was inquiring if a Papist
could not possess and bequeath land in the territory
of Lausanne.   He urged secrecy on de Brenles ; and
entered fully into money matters.   If he bought land,
it was to be in the name of his niece, Madame Denis.
There was a danger throughout these months of that
bomb the ' Pucelle ' bursting—into print—' and killing
me.'   That fear made the Swiss arrangements go forward with a will.

On October 23, Voltaire went to supper at a poor
tavern of Colmar, called the ' Black Mountain,' with no
less a personage than his friend Wilhelmina of Bayreuth.
She overwhelmed him with kindness and attention ;
asked him to stay with her ; begged she might see
Madame Denis, and made a thousand excuses for the
bad behaviour of brother Frederick : so that impulsive
Voltaire jumped once more to that favourite conclusion
of his that ' women are worth more than men.'   To be

sure, if he had seen an account of the interview his clever Princess wrote to her brother, he might have thought something less highly of her and her sex. But he did not see it; nor Frederick's bitter reply. If he had, neither flattery nor opprobrium would have moved him now from one fixed resolve—to shelter in Switzerland.

On November 11, Voltaire, Collini, Madame Denis, a lady's maid, and a servant left Colmar to visit the Duke of Richelieu at Lyons. Voltaire had lived at Colmar on and off for thirteen months—among Jesuits who five years earlier had publicly burnt the works of Bayle, the prophet of tolerance. He could not have left with regret. Just as they were starting off, Collini declares that his master, finding the travelling carriage overladen with luggage, gave orders that everything should be taken out except his own trunk and Madame Denis'; and that he told Collini to sell *his* portmanteau and its contents. The hot-tempered young Italian refused to do so, and gave notice on the spot. On his own showing, his impetuous master made at once the handsomest apologies for his little burst of temper; gave the secretary generous presents of money as a peace-offering; and made him re-pack his portmanteau and put it back in the carriage. The storm blew over; but Collini, like almost all Voltaire's servants, was beginning to take advantage of his master's indulgence, and to trespass on a kindness which Voltaire made doubly kind to compensate for his irritability.

By November 15, the party were installed in a very bad inn, called the 'Palais Royal,' at Lyons. Voltaire complained that it was 'a little too much of a joke for a sick man to come a hundred *lieues*

to talk to the Maréchal de Richelieu.' But he and
Richelieu were not only very old friends but, in spite
of little disagreements such as that affair of the
' Panegyric of Louis XV.' at Court in 1749, very
faithful friends. The brilliant author and the brilliant
soldier had still for each other the attraction which had
been potent twenty years earlier in those June days at
Montjeu, when Voltaire had negotiated the marriage
between Mademoiselle de Guise and the gallant Duke.
The charming wife had died young ; and her husband
and Voltaire had met little of late. But Voltaire
received Richelieu in the bad inn, and clever Richelieu
made the five days he stayed at Lyons so infinitely
soothing and agreeable for his much tried and
harassed friend, that when Richelieu left, Voltaire
said he felt like Ariadne in Naxos after the desertion of
Theseus.

While he was at Lyons the enterprising traveller
also went to call on Cardinal de Tencin, head of the
Church there, uncle of d'Argental, and brother of that
famous Madame de Tencin who had played Thisbe to
Voltaire's Pyramus when Voltaire was in the Bastille
in 1726. The wary Lord Cardinal stated to M. de Voltaire that he could not ask a person in such ill-favour
with his Majesty of France to dine with him. Voltaire replied that he never dined out, and knew how
to take his own part against kings and cardinals ; and,
so saying, turned his back on his Eminence and went
out of the room. As he and Collini were returning
from that brief visit, the visitor observed absently that
this country was not made for him. The officer in
command of the troops in Lyons received him in much
the same way. All the authorities were cold, in fact,
to propitiate that Highest Authority at the Court of

France, who was colder still.   However, their disap-
proval was not very afflicting.   The town of Lyons
saw Voltaire with bolder eyes.   It acted his plays
at the theatre; and when he appeared in his box
there, loudly applauded him.   On November 26 he
formally took his seat in the Lyons Academy, of which
he had long been an honorary member.   Then, too,
Wilhelmina was in Lyons ; and Wilhelmina used her
shrewd influence with de Tencin, and at a second interview, behold ! the Church and Deism on quite friendly
terms.

As a whole, the Lyons visit was a success ; or would
have been but for Voltaire's ill-health and 'mortal
anxieties ' about ' that cursed Pucelle.'   He was afraid
that it was in the possession of Mademoiselle du Thil,
once companion to Madame du Châtelet, who had
found it among Émilie's effects.   The ill-health, too,
which took the form of gouty rheumatism this time,
was so painful and annoying that many of his friends
had strongly recommended him to try for it the waters
of Aix-in-Savoy.   In the meantime he had been
lent ' a charming house halfway.'   On December 10,
1754, he, Madame Denis, and Collini left Lyons for
ninety-three miles distant Geneva, which they reached
on December 13 and found gaily celebrating a victory
gained in 1602 over the Duke of Savoy.   The gates
of the city were shut for the night when they arrived.
But the great M. de Voltaire was expected: and
they were flung open for him.   He supped that night
in Geneva with a man who was to be till his death one
of the best and wisest friends he ever had, the famous
Dr. Tronchin.

No account of Voltaire's life in Switzerland could
be complete without mention of that honourable and

celebrated family, who in the eighteenth century nobly filled many important posts in the Swiss republic and whose descendants are well known in it to the present day.   One Tronchin, the Swiss jurisconsult, is cele- brated as having provoked, by certain 'Letters from the Country,' the famous ' Letters from the Mountain ' of Jean Jacques Rousseau.   Another, the Councillor François Tronchin, the most delightful and hospitable of men, was at once the constant correspondent, the legal adviser—in brief, the factotum of Voltaire.

But the most famous of the family, as well as the one most intimately associated with Voltaire, was Theodore Tronchin, the doctor.   Handsome face, noble mind, fearless spirit, with the stern uprightness of the Puritan, and an infinite benevolence and compassion all his own—if greatness meant only goodness, friend Theodore was a greater man than his great patient, Voltaire.

Yet, though no spark of the Voltairian genius was in him, he was the most enlightened doctor of his age. It is not only as the intimate of that 'old baby' as he called him, the Patriarch of Ferney, that Tronchin may well interest the present day : but as the earliest discoverer—after eighteen centuries of stuffiness—of the value of fresh air ; as the first of his class who preached the Gospel of Nature ; recommended tem- perance, exercise, cleanliness in lieu of the drugs of the Pharmacopœia ; and, after years of labour, taught the woman of his age to be very nearly as good a mother to her children as is the lioness to her cubs. Tronchin deserves to be famous.

It was he who discountenanced the idea of Voltaire trying the waters of Aix.   Tronchin's diagnosis always went through the body to the soul.   No doubt he saw that this *vif*, irritable, nervous patient—torn to pieces with the quarrels and the excitement of the last five years—wanted, not the waters of Aix, but of Lethe : peace, quiet, monotony, and a home.

After four days' stay in Geneva, Voltaire and suite reached the 'charming house' which had been lent him, and which was ten miles from Geneva and called the Château of Prangins. It stood on very high ground, overlooking the lake from thirteen immense windows. There was too much house and too little garden. The house was only half furnished, and beaten by every wind that blew. And it was mid-winter in Switzerland. Was it really so charming? Madame Denis was volubly discontented. Italian Collini, who felt he had been cheated out of going to Paris, was extremely cross and cold. His master and mistress were always calling him to make up the fires, shut the windows, and bring them their furs. The draughts were really abominable. And what was one to do here? 'Be bored ; in a worse temper than usual ; and write a great deal of history ; be as bad a philosopher as in the town ; and have not the slightest idea what is to become of us.' This was discontented Collini's account of Prangins. He was pluming his wings for flight, and not at all in the mood to make the best of things.

It was Voltaire who did that. Between the grumbling niece and secretary, acutely sensitive him-self to physical discomfort, not a little worried by the memory of that 'abortion of a Universal History,' compelled to wait for a package of absolutely necessary books that ought to have come from Paris and had not, so ill that by January 3, 1755, he could not even hold a pen, he was still, in spite of angry Collini's insinuations, the same true philosopher who had astronomised with Madame du Châtelet sitting by the roadside on a January evening on the cushions of their broken-down carriage. He was still busy and cheerful. ' *They* have need of courage,' he wrote of his companions, very justly. As for himself, he worked and forgot the cold. It was in these early days of his life in Switzerland that he arranged with the Brothers Cramer, the famous publishers of Geneva, to bring out the first complete edition of his writings. Then he heard from d'Argental that the public of Paris resented his exile. What warmth and comfort in that! ' Nanine ' was played there with success ; and a play of Crébillon's was a failure. That would have made one glow with satisfaction in any climate. And if Prangins was cold, two at least of the influential persons in the neighbourhood had written warmly to assure the famous newcomer of their good offices.

And better than all, better a thousand times, through this chill, discontented January, Voltaire was eagerly looking for a house and property of his own, in this free little Switzerland, where he might settle down at last and be in peace. On January 31, 1755, he was in active negotiation about two houses. On February 1 there appeared in the Registers of the Council of State of Geneva a special permission to M. de Voltaire—who alleged the state of his health and the necessity for living near his doctor, Tronchin, as a reason for wishing to settle in Switzerland—to inhabit the territory of the republic under the good pleasure of the Seigneury.

On February 8 or 9 the Councillor Tronchin bought a property quite close to Geneva, called Saint-Jean, which he let on a life lease to Voltaire, and which, in a characteristic enthusiasm and before he had had any practical experience of it, Voltaire re-christened ' Les Délices.' Thus he was enabled to evade the law of the republic, and, Papist though he nominally was, to live and hold property under the Genevan republic.

A few days later, he acquired a second house, called Monrion, on the way from Lausanne to Ouchy.

He was now sixty-one years old. Strong in his heart all his life had been his love of a home. For a while Cirey had seemed like one. But it had never belonged to him. It was, too, in France ; and there had been often the painful necessity of leaving it as quickly as possible, and without any surety of being allowed to come back again. The man's whole life had been a buffeting from pillar to post.

But the fretted youth in Paris, the restless middle age at Lunéville, Brussels, Cirey, and the angry hurry of Prussia were over for ever.

When he settled in Switzerland Voltaire took a new lease of his life. He entered upon its last, greatest, noblest, and calmest epoch.

CHAPTER XXVIII

THE DÉLICES,
AND THE ' POEM ON THE DISASTER OF LISBON '

In 1755 the little republic of Geneva contained twenty
thousand of some of the most simple, honest, frugal,
and industrious persons in the world.   Calvin had been
dead two centuries.   But his influence yet lived in laws
which regulated not only the worship but the food
and the drink of his followers ; which bade them rise at
five in summer and at six in winter, under penalty of a
fine ; allowed but two dishes at their tables ; and made
more than one fire in a house appear unjustifiable ex-
travagance.   In many respects the Genevan Calvinists
of the time of Voltaire were not unlike a certain section
of Scottish society.   Austere in morals, and shrewd in
mind, narrow, laborious, economical, equally exempt
from degrading poverty and degrading luxury, content
with stern pleasures, and a brief and rigid creed—the
Calvinist was but a severer Presbyterian after all.   By
the middle of the eighteenth century, indeed, one party
of the Genevans had been influenced not a little, on the
side of their intellect, by the new science, the new
literature, the new philosophy, which were remoulding
Europe ; and beneath the Calvinistic gloom still felt
the gay heart-beats of the Frenchman.   But the other
and larger party were Puritan to the marrow—who

believed, with all the morbid intensity of their founder, that enjoyment was sinful, musical instruments had been invented by the devil, and play-acting was the abomination of desolation.

It was among such a people that this cynic Voltaire, whose motto was 'Rire et fais rire,' whose darling amusement was the drama, and whose incorrigible indulgence was the 'Pucelle,' had elected to live.

On the very day, February 9, 1755, when he completed his negotiations for buying the lease of Délices, a certain Pastor Vernet wrote to him, begging him to respect religion, and saying that the serious persons of the neighbourhood were not without their apprehensions on that count. But when it came to writing, Voltaire was more than a match for any pastor who ever lived. He responded by a letter brilliantly ambiguous ; to which Vernet could take no exception, but in which he must have found much food for thought.

Les Délices stood on the top of a hill on the Lyons road and quite near to the town of Geneva. It was therefore in that republic, while it was ten minutes' walk from the Sardinian province of Savoy, half an hour's ride into France, and an hour's ride into Vaud. Altogether, a most prudent situation for a Voltaire. Lake Leman lapped to the foot of its terraces. It was surrounded by gardens, whose beauty was only marred by high walls which shut out the lovely surrounding country. His signature on the lease was still wet when this enthusiastic Voltaire began pulling down those walls that he might look uninterruptedly upon one of the most beautiful views in Switzerland—across the city of Geneva, the junction of the rivers Arne and Rhone, to the Jura and the Alps. He called the place

the Délices, he said, because 'there is nothing more
delightful than to be free and independent.' Certainly,
the Delights were his torments in some respects. He
complained that the architect of Prangins had forgotten
to make a garden, and the architect of Délices had
forgotten to make a house. Its builder had built for
himself ; and the guest-rooms were inadequate and
uncomfortable. But such defects could be remedied.
The last occupant of Délices was the son of that
Duchess of Saxe-Gotha who had inspired the 'Annals.'
That seemed like a good omen.

Monrion, the second purchase, was on the way from
Lausanne to Ouchy—at the other end of the lake from
Délices. 'Les Délices will be for the summer, Monrion
for the winter, and you for all seasons,' Voltaire wrote
to Lawyer de Brenles, the very day he acquired Délices.
'I wanted only one tomb. I shall have two.' Monrion
was comfortable and 'sheltered from the cruel north
wind '—'my little cabin,' 'my winter palace '—a 'clean,
simple house ' such as its master loved. After his time
it was inhabited by Tissot—a celebrated doctor, only
second in reputation to Tronchin.

It is pleasant to see the keen youthful enjoyment
and ardour with which Voltaire turned to the improve-
ment of his new homes. The first letter he wrote from
Délices is dated March 5, 1755, but, as has been noted,
even before that date he was enthusiastically pulling
down walls in the garden and planning new rooms for
the house. By March 24, he and Madame Denis were
actually in the midst of building the 'accommodation
for our friends and our chickens—planting oranges and
onions, tulips and carrots. One must found Carthage.'
The new fascination—the safest and best he had ever
known—the fascination of home and garden, of country

life, of pride in simple things—took possession of the
most susceptible of men.   He said, with his cynic
smile, that he 'was born faun and sylvan.'   He was at
least strangely free from love of the pavement for a
man who had spent on it all the most pliable years of
his life.   He wrote in this March that his whole conversation was of 'masons, carpenters, and gardeners.'
Even Madame Denis, whose 'natural aversion to a
country life' her poor uncle was to have bitter cause
to lament, liked the hurry and bustle of moving, and
was for a while content.

There was much to be done, too, within doors.   For
himself, Voltaire's own tastes were always quite frugal
and simple.   He wanted neither fine furniture nor
many servants.   And as for rich eating and drink, from
that, if he had ever desired it—which he had not—his
health would have precluded him.   His sternly frugal
fare and love of simplicity about him should have
pleased his Calvinistic neighbours.   But he was a friend
before all things.   And Délices and Monrion were to
be open to all his friends—who must be received with
every hospitality and with every generous comfort of
which their host could think.   For them, he would live
like a rich man.   For them, he began spending that
comfortable fortune he had acquired with so much
sagacity, and very often with so much self-denial.   He
bought half a dozen horses and four carriages.   He
kept a couple of lackeys, a valet called Boisse, a French
cook and a cook's boy; maidservants, coachmen, a
postillion, and gardeners; besides Collini, whose duties
were only less universal than Longchamp's had
been.   That French cook soon had to provide a great
many dinners for a great many diners; and generous suppers after evening theatricals.   The carriages

had to be sent to bring the economical, quiet-going
neighbours to and from the dinner parties. The
carriage Voltaire kept for his own use was of antique
build, with a blue ground speckled with gold stars ; but
it was his fancy always to drive this remarkable
equipage into Geneva with four horses in it—to the
great excitement and astonishment of the grave little
republic. On one occasion the people so crowded
round him to see him alight from this extraordinary
conveyance, that he called out, 'What do you want to
see, boobies ? A skeleton ? Well, here is one,' and he
threw off his cloak. The establishment of Délices was
further completed by a tame bear and a monkey. The
monkey, who bit the hand that caressed him, was called
Luc. So in his letters of the time Voltaire soon began
to allude to a certain royal friend as Luc too.

Voltaire had been established at Délices about a
month, when in April his first visitor, Lekain the actor,
came to stay with him. Lekain, who in 1750 had
been nobody at all but a clever young dependent on
the bounty of the famous M. de Voltaire, was himself
famous now, as one of the best tragedians in Paris.
Of course the amateur dramatic talent of Délices took
advantage of the professional genius of Lekain. ' Zaire '
was rehearsed ; and then read aloud in one of the large
rooms of the house. Denis and Lekain were in the
principal parts. Voltaire took his favourite *rôle* of
Lusignan, and declared gaily that no company in Europe
had a better old fool in it than himself. The frigid
Calvinists and the Tronchins, who formed the audience,
were in tears. Lekain had more sentiment than voice,
said Voltaire ; and was so moved sometimes as to
be inaudible. But then he moved his audience too.
That was the great thing. He and his amateurs also

read some part of the new play, ' The Orphan of China ' ;
and when Lekain left he carried away most of it in his
box with the view of producing it in Paris.

But even at Délices the man who had written the
' Pucelle ' could not long expect to find only the pleasures
of play-acting and the agreeable troubles of an estate.
Since he began it, in 1730, the thing had been copied,
and miscopied, read, re-read, quoted, and travestied
a thousand times. It had been imitated by King
Frederick in the ' Palladium ' ; and read aloud to the
Prussian princesses and the Duchess of Saxe-Gotha.
It had been transcribed *for* Prince Henry, and *by*
Longchamp. It was everybody's secret : but still it
was a secret. There was one indecorum it had not yet
committed—that of print.

And in this January of 1755 had come that unpleasant news that a manuscript *was* in the possession of Mademoiselle du Thil ; and then, like a clap of
thunder, the announcement that the thing ' was printed
and being sold for a louis in Paris.'

The publication of such a work would have been
disastrous for Voltaire at any moment ; but it was
doubly disastrous now. Here he was just settling down
upon his estate as a sober, respectable, country gentleman, very much minded to stand well with his straitlaced neighbours, very fond of his new home, not at all
inclined to leave it, and having nowhere to go if he did
leave it—yet holding his land and his right to live on
it only at the ' good pleasure ' of a very strict Seigneury.
To make matters worse, the printed ' Pucelle ' was (of
course) full of errors ; and while it was much less witty
than the original, was not at all less indecent. At first
there seemed to be nothing to be done but to follow the
old, old plan. The thing is not mine at all ! Here, for

Le voila donc connu, ce secret plein d'horreur !

Dedié, par l'Amour Filial
aux Manes de Henri Louis Le Kain,
Pensionnaire du Roi.

LEKAIN.

From an Engraving after a Painting by S. B. Le Noir.

instance, is a passage abusing Richelieu—and Richelieu
is my friend ! And then, to make assurance doubly sure,
Voltaire tried another very artful and most characteristic *ruse*. He employed hundreds of copyists in Paris
to copy it as incorrectly as possible. Then all his
friends, as well as himself, denied loudly and vehemently
that he was the author thereof. A Voltaire write such
bad verse—so *fade*, so *plat*, so prosy! Impossible!
At the same time, Voltaire sent copies of such a
'Pucelle'—or such parts of *the* ' Pucelle '—as he wished
to avow, to all his acquaintance and all persons in
authority. It was a very good idea. It cost a great
deal of money, and a great deal of trouble ; and might
have been of some use if M. de Voltaire's character
and writings had not been known and feared these forty
years.

On July 26, Grasset, a publisher of Lausanne,
appeared at the Délices and kindly offered to sell
M. de Voltaire the incorrect copy of his own ' Pucelle '
for fifty louis. Voltaire had already written to Grasset
to tell him in no mild terms that those ' rags of manuscript' were not his ' Pucelle ' at all, but the work of
some person who had neither ' poetic art, good sense,
nor good morals ;' and that of such a thing Grasset would
not sell a hundred copies. His rage, therefore, may be
imagined. He denounced Grasset to the Genevan
authorities ; and had the satisfaction of seeing that
misguided person made fast in prison—for a time.
On July 27 factotum Collini was sent up to Paris to see
if he could not better matters there. But Paris burnt
the ' Pucelle.' The Pope prohibited it : and it sold
lustily. It is not a little curious that Voltaire himself
never in all his life suffered anything worse from it
than frights ; though of those he had enough and

to spare. In 1757 a Parisian printer was sentenced
to nine years at the galleys for printing an edition.
Geneva—pretending to believe, and trying to believe,
that M. de Voltaire was not its author—burnt the
accursed thing as Paris had done; knowing that M.
de Voltaire could only be glad to see the destruction
of such a wicked travesty of his respectable poem.
With what a wry smile he must have watched that
bonfire!

The republic, however, for the moment, ostensibly
gave him the benefit of the doubt. And then in this very
July, just when he ought to have been most cautious
and circumspect, if this imprudent, mischievous person
does not begin making a stage of inverted wine barrels,
painting scenery, getting together theatrical costumes,
flashing sham lightning in a dustpan, preparing sham
thunder by means of the rims of two cartwheels—
and, worse than all, a thousand times worse—recruit-
ing a theatrical company from among the young
people of Geneva! The young people were only too
willing. The Council of State had swallowed—in
disapproving silence—that reading of 'Zaire' when
Lekain had reduced 'Tronchins and syndics' to tears.
But this was a little too much. So on July 31 the
Council met, and, as the result of a solemn confabulation,
reminded M. de Voltaire that the drama, played publicly
or privately, was contrary to their regulations, and that
no Calvinists were allowed to take part in, or to witness,
the same. Voltaire replied with a suspicious meekness
that his only desire was to obey the 'wise laws' of the
government. He further wrote to Councillor Tronchin
in terms quite abject. 'No man who owes to your
honourable body the privilege of living in this air ought
to displease anyone who breathes it.'

In brief, there was a different and quite as good an
air in Lausanne, where the 'wise laws' of Geneva
had no sway. Lausanne loved play-acting ; and M. de
Voltaire had a house at Monrion.

In Paris, too, on August 20, 'The Orphan of
China' was performed with brilliant success. Here
was excellent consolation for the solemn resolutions
of Genevan Councils. They might take offence at
'Zaire,' but Paris applauded 'my Chinese baboons' to
the echo. Poor Marie Leczinska, indeed, who not
unnaturally saw evil in everything this sceptic, this
Pompadour's favourite, did, saw it here too. But
even her objections, that the piece contained lines
hostile to religion and to the King, were too obviously
unjust to harm it. The censor had passed it. Its first
performance declared it Voltaire's greatest success
since 'Mérope.' If Lekain *did* fall into his old fault
and speak dreadfully indistinctly, Mademoiselle Clairon
made the most charming of heroines, and the play was
'all full of love '—tender, graceful, picturesque. It was
played twelve or thirteen times in Paris ; and when it
was moved to Fontainebleau the Court delighted in it
as much as the capital had done. In the annals of the
French stage it is still remembered as the first play in
which the actresses consented to forego their *paniers*.

Collini was present on the opening night. Even his
grumbling pen allows that his master had made a
very palpable hit. The pleasure-loving secretary had
spent six weeks in Paris, almost entirely engaged in
enjoying himself, before Voltaire recalled him in the
friendliest of terms.

On August 30, 1755, Voltaire wrote from Délices
one of his most famous letters ; perhaps one of the
most famous letters in the world. It was to Jean

Jacques Rousseau, and thanked him for the 'Discourse on the Origin of Inequality among Men,' which Rousseau had written as a prize essay at the Academy of Dijon, and now sent for the approval of the great master. The 'Discourse' was nothing but an elaboration of Rousseau's famous theory—the advantage of savage over civilised life. Years before, at the French Court in 1745, Voltaire and Rousseau had had dealings with each other. They now renewed that acquaintance. Voltaire's letter began, 'I have received, Sir, your new book against the human race. . . . No one has ever employed so much wit in trying to make us beasts : one longs to go on four paws when one reads your book, but, personally, it is sixty years since I lost the habit, and I feel it is impossible for me to resume it.' He went on to agree with Jean Jacques that literature and science brought many troubles to their votaries ; and instanced his own case with as quick a feeling as if all his wrongs were of yesterday. But, 'literature nourishes, rectifies, and consoles the soul . . . one must love it, in spite of the way it is abused, as one must love society, though the wicked corrupt its sweetness; as one must love one's country, though one suffers injustice from it ; and one's God, though superstition and fanaticism degrade His service.'

On September 10 Rousseau replied from Paris in warm terms of friendship, and agreeing with the superior wisdom of his master's argument. As yet, each could see the other's genius—and reverence it. They could disagree and be friends.

The autumn at Délices was further marked by the visit of Patu, a poet, who was a friend of David Garrick's and wrote him an ecstatic account of his

boyishly energetic host ; and by a *fracas* with Madame
Denis.

The facts that that foolish person was fat, short,
forty-five years old, and squinted, did not, it has been
said, make her less fond of admiration from the
opposite sex, or less prone to make a fool of herself in
a flirtation when opportunity offered.

In the present case Uncle Voltaire suspected her of
being a party to a theft her old admirer, the Marquis
de Ximenès, had made of some manuscript notes for
Voltaire's ' Campaigns of the King.' Ximenès had sold
the notes to a publisher. Madame Denis's voluble
denials would certainly prove nothing. Voltaire was
already quite aware of what Madame d'Épinay discovered after a very short acquaintance with her, that
his niece was constitutionally a liar.

And then, on November 24, came news which
staggered Voltaire's soul ; and beside which all petty
trouble seemed shameful. On November 1, 1755,
Lisbon was destroyed by an earthquake. It was All
Saints' Day, and the churches were full. In six
minutes, fifteen thousand persons were dead ; and
fifteen thousand more were dying.

In these days, when every morning has its ' crisis '
and every evening its ' appalling disaster,' it is difficult
to realise the effect of the earthquake at Lisbon
upon the eighteenth century. The less news there
is, the more is that news felt. In the eighteenth
century, too, all thoughtful persons saw signs in the
heavens and the earth of some great change ; and felt
in the social order throes, which might be the death
pangs of the old world, or the birth pains of a new.
Further, men had begun to think and to reason for
themselves : to ask why ? from whence ? to what

end ? and to brush aside the answers of the old theologies to those ancient questions as trite, unproven,
and inadequate.

And if this was the temper of mind of most thoughtful persons, how much more of a Voltaire !

The news took nearly a month to reach him.   For
many months after he received it, there is hardly one
of his letters which does not allude to it in terms of a
passionate horror or a passionate inquiry.   'The best
of all possible worlds ! '   'If Pope had been there
would he have said "Whatever is, is right "?'   'All
is well seems to me absurd, when evil is on land and
sea.'   'I no longer dare to complain of my ailments :
none must dare to think of himself in a disaster so
general.'   'Beaumont, who has escaped, says there is not
a house left in Lisbon—this is *optimism.*'   Over and
over again he reverts to the comfortable dogmas of
Mr. Pope's 'Essay on Man '—conceived sitting safe
and easy in a Twickenham villa.   The stories of the
earthquake reached Voltaire exaggerated.   But the
bald truth was enough.   'Voltaire,' said Joubert, 'is
sometimes sad ; he is moved ; but he is never serious.'
He was serious once—over the Earthquake of Lisbon.

When the horrors were still fresh in his mind,
when the burning questions to which they gave rise
were still loudly demanding an answer, he wrote the
most passionate and touching of all his compositions ;
one of the most vigorous and inspired works of any
author of the age.

The ' Poem on the Disaster of Lisbon ' is only two
hundred and fifty lines long ; but it contains a statement of almost all those searching problems which
every thinking man, of whatever belief or unbelief he
be, has to face at last.

What am I? Whence am I? Whither go I? What is the origin of evil? What end is accomplished by the suffering and sorrow I see around me? ' Why is Lisbon engulfed while Paris, no less wicked, dances?' Your ' whatever is, is right ' may be an easy doctrine for the happy, the rich, the healthy; but a hard saying for the poor, the sick, and the wretched. I will none of it! All nature gives it the lie. The lips that utter it in prosperity to-day will deny it in misery to-morrow. At the end, the note of consolation is struck in the story of the caliph who, dying, worshipped God in the prayer ' " I bring to Thee all that which Thou hast not in Thy immensity—faults, regrets, evils, ignorance." He might have added also Hope.'

The philosophy of ' The Disaster of Lisbon ' is the philosophy of ' In Memoriam.'

> Behold, we know not anything ;
>   I can but trust that good shall fall
>   At last—far off—at last, to all,
> And every winter change to Spring.

Voltaire's poem has not the tender beauty of the other : but it is not less reverent, and not less religious.

One line of it, at least, has found a place in the immortalities of poetry :

> Que suis-je, où suis-je, où vais-je, et d'où suis-je tiré ?

and one phrase, ' Autres temps, autres mœurs,' has become part not only of the French language, but of our own.

On January 1 of the new year 1756 Voltaire sent an incomplete copy of the poem to the Duchess of Saxe-Gotha. On the margin he wrote the word ' Secret.' But on January 8 he was telling d'Argental,

' My sermon on Lisbon was only for the edification of
your flock. I do not throw the bread of life to dogs.'
So many confidences and so many confidential friends
had their usual result. ' The Disaster of Lisbon '
appeared in Paris. With it was also published the
' Poem on Natural Law,' begun in Prussia in 1752.

CHAPTER XXIX

'NATURAL LAW,' THE VISIT OF D'ALEMBERT, AND THE AFFAIR OF BYNG

THE ' Poem on Natural Law' was an answer to Frederick the Great's version of the stupendous question of Pilate—'What is truth?' The poem is in four short parts and an 'easy and limpid versification.' In it, Voltaire calls it a 'seeking for the law of God.' Condorcet says it is 'the most splendid homage man ever paid to Divinity.' Desnoiresterres speaks of its 'incontestable orthodoxy.' At once profound and simple —the simple expression of profound problems— 'Natural Law' and 'The Disaster of Lisbon' are almost the only works of the man who has been called the Prince of Scoffers which are completely reverent. They are pre-eminently *not* the writings of an atheist, but of one who gropes for a God he knows to exist, though he knows neither how nor where.

But, not the less, the whole world and all the Churches fell upon them both, tooth and nail. In 1759 'Natural Law' was publicly burnt by the hangman in Paris ; and immediately after it appeared, the pious Genevans begged J. J. Rousseau to refute the horrible heterodoxy of 'The Disaster of Lisbon.' In July 1757 Marie Leczinska, going to mass, saw a copy of ' Natural Law'—which was then commonly entitled ' Natural

Religion '—on a bookstall.   On her return from
church she took the pamphlet and tore it across, and
told the astonished shopwoman (' who had supposed,
from its title, the work to be one of edification ') that if
she sold such things her licence should be taken from
her.   It is true, there was a smile for Voltaire and all
the world in such stories.   There is a smile still in the
fact that works far more free-thinking than ' Natural
Law ' and ' Lisbon ' are avowed now by persons who
continue to call themselves not only Christians, but
orthodox Catholic churchmen.

The January of 1756 passed quietly at Monrion,
where Voltaire had arrived for the winter at the end
of December.   In spite of his opinions, Lausanne
ministers, always more liberal-minded than the Genevans, came much to see him.   He liked them not a little.
' They are very amiable and well read,' he wrote.   ' It
must be granted there is more wit and knowledge in
that profession than in any other.   It is true I do not
listen to their sermons.'   Other visitors were Lawyer
de Brenles and his charming young wife.   Voltaire,
disappointed of his play-acting in Geneva, had greatly
encouraged a scheme for building a theatre here in
Lausanne.   But the earthquake had made all men
thoughtful.   They mistrusted their love of the drama,
and filled the churches instead.

That wave of austerity swept also over Paris and the
Court.   They were in the vanguard of this new mode
of seriousness, as of every other.   To quite propitiate
an angry heaven Madame de Pompadour renounced
her connection with the King.   His private entrance
to her apartments was closed ; and in February Madame
was created Maid of Honour (of honour !) to the
Queen.

Voltaire had dedicated ' Lisbon ' to a certâin courtier
friend—the Duc de la Vallière—grandson of the hapless
Louise de la Vallière, the mistress of Louis XIV.   In
return, possibly, for the compliment of that dedication
the goodnatured Duke consented to be the emissary of
the Pompadour, and to write from Court on March 1
to make a really most advantageous proposal to M. de
Voltaire.   We are all serious here now, you know !
Can you not take advantage of our seriousness and versify
some of the Psalms which I, the Duke, will at once
have printed at the Louvre ?   The typical wit of the
eighteenth century has no doubt lost something by the
fact that Voltaire's two letters in reply to this proposal
are missing.   He did not versify the Psalms.   Condorcet
says that he could not be a hypocrite even to be a
cardinal.   It seems, if not certainly, at least very likely,
to be true that a red hat *was* held out to him—in those
fairest of white hands—as an inducement to fall in
with the grave vogue of the Court and employ that matchless irony and that scathing wit for, instead of against,
the established religion.

It was the chief duty of the mistresses of Louis XV.
to keep him from being bored ; and the Pompadour
knew her business to perfection.   What reason was
there why Voltaire, who could do it so well, should not
help her to ' *égayer* the King's religion '—for a reward ?
That age had had worse cardinals than he would
have been.   It still remembered Iscariot Dubois,
traitor, usurer, debauchee ; and Mazarin, that synonym
for lies.

Carlyle, who, by every instinct of his character and
every racial trait, was necessarily out of sympathy with
such a man as Voltaire, said of him, ' that he has never
yet in a single instance been convicted of wilfully

perverting his belief ; of uttering in all his controversies one deliberate falsehood.'

He was at least too honest a man to be a cardinal. A little later he did write ' a free, too free imitation ' of Ecclesiastes and the Song of Solomon. But he cannot be charged with pandering in these works to the popular creed. His Notes on his paraphrases are profane and coarse ; and the paraphrases themselves miss all the dignity and beauty of the original. The only merit they have is that they truthfully express the unpalatable opinions their writer held—to his loss.

In May, Voltaire paid a brief visit to Berne. On June 12 Collini left his service. He had been with him four years. Bright-witted, quick-tempered, too fond of pleasure, and ' loving women,' said Madame Denis, ' like a fool,' Collini had never been a satisfactory servant. It is only a very noble character which can remain unspoilt by spoiling. Voltaire certainly did not understand the Napoleonic principle of government—to be feared before you are loved. He had apologised to Collini. He had forgiven him a hundred times ; nay more, when it was the servant who was in the wrong it was the master who had won him back to good temper by a thousand injudicious indulgences. Voltaire was lax enough on the subject himself, heaven knows ; but now his foolish secretary must needs conduct himself in a love affair in a manner which offended even this easy-going master. Then, Collini speaks ill of us behind our backs ! That seemed one of the worst failings in the world to a man who understood the art of friendship so completely as Voltaire. And then—then—the foolish secretary—called away suddenly to get a carriage for Madame de Fontaine, who was just going to arrive at Délices from Paris—

leaves open on his desk a letter in which he had laughed
at Madame Denis; and Madame Denis's maid, coming
in, reads the letter and carries it to her mistress.
Voltaire had been infinitely loyal to Madame du Châtelet.
He was not less so to this chattering *bourgeoise* of a
niece. He gave the secretary his *congé* the next day
—sadly, but firmly at last—as a decision that admitted
of no appeal. Collini must go! Collini implies in his
Memoirs that a kind of flirtation between himself and
Madame Denis was one of the causes of his dismissal.
Madame Denis was certainly foolish enough. It is
also on his testimony that when his master said Good-
bye to him, he talked with him for more than an hour
and asked if he had enough money for his journey to
Paris—' and to last some time.' As he spoke Voltaire
went to his desk and took from it a *rouleau* of louis,
saying ' Take that : one never knows what may happen.'
And Collini adds, ' with tears in my eyes I left the
Délices.' Three years later, Voltaire procured a post
for him at the court of the Elector Palatine, which
Collini is believed to have kept till his death. Written
long after their parting are many friendly letters from
the master to the servant.

Collini had his significance and his uses. From
his ' Séjour auprès de Voltaire,' where he tries to make
Voltaire appear as faulty and himself as faultless as
he can, the master still comes out better than the
servant. There is no more reliable testimony to
character than that wrung out of an unfriendly witness. On one point at least the ill-tempered young
Italian has cleared his master's reputation for ever.
' Stinginess never had a place in his house. I have
never known a man whose servants could rob him with

greater ease. I repeat it, he was a miser of nothing
but his time.'

Collini's place was at once filled by Wagnière, a
Genevan boy, now sixteen years old, who had been in
Voltaire's service since 1754. As if he had nothing
else to do in the world, Voltaire taught him Latin
and trained him in his duties himself.

Collini's departure for Paris seems to have suggested
to his master that he too would like to pay a visit to the
capital—just a very flying visit to see about some
business. So he wrote off to one d'Argenson, to ask
him to get the requisite permission from the other
d'Argenson, the Secretary of State. But in spite of
that old school friendship, the minister was not at all
too friendly just now to this presumptuous exile. The
permission was refused : and Voltaire revenged himself
by an epigram. He had a richer revenge, if he had
wanted it, in the January of the next year, 1757, when
the Secretary was banished to please her Mightiness
the Pompadour. But he did not want it. The spiteful epigram relieved his feelings and his temper. And
it will be remembered of an earlier Voltaire, that from
the moment an enemy became unfortunate, this inconsistent person could not help regarding him as a
friend.

In August, J. J. Rousseau wrote, as the Genevan
ministers had asked him, to remonstrate with Voltaire
on that unorthodox ' Disaster of Lisbon.' Jean Jacques
permitted himself to admire the grace and beauty of
M. de Voltaire's poem, while continuing to find the
optimism of Mr. Pope much more consolatory, and
deducing from the earthquake a splendid argument for
his darling theory of the advantages of savage over
civilised life. Do you not see, my dear M. de Voltaire,

that if people did not build themselves houses seven
stories high and huddle together in great towns, earth-
quakes really would not be nearly so disastrous ?

The letter was scarcely one which called for a
serious reply. But it was instinct with all the glow
and passion of that matchless style which made men
forget to examine the common-sense of the ideas it
clothed ; and it fitted in admirably with the fashionable
optimism which was naturally popular with the well-
to-do and the powerful. The world *did* take it gravely.
And in September M. de Voltaire sent a reply of airy
badinage.

'Madame de Fontaine has been in danger of her
life, and I have been ill too ; so I am waiting till I
am better and my niece cured, to dare to think as
you do.'

The note was a little trifling, certainly ; but Rousseau wrote to Tronchin that he was charmed with
it. As for Voltaire, the very idea of that further
scathing rollicking answer that was to come had not
yet even occurred to him. He had as little time as
desire to quarrel with anybody at the present moment.
Besides all his new duties as a landed proprietor, a
tragedy, history, verses, correspondence, he was engrossed with d'Alembert as a visitor and the 'Encyclopædia ' as a hobby.

The story of the foundling who, thirty-nine years
earlier, had been discovered on the steps of a Parisian
church, is hardly less familiar to our own century than
it was to the eighteenth. Brought up by a com-
passionate poor woman, a glazier's wife, it was not
until he had become the great d'Alembert, the first
geometrician and philosopher of the day, that the
false mother who had borne and abandoned him—

Madame de Tencin, the old acquaintance of Voltaire—
would fain have avowed a child so creditable. But
that child had not a characteristic in common with her.
He denied her. He had no mother but the glazier's wife.
In her home he grew up to be one of the wisest and
gentlest of great men. In her home he learnt the
blessings of peace and privacy, of work and obscurity.
'Simple, sober, and proud,' too well acquainted with
Poverty to be afraid of her, he always shunned a
society which could give him nothing and might rob
him of the time to work out the work of his life.
Above that glazier's shop, after long throes and travail
of delightful pain, he brought forth in 1750 the first-
born son of his genius, the Preliminary Discourse of
the great 'Encyclopædia.' In 1756 he became a member of the French Academy. In 1772 he was made its
perpetual secretary. His long passion for that most ardent and unhappy woman, Mademoiselle de Lespinasse,
was for eleven years of his later life at once its consolation and its despair. As a writer his style has all
the clumsiness of the *savant* who has so much to say
that he has no time to take care how he says it, and
all the coldness of the mathematician. But it was
only his writing that was cold.

For all his 'stately irony,' for all his recluse student
ways and frugal life, d'Alembert inspired his century
not so much with admiration as with love. Once,
when Voltaire was asked to write something in an
album, he saw in it the name of d'Alembert. Beneath,
he wrote his own—*Hic fuit Dalemberti amicus.*

D'Alembert arrived at Délices some time about
August 10, 1756. He stayed five weeks. It must
have been a delightful visit. Voltaire had that rare
combination of qualities as a host—he knew both how

to amuse his guest and how to leave him to amuse himself. It was during this stay that at a dinner party at Délices, at which Dr. Tronchin and others were present, the company began telling robber stories. Each anecdote was more thrilling than the last. Then Voltaire looked up—' Once, Gentlemen, there was a Farmer-General . . .' and he relapsed into silence, with the honours of the evening. That ancient story still has point. How much more it must have had when it was new—in 1756 !

The five weeks passed only too quickly. Summer was on that beautiful country. Madame de Fontaine was also staying at Délices. She was now a widow of about forty, rather tall and good-looking, and with a taste for painting—the subjects not too decorous, for choice. Madame was not exactly decorous herself. When she arrived at Délices she had brought with her the Marquis de Florian, her lover. Uncle Voltaire accepted that intimacy with perfect nonchalance and amiability. On the present occasion Madame de Fontaine was useful to keep Madame Denis company, and so leave Voltaire and d'Alembert to themselves.

They had much to do and to say. From 1746 they had been correspondents ; but the ' Encyclopædia ' was a link which had bound them closer far. Founded on the ' English Encyclopædia' of Chambers, which had been translated into French about 1743, the ' immense and immortal work ' of Diderot and d'Alembert wholly eclipsed its prototype. It was, is, and will be, not *an* 'Encyclopædia,' but *the* ' Encyclopædia.' It includes, indeed, neither history nor biography : the vast discoveries of modern times make men smile to-day at its science ; and its hardy philosophy seems timid to our bolder age.

But it was not the less the Guide to the Revolution, the first great public invitation to all men to drink of that knowledge which enfranchises the soul. To it Grimm, Rousseau, Holbach, Marmontel, and Condorcet were contributors. There was not an enlightened man in France who did not recognise it as the primer of a new language—the handbook to a better country. The authorities burnt it. Voltaire loved it. It suggested to him his own Philosophical or, as he called it, ' pocket Dictionary.' To the ' pocket Dictionary ' could be relegated what was too bold even for the Encyclopædia. It has been seen that in Prussia he wrote articles for it, and reams of letters about it. It was not his own. He called himself ' the boy in your great shop ; ' and his contributions to it ' pebbles to stick into the corners of the immortal edifice you are raising.' But he loved it as if it had been his own, and as he loved the d'Alembert who had created it.

That summer visit at Délices was the cause of the most famous and fought-over article the Encyclopædia contains. Geneva delighted in d'Alembert. Besides being gentle, modest, and accomplished, it also knew him to be hostile to the Church of Rome ; and naturally concluded that hostility to Rome meant friendliness to Calvin. The ministers flocked to Délices, and gave parties themselves for their host and his guest. The guest was quite as charmed with them as they were with him. They were so free from superstition, so learned, tolerant, and open to reason ! It was equally pleasant and surprising to find a religion—and the ministers of a religion—nearly as agnostic as the philosophers themselves.

The next thing to do when I get back to Paris is to write an article on Geneva and compliment the children

of Calvin on their freedom of thought!   There is no
doubt that d'Alembert talked over that proposed article
with his host.   Nor is there any doubt that Voltaire
knew perfectly well that such compliments would set
all the Calvinists in Geneva by the ears and create a
fracas which would ring through Europe; nor that he
anticipated that fight with the richest enjoyment, and
secretly and gleefully rubbed his hands together at the
prospect of it.

And as you *are* going to write the article, my dear
d'Alembert, can you not put in just a few lines to say
that the only thing the Genevans really need to make
them entirely delightful is to permit theatrical represen-
tations among them—not for enjoyment, of course, but
just to 'improve their taste' and give them 'tact and
feeling'?

The amiable d'Alembert naturally agreed to oblige
his host on so small a matter.

In September he packed up his boxes and went
back to Paris with the article on Geneva much in his
mind; and those casual observations on play-acting, not
to be forgotten.

He was missed at Délices.   Madame de Fontaine
was ill there in the autumn.   Her uncle's cook was
too good for both her and her sister, who were always
calling in Tronchin to cure them of 'a little indigestion.'   And of course Voltaire (though certainly not
from the same cause) was ill himself.   'We have been
on the point, my dear universal philosopher,' he wrote
to d'Alembert on October 9, 'of knowing, Madame
de Fontaine and I, what becomes of the soul when
separated from its partner.   We hope to remain in
ignorance some time longer.'

On December 9 Voltaire received a visit from

an old friend, George Keith, Earl Marischal of Scot-
land.

He did not come as the emissary of Frederick; or
to recall, though no doubt he did recall, to Voltaire
those early golden days of the Prussian visit when they
had sat together at the most famous supper table in
the world. He introduced many of his countrymen to
the 'old owl of Délices.' But that was not the reason
either of his visit. He came to plead the cause of
Admiral Byng.

Richelieu had just taken Minorca from the English.
The fleet sent by England to its relief retired under
Byng, before the French. Paris went mad with
delight as only Paris can, and sang the exploits of
Richelieu in one of those national songs whose glow
and vigour keep them fresh for ever.

> Plein d'une noble audace
> Richelieu presse, attaque la place——

Voltaire was nearly as enthusiastic as Paris. He had
prophesied such splendid things of his hero! And
it would have been very damping to his ardour to have
had his prophecies and hero-worship proved wrong.
Then, too, England had been so confident of victory;
and so dreadfully rude and aggressive in her confidence.
Such pride deserved a fall; and great was the fall of it.
To be beaten on the sea by the French seemed to
Britain like being struck across the face by the open
hand of insult. She forgot that love of fair play which
she has some right to call her national instinct. She
did what, with all her faults, she very seldom does—she
hit a man when he was down, and wreaked upon him,
in the bitterness of her disappointment, the anger she
should have kept for the blundering ministry who had

commanded him impossibilities.   Byng was arraigned
on a charge of treason and cowardice.   But he had a
friend—and the friend remembered Voltaire.   True,
Voltaire was a Frenchman, and the closest intimate of
Richelieu.   But Keith knew that he was first of all
a humanitarian ; and that he had a passion for justice
and a rage against tyranny which made him love his
enemies if they were oppressed, and hate even his
friends if they were oppressors.   On December 20
Voltaire wrote to Richelieu telling Byng's story.
Richelieu replied in an open letter which generously
vindicated the character of his foe.   Had Byng continued the fight, the English fleet must have been
totally destroyed.   A clever sailor and a brave man,
his misfortunes were from the Hand of God—and the
valour of the French.

Voltaire sent that letter to Byng with a letter of his
own.   He had known the Admiral as a young man,
when he was in England ; but he judged it better not
now to mention that they were acquainted, lest his
interference might be attributed to personal partiality.
The sequel is very well known.   The miserable
ministry wanted a scapegoat.   Though Byng was recommended to mercy by the court which tried him, he
was shot on March 14, 1757, meeting his death with
the courage with which his foes declared he had met
them.

He left grateful messages to Richelieu and to Voltaire ; and to Voltaire a copy of his defence.

The author of ' Candide ' added later to that famous
satire a few stinging and immortal lines on this *cause
célèbre*.   ' In this country it is good to put an admiral
to death now and then, *to encourage the others*.'

Voltaire's part in the affair of Byng is not only of

importance as being of interest to English people. It began a new era in his life.

The scoffer, the jester, the uprooter had found nobler work for his hands at last. The defender of Byng became the avenger of La Barre, of Sirven, of Montbailli, and of Calas.

CHAPTER XXX

THE INTERFERENCE IN THE SEVEN YEARS' WAR, THE 'GENEVA' ARTICLE, AND LIFE AT DÉLICES

On January 5, 1757, Damiens, an unfortunate lunatic, made a very feeble attempt upon the life of Louis XV. As is usual in such cases, the King was accredited with infinite calm and courage, though his heroism had consisted entirely in being the unwilling victim of a very small wound from a very small penknife. However, he took the penknife to be the chosen instrument of the wrath of heaven; went to bed; sent a contrite message to the Queen; and for ten days declined to have any dealings with the lively Pompadour.

On January 6, d'Argenson wrote Voltaire a very courtier-like account of the affair. To say that when Voltaire heard that a New Testament had been found in the poor lunatic's pocket he was delighted, is to express his sentiments feebly. A Testament! I told you so! All assassins have 'a Bible with their daggers.' But have you ever heard of one who had a Cicero, a Plato, or a Virgil?

He turned, twisted, and tossed the subject with all that gibing buffoonery which was his *forte* and other men's fear. Damiens died under tortures which were a disgrace to civilisation. D'Argenson, Secretary of State, and Machault, Keeper of the Seals, who had been

bold and foolish enough to suppose that the King would
be able to kill time without his Pompadour, united, in
her brief disgrace, to crush her. With her return to
power, she crushed them. On February 1 they were
both exiled. A few days earlier, the other brother
d'Argenson (the better friend of the two to Voltaire)
had died. Voltaire might well say that his own fate was
more worth having than that of a Secretary of State
who was banished ; and that he would rather scold his
gardeners than pay court to kings. In February he
received a very flattering invitation from Elizabeth,
Empress of Russia, to go to Petersburg to write ' The
History of Peter the Great,' her father. He undertook
to write the history. But he declined the invitation.
Frederick, too, was trying coquetries on him—such a
tender letter, for instance, from Dresden on January 19 !
But here again he was firm : ' I want neither king nor
autocracy. I have tasted them . . . that is enough.'

The early months of the year 1757 were passing,
indeed, not a little pleasantly at Monrion.

The society of Lausanne, living up to its character
of being more liberal than that of Geneva, was only too
delighted to welcome such an amusing person as Voltaire in its midst. Many Lausannois were French—
all French in their social charms and their language—
and only Swiss in their sincerity and simplicity. Voltaire said that, as an audience, there were a couple of
hundred of them who were worth the whole *parterre*
of Paris, and who would have hissed Crébillon's
' Catilina ' off the stage. What higher praise could he
have given to anybody ? Lausanne, indeed, would
not have been Swiss if there had not been a certain
section of its society who held themselves aloof from
this volatile Deist and his more volatile entertainments.

Nor would it have been a country town if there had
not been in it some touchy and discontented persons
who were offended with M. de Voltaire because he had
not asked them often enough or had asked someone else
too often.   Voltaire gaily divided the society into two
parts : first, the Olympe, which included both the straitlaced and the offended ; and, second, the Sensible People.
That classification spoke for itself.   He was not a little
amused one day when, hearing that an Olympe lady had
had a parody of ' Zaire ' acted at her house, he said to a
young girl of the same name, ' Ah ! Mademoiselle, it is
you who have been laughing at me ! ' and the naïve girl
replied, ' Oh no, Monsieur, it was my aunt ! '

But, Olympes notwithstanding, Lausanne as a whole
was only too delighted to come to M. de Voltaire's theatricals, and the excellent suppers prepared by his first-
rate cook.   It did not expect him to pay visits, which he
hated.   So he and Madame Denis spent all their leisure
hours learning parts and coaching their company.
Madame Denis lived in a whirl of ' tailors, hair-
dressers, and actors,' and being well amused was entirely amiable.

The plays acted were ' Zaire,' ' Alzire,' and the
' Enfant Prodigue,' and a new play of Voltaire's which
he now called ' Fanine ' and which was afterwards called
' Zulime.'

Voltaire persistently declared that Madame Denis
acted ' Zaire ' infinitely better than Gaussin, ' though
she has not such fine eyes ; ' which was a very delicate
way of describing her squint.

In March they ' preached the " Enfant Prodigue,"
with an opera-bouffe (" Serva Padrona ") for dessert.'
Also in March, they played ' Zulime ' ' better than it
will be played in Paris,' said its author.   He proudly

numbered among the audience on its first night twelve
Calvinist ministers and their young students, studying
for the Church.   Here was liberal-mindedness indeed !
Besides acting plays, there was the house to improve
or to alter.   Its master was surrounded with workmen.   He had, also, a parrot and a squirrel.   He had
turned to play-acting, he said, because though 'tranquillity is a beautiful thing—ennui is of its acquaintance
and family.'   But he knew too well, by that old courtly
experience, that the worst of all boredoms is perpetual
amusement.   He was happy at Monrion because there,
as everywhere, he knew how to work as well as to play.
In articles for the 'Encyclopædia,' rewriting 'Zulime,'
and beginning 'The History of Peter the Great,' he
justified his existence.   He had much to do, so he
enjoyed his theatricals and the lovely country in which
he found himself, as only the busy can enjoy anything.
'From my bed I can see the lake, the Rhone, and
another river.   Have you a better view ?   Have you
tulips in March ? . . .   My vines, my orchard, and myself
owe no man anything. . . .'

Was it glamour again ?   If it was, it was a better
glamour than had made him dream Prussia heaven,
and Frederick the Great a faithful friend.

On June 3 he went back to Délices for the summer.
Madame Denis was still in high good-humour—fur-
nishing the house, entertaining, acting.   Voltaire said
she was 'a niece who made the happiness of his life.'
Everything was *couleur de rose.*   Switzerland had
proved a successful venture indeed.   By August the
man who now signed himself the Swiss Voltaire had
acquired yet another house in Lausanne—Chêne, in
the Rue de Lausanne, which was the last street in
the town on the Geneva side, and from where he had

exquisite views of the lake. He rented it for nine
years. Quite near it was a house called Mon Repos,
which belonged to two of Voltaire's amateur dramatic
company, the Marquis and Marquise de Genlis. Very
soon these two enthusiasts made, in a barn adjoining their house, a theatre which practically belonged
to Voltaire, and where in future nearly all his theatricals were held. His first letter from Chêne is dated
August 29, 1757. Here he soon received with great
gravity the Lord Bailiffs of Berne : good, sober, pompous people, with a very amusing idea of their own
importance, and a strictly limited sense of humour.
' What the deuce, M. de Voltaire,' said one of them one
day, ' are you always writing verses for ? What is the
good of it, I ask you ? It leads to nothing. Now *I*,
you see, am a Bailiff.' And another day, a second observed solemnly, ' They say you have written against
God. That is bad, but I hope He will pardon you ; and
against religion, which is worse ; and against our Lord,
which is worse still : but He will forgive you in His
mercy. Only take care, M. de Voltaire, you do not write
against their Excellencies the High Bailiffs, for *they*
will never pardon you ! ' It is not difficult to imagine
the zest and delight with which Voltaire repeated these
stories.

These good Swiss had not only charming scenery,
cultivated society, and some kind of freedom, but they
were also, without intending it, positively amusing !
It would have been well for Voltaire's peace of mind
if he could have engrossed himself entirely in their
small world, and forgotten wholly that vaster, louder
one, which stretched wide beyond Délices, Monrion,
and Chêne. But he had ever itching fingers for a
fight.

In the August of 1756 had begun the third, longest,
and greatest struggle for Silesia, the Seven Years' War.
Voltaire did not choose to remember that, though he
had tried diplomacy before, he had never tried it successfully.   He flung himself, head foremost in every
sense, into the contest. He began in the spring of 1757
by inventing a war machine : ' an engine of massacre
upon the plan of the Assyrian war chariots of old.'
Certainly, he was a peace advocate. But if men must
destroy each other, let them do so by the best and
quickest of possible means.   He had, too, had a dozen
careers already without adding to them that of a
scientific inventor. It is marvellous, but true, that
this ' paper smudger's ' idea—the appellation was his
own—was really very excellent.   The machine was
also intended to carry ammunition and forage.   The
Minister of War thought well of it.   The inventor
recommended it highly to Richelieu.   The Assyrian
chariots were not tried until they were used for
carrying grape-shot, but they were not the less an
uncommonly bright, ingenious, and Voltairian invention.

The inventor relinquished the idea of their immediate use rather sadly. But the war, considered apart
from war chariots, was becoming of personal moment
to him.

In the spring of 1757 the Petticoats, which were
the damnation of France, swept her into it.

In his old Paris days, Voltaire had known, and
scornfully liked, a certain rosy-cheeked *bon conteur* of
an abbé, called Bernis. Verse-maker and *bon-vivant*,
without morals, without brains—or rather with just
enough to enable him to court the right person at the
right moment—Voltaire had named the abbé the

flower-girl of Parnassus, or Babet, after a famous
pretty flower-seller of the day; and loved to tease him
on those rosy cheeks and that cheerful air.   Babet,
who was nothing if not audacious, had asked Boyer
(the âne of Mirepoix, who had died in 1755) for a post:
and when Boyer told him that as long as he was in
power a Babet had nothing to hope for, replied, ' Sir,
I shall wait.'   The answer ran through Paris.   It was
the beginning of success.   The Pompadour turned her
smile on this round-faced wit; pensioned him; installed him in the Tuileries; and made him ambassador
to Vienna, and Secretary for Foreign Affairs.   Frederick,
who had received the mistress's kind regards, sent
through Voltaire, with that curt ' I do not know her,'
had also laughed at Bernis-Babet in the fatal ' Œuvre
de Poëshie du Roi Mon Maître.'

Therefore, on May 1, 1757, ' the first minister of
the state,' Pompadour, made her willing tool, Bernis,
sign an offensive and defensive treaty with the ambassador of Austria against Frederick the Great, and
plunged France into the blood of the Seven Years'
War.

Voltaire's interest in it was varied and conflict-
ing.   He was the friend of Richelieu, of Babet, and
the Pompadour: and he was a Frenchman.   He
had strong sympathy with brave Maria Theresa and
with Austria—the allies of his country.   Her great
enemy, Frederick, was both his friend and his foe:
still loved, still admired, and still unforgiven.   All
through these seven years one sees that fatal affair of
Frankfort rankling in Voltaire's heart; struggling
with his admiration for Frederick as a king and
a soldier: with his pity for him when beaten, with
his pride in him when victorious.   All through the

war Frederick wrote him prose and verse ; the deepest sorrows of his soul, reproaches, confidences, yearnings. And Voltaire answered half bitterly and half tenderly, with angry allusions to the past, and brave words to comfort the King's sore heart for the future : never consistent, not seldom spiteful, and yet touched, affectionate, and sympathetic.

Explain the attitude who can.

In July 1757 Voltaire wrote to Richelieu begging him, if he passed by Frankfort, to send the four ears of those two *coquins*, Freytag and Schmidt.

In August he was busy trying to bring about peace, through the medium of the Margravine of Bayreuth and Richelieu, between Freytag's master and France. This first diplomatic interference of Voltaire's in the war was not badly planned. In his own words, he ' wanted Richelieu to add the quality of arbitrator to that of general.' The scheme was so far a success that, on August 19, Wilhelmina replied that her brother was as grateful for such a proposal as herself. The moment for it was opportune. Frederick was still bruised and broken by the crushing defeat he had suffered at Kolin on June 18. He wrote direct to Richelieu on September 6, asking him to act as an arbitrator ; and Richelieu replied that he was very willing. Did the hermit of Délices rub his lean hands and congratulate himself on a good piece of work? Perhaps he knew the temper of an offended woman and a piqued Babet too well. The blood of her children was as water to these rulers of France. The Court declined arbitration.

The unhappy Margravine wrote to Voltaire on September 12 that Frederick was reduced to frightful extremities. She might well so write. In October

Voltaire sent to the King one of the wisest and kindliest letters which he ever penned. He dissuaded Frederick from a contemplation of suicide. He stimulated him by admiration. He deterred him by insisting that such an act would not only sadden his friends, but please his foes. When, in this same month, Voltaire read some dismal verses Frederick had written to d'Argens on the same unhappy topic, he wrote a second letter to the King, diplomatically lauding the verses to the skies, and again passionately dissuading such a poet, and such a man, from the disgrace of suicide.

In those fatal ' Memoirs ' (meant to be secret) he was now writing at Délices, Voltaire, indeed, avenged himself for Freytag and Frankfort by declaring that much of that Epistle to d'Argens was stolen from Chaulieu and from himself ; while that love of justice which was always getting the better of his malice, in spite of himself, made him add that, under the circumstances, it was wonderful for a king to have written two hundred verses at all.

On October 8 dismal Luc confided to Wilhelmina that he had ' laughed ' at the exhortations of Patriarch Voltaire ; and the very next day wrote to the Patriarch a letter owning that those admonitions had had effect, and ending :

> Though the storm beats high
> I must fight, not fly,
> And a King live and die.

Meanwhile, at Délices, busy Voltaire was trying his hand a second time at peace negotiations. This time his medium was de Tencin—that crafty and haughty Cardinal, who, three years before, at Lyons, had found

it impolitic to invite Voltaire to dinner. But the
Cardinal loved intrigue, and hated Austria and the
Austrian alliance with France, from his soul. When,
on November 5, 1757, Frederick beat French and
Austrians at Rossbach with 'the most unheard-of and the
most complete defeat in history' (the vigorous words
are Voltaire's), all angry France shared the Cardinal's
hatred of the rosy-cheeked Babet's treaty with the Court
of Vienna. De Tencin allied himself with the man
he had despised—Voltaire—' to engage the Margravine
to confide to him the interests of her brother the King,'
and so to procure peace between France and Prussia.
Prussia was willing enough. Voltaire was the inter-
mediary through whom all the letters passed. He said
malignly that he enjoyed the post because he foresaw
the disappointment the Cardinal was preparing for
himself. In reality, he was something less Machia-
vellian, and really thought the peace he hoped for
might be brought about. De Tencin communicated
directly with Louis XV.; and sent him a letter of the
Margravine, written to be so sent. But Maria Theresa
had bowed her pride to flatter the Pompadour; while
Frederick had said 'I do not know her.' The Pompadour's kingly slave answered de Tencin icily that
the Secretary for Foreign Affairs would instruct his
Eminence of the royal intentions. So Babet, the
'flower-girl,' the verse-maker, the *bon-vivant*, dictated
to the astute Cardinal the unfavourable reply he was
to make to the Margravine. De Tencin had to sign
it. He died only a fortnight later—of mortification,
said Voltaire.

Thus ended Voltaire's second interference in the
Seven Years' War. Both were useless. His interest
in the affair was very far from being ended, or even

weakened. But in the meantime there were disturb-
ances nearer home.

It was sixteen months since d'Alembert had stayed
at Délices, and been charmed by the liberal-mindedness of Calvinism. The result of that visit was, as has
been noted, the famous article entitled ' Geneva ' in
the storm-breeding ' Encyclopædia.' In this December
of 1757 the pious pastors of that town heard that
they were therein complimented as no longer believing
in the divinity of Christ or in hell ; as having in many
cases no other religion than ' a perfect Socinianism,'
rejecting all mystery ; as, among the learned at least,
having a faith which had reduced itself to belief in one
God, and which was alone distinguished from pure
Deism by a cold respect for the Scriptures and for
Christ.

It is not difficult to fancy what an effect such
statements, uttered by a d'Alembert, and in what was
then the most famous book in the world, would have
on that strict, simple, pure-living sect. Was it true ?
Could any of it be true? The dreadful fear that it
might be—that that stern, narrow creed, with its brief
assertions and its wide negations, might lead, or
tend, unknown to its followers, to something very like
a barren Deism—appears to have taken possession of
their souls.

On December 12, Voltaire, who had been waiting
sixteen months for this *dénouement,* began to enjoy
himself. ' These droll people,' he wrote to d'Alembert
' actually dare to complain of the praise you have given
them—to believe in a God and to have more reason than
faith. Some of them accuse me of having a profane
alliance with you. They say they will protest against
your article. Let them, and laugh at them.'

On December 23, at a meeting of Calvinistic pastors, they made, with deep heart-searchings, a formal inquiry to assure themselves that none of them had given ground for d'Alembert's—compliments. They then drew up a commission, which appointed Dr. Tronchin, not less a sincere Christian than he was a sincere friend of the Deist Voltaire, to reply to the article in the ' Encyclopædia ' and ' to wipe away the stain ' that d'Alembert had affixed to their character. It was Tronchin's charm as a writer that he touched the heart as well as appealed to the head. He refuted the imputations of d'Alembert in terms not a little touching. From Paris, on January 6, 1758, d'Alembert replied, as he could but reply, that he was convinced of the truth of his words : and what he had written, he had written. When Geneva further asked him to name the pastors who had given rise to such opinions, he very honourably declined. On February 8 the commission produced its Confession of Faith. As it did not insist on the doctrine of Everlasting Punishment, or declare that Christ was equal to His Father, or lay stress on the worship of Him, Voltaire said with some truth, when he wrote to d'Alembert, that they had declared themselves Christian Deists after all, and justified the article in the ' Encyclopædia.'

' Geneva,' in fact, brought home to the thoughtful Calvinist the logical outcome of his religion. The shock was great. To stand face to face with the ultimate consequences of their belief would indeed startle the votaries of many other creeds besides Calvinism.

Their difference on the most vital of all subjects did not affect the friendship of the great Voltaire and the great Tronchin.

During this winter of 1757–58 the Doctor was, for the time being, almost the greater man of the two. He had just returned from Paris, where he had prescribed for all its rank, wit, and fashion ; and where he and his inoculation had become a *furore* and the mode. In Geneva he now started a cure, to which flocked all the *mondaines* of Paris to learn the rudiments of hygiene, of temperance, and of common-sense ; to be taught for the first time in their lives the value of simple living ; and to undergo inoculation.

Voltaire always loved the bold and sensible regimen of this good physician. Like the women, he was also not a little influenced by the great Doctor's charming manner, handsome face, and splendid six feet of height. Then, too, supposing ennui *should* be ' of the acquaintance and family ' of retirement, this ' cure ' brought half the wit of the capital to the very doors of the Hermit of Délices. The year 1757 was not over, and their acquaintance was of the briefest, when Voltaire, with his usual impulsiveness, was already in the midst of a delightful intimacy with one of the cleverest and most sympathetic of the Tronchin patients, Madame d'Épinay. Bright, black-eyed, about two-and-thirty years old, the ill-treated wife of a Farmer-General, the head of a salon, and the coquettish friend of Rousseau, Madame d'Épinay reflected in her sparkling little French mind the cleverness of a clever age, and, without ever saying or doing anything which gave substantial evidence of a superior intelligence, had a great deal of that vague quality which is now called culture. Voltaire delighted in her ; played with her ; laughed with her ; talked with her ; called her his Beautiful Philosopher ; wrote her innumerable little

notes about innumerable little nothings; welcomed
her constantly at Délices; and in January 1758 had
her to stay there for two or three days with her doctor.
Madame's complaint was of the nerves, and the very
best cure for that kind of disease is to be amused, as
everybody knows. So she was delighted to come to
Délices, where Madame Denis was 'entirely comic,'
and 'fit to make you die of laughing;' short, fat,
ugly; quite goodnatured; a liar, simply from habit;
clever enough to seem so without being so; always
gesticulating, talking, and arguing, especially when that
'Geneva' article—just now very much on the *tapis*—
was mentioned: when she threw her arms and hands
about, abused republics and their laws with a fine
generality, and was entirely absurd.

The little, shrewd, shallow visitor was not quite so
sure about the great Voltaire. He might have been
fifteen, he was so gay, lively, and inconsequent! But
then he had a number of quite childish prejudices; and
an air of laughing at everybody, even himself. Madame
d'Épinay was not at all certain she liked *that*. In
Paris she had been taken gravely as a clever woman.
The owl of Délices, looking at her through those little,
cynic, half-shut and all-seeing eyes of his, regarded her
as an ingenious little mechanical toy, whom it amused
him to set in motion. That he was very gallant with
her was true enough. But gallantry is hardly a
compliment to a woman who wants to be looked upon
as *savante*.

Madame d'Épinay was not the only one of Tronchin's patients who visited Voltaire. Almost all of
them came to peep at him. Here was the Marquise
de Muy—'a very little soul in a very little body much
debilitated by remedies,' said Tronchin—but the *chère*

amie of Choiseul the minister, and so to be cultivated by a far-seeing Voltaire.

Here, too, came the nephew and niece of de Tencin, the Montferrats—whom Voltaire received very kindly though he liked neither them nor their uncle.

Among neighbours who were not of Tronchin's ' cure,' Huber, celebrated as a painter and wit, had been one of the most constant visitors at Délices from the first, and was fast dropping into the position he never afterwards relinquished, of *ami de la maison.* Madame Tronchin—as plain and disagreeable as her husband was handsome and charming—was a guest too. ' Et que fait Madame Tronchin ? ' said someone one day to the sprightly Madame Cramer, herself a visitor ' Elle fait peur ' was the answer. Madame Cramer, as the wife of Gabriel Cramer, one of Voltaire's publishers, and as, in her own person, gay, naïve, and witty, was always a *persona grata* at Délices. Her husband and brother-in-law were as successful socially as in their business ; acted in their client's theatricals, and were delightfully good-looking and pleasant.

Voltaire's nearest neighbours at Délices, a Professor Pictet and his wife and daughter, were constantly of his parties. The daughter Charlotte was a gay and pretty little person, who had aroused the jealousy of Madame Denis by embroidering Voltaire a cap to wear on the top of the great peruke he always affected. Voltaire repaid the present by trying to find Mademoiselle what he always considered the *summum bonum,* a husband ; and Madame Denis was not precisely pleased when Charlotte married a handsome major of eight-and-twenty, for whom the foolish niece herself had had a *tendresse.* In 1757 a Baron Gleichen who wrote Souvenirs, also visited Délices.

It is no contradiction to say of Voltaire that he was all through his life both the most unsociable and the most sociable of men.

At Délices there were nearly always seven or eight persons to supper. On one occasion at least, the house was so full of guests for theatricals, that Madame Denis, having no bed, sat up all through the night playing cards. When he met his guests, no host could have been more agreeable than Voltaire. He had a hundred stories to tell. He made so many *mots* that half the *mots* of the eighteenth century have been fathered upon him by posterity. Sometimes he read aloud, or quoted from memory. He was inimitably gay, goodnatured, and courteous. One woman (who did not love him) said that he alone of his age knew how to speak to women as women like to be spoken to. That old quality which had made him revere the intellect of Madame du Châtelet made him respect now whatever was respectable in the intellect of his female companions. That surest sign of inferiority— to be afraid of mental superiority in the weaker sex— was certainly never to be found in Voltaire. If he toyed with a d'Épinay, it was because she was but a toy after all. He searched so diligently for cleverness in his nieces that he actually thought he had found it. Some of the best and most careful letters he ever wrote are those to Madame du Deffand—who was old, poor, blind—but splendidly intelligent.

He certainly took very good care during this social winter of 1757–58—as in all other social winters and summers—not to see too much of his guests, male or female. He worked twelve or fifteen hours a day; and generally kept his secretary writing part of the night as well. He never suffered himself to be

interrupted in the mornings; and was fond of saying
that he believed less in optimism at that time than at
any other.

As in the old days at Cirey, he was often too busy
to join his friends at dinner, and ate 'no matter what,
no matter when,' instead.

In January 1758 he migrated to Chêne, his newly
acquired house in Lausanne; and, in the formal phrase
of one of his guests there, by ' his wit and his philosophy, his table and his theatre, refined in a visible
degree the manners' of that town. That guest was
a certain fat-faced English youth called Gibbon, who,
having been led into Roman Catholicism at college, had
been sent to a minister at Lausanne to be led out of
it again—by Calvinism. In the intervals of falling in
love with the *beaux yeux* of a certain Mademoiselle
Curchod (afterwards Madame Necker), the self-satisfied
young gentleman found time during two winters to
pompously approve of M. de Voltaire in various *rôles*
—in ' Zaire,' 'Alzire,' 'Fanine,' and the 'Enfant
Prodigue,' played in that theatre in the granary of
Mon Repos. Gibbon wrote hereafter, in that solemn,
polished, rewritten, immortal autobiography, that
M. de Voltaire's 'declamation was fashioned to the
pomp and cadence of the old stage, and he expressed
the enthusiasm of poetry rather than the feelings of
Nature;' while Voltaire, in the gay impromptu of
his style, declared of himself he was ' the best old
fool in any troupe. I had rage and tears—attitudes
and a cap.' He added that Madame Denis was
splendid in the *rôle* of mothers; and a little later
quite seriously announced that though she had not *all*
the talents of Mademoiselle Clairon (!) she was much
more pathetic and human! The observing English

youth in the audience considered, on the contrary, that
the ' fat and ugly niece ' quite ruined the parts of ' the
young and fair,' and was not nearly clever enough to
make the spectators forget the defects of her age and
person.   When she was playing the heroine in ' Zaire '
she did herself say, hoping for a compliment, ' To take
such a part one oug̃ht to be young and beautiful ! ' and
a well-meaning *gauche* person replied ' Ah ! Madame,
you are a living proof to the contrary ' ! Uncle Voltaire
would have been very *vif*, no doubt, if he had known
of Gibbon's unflattering criticism on his niece.   As
it was, he was not too pleased on his own account
when this heavy young genius must needs, after having
heard them only twice, remember and repeat certain
lines which Voltaire had written in the first enthusiasm
of settling at Délices, and which (of course) contained
an allusion which would offend somebody.   M. de
Voltaire may be forgiven if he wished this blundering
Mr. Gibbon and his prodigious memory—in England.

In May, after the *ménage* Voltaire had moved back
to Délices, another visitor came to it. She was Madame
du Boccage, famous for her learning, as modest as she
was accomplished, and a woman quite after her host's
heart.   He put off a visit to the Elector Palatine to
receive her.   He gave up his bed to her as being the
most comfortable in the house ; and got up plays
for her benefit.   As for Madame, she found him
everything that was kind and agreeable, surrounded
by the best company—that is, the intellectually best
company—and always singing the praises of his rural
life. In fact, the only thing she had to complain of was
that he was so very hospitable that, like the nieces, she
was always having indigestion.   She left after a visit
of five days, and long corresponded with her host.

Between work and play, the Délices, Monrion, and Chêne, Voltaire had spent more than three years in Switzerland. That they had been happy enough to have made him altogether forget that a Paris, a Louis, and a Pompadour existed—and neglected him—is true enough. But he never forgot. If on one side of his character he was splendidly a philosopher, on the other he was always an ' old baby ' crying for the moon.

CHAPTER XXXI

'THE LITERARY WAR,' AND THE PURCHASE OF
FERNEY AND TOURNEY

ON June 21, 1758, Voltaire was writing delightedly to
his Angel to tell him that through the offices of
the pink-cheeked Babet, Louis XV. had been good
enough to give a formal permit for the greatest Frenchman of the age to retain his title of Gentleman-in-
Ordinary.

Frederick said, obviously enough, '*That* will not be
the patent that will immortalise you.' But the Gentleman himself was quite naïvely delighted. He had
always been miserable at Court and in Paris, but he
so much wished to feel he could go back there, if he
liked! He seems to have regarded this formal permission to keep his title as the thin end of the wedge.
But it was not.

'Let him stay where he is,' was the Bien-Aimé's
sole comment on Voltaire's exile. Marmontel suggested
to the Pompadour that it was for *her* to recall him; but
Madame could only reply, perhaps not untruthfully,
'Ah, no! it does not rest with me.'

In July Voltaire visited another Court, which had
never looked askance at him. He spent a fortnight
with his old friend the Elector Palatine, at Schwetzingen. The Elector had arranged some money matters

for Voltaire greatly to his advantage, so the visit was
one of gratitude.   It has no importance, except that
the story runs that here the guest was so engrossed by
a mysterious Something he was writing that he shut
himself up in his room for three days, only opening his
door to have food and coffee passed in.   On the fourth
day Madame Denis forced an entry.   Voltaire threw
a manuscript at her, saying, ' There, curious, that is
for you.'   It was the manuscript of ' Candide.'

The only drawback to the little anecdote is that
Madame Denis was not at Schwetzingen at all—having
been left behind at home with her sister, learning parts.
' Candide ' may have been written at the Elector's ;
but the time for its appearance was not yet ripe.

The summer of 1758 passed without much incident at Délices.   Elsewhere, there was only too
much.   The Seven Years' War—' the most hellish war
that ever was fought,' said Voltaire—raged with un-
abated fury.   Frederick had recovered Silesia by a great
victory at Leuthen on December 5, 1757, when he
beat an army of Austrians three times as large as his
own.   On August 25 of this 1758 he beat the Russians
at Zorndorf.   And then his evil star rose again.   On
October 14 he was taken by surprise and defeated with
great loss at Hochkirch.   But he suffered a still greater
loss that day in the death of Wilhelmina, Margravine
of Bayreuth.   Worthy in courage to be the sister of
Frederick, and in intelligence to be the friend of Voltaire, both men mourned her as she deserved to be
mourned.   Frederick wrote that there are some troubles
against which all stoicism and all the reasonings of the
philosophers are alike useless.   He was face to face
with such a trouble now.   Voltaire, at the King's
request, wrote to her memory an ode beginning ' Dear

and illustrious shade, soul brave and pure.' But it is
not always when the writer is himself most moved that
his writings are most moving. There are some griefs
which paralyse the brain and make every utterance
cold. Voltaire was no more satisfied with his poem
than was Frederick. He wrote another, which gave
the unhappy brother the first moment of comfort he
had had, he said, for five months. For a time their
mutual loss and grief drew the two friends together as
of yore. They put away their grievances. The ' old
need of communication, of finding each other again,
at least in thought,' was powerfully present. Over
Wilhelmina's grave they forgot for a while Maupertuis
and Akakia, Freytag and Frankfort.

Voltaire would have known himself forgotten and
obscure if he had ever lived six consecutive months in
his life without being plunged in some or other kind of
quarrel. That ' Geneva ' article was still a tree of discord bearing fruit. It will not be forgotten that to
oblige the most hospitable host in the world, d'Alembert had introduced into it a few remarks on the
beneficial effects of play-acting in general, and the
peculiar benefits which would accrue from it to Geneva
in particular.

In the October of 1758, from the depths of his forest
of Montmorency, Jean Jacques Rousseau—intense,
morbid, bitter, with so much amiss in himself that he
supposed all other men to be unreasonable and out of
gear—wrote to d'Alembert his famous ' Letter on
Plays.'

He had ' tried his wings ' against d'Alembert's friend,
in his reply to the ' Poem on the Disaster of Lisbon,'
and Voltaire had laughed at him gaily and civilly
enough. If Jean Jacques' impetuosity had ever waited

for reason, there would have seemed none now why he
should not enter the lists again, and tilt once more with
this active, mocking, sprightly little opponent, whom
everybody knew to have inspired d'Alembert's sentiments.

Jean Jacques, it is true, was a strange person to
write against plays. He had written them himself.
He had a genuine admiration for M. de Voltaire's. If
all plays were but like his! But, then, they are not.
So he brought to bear against them all the magic and
the fervour of his style, and flung on to four hundred
pages of paper his astonishing views not only on play-
acting, but on women, on love, and on literature.

No one reads 'La Lettre sur les Spectacles' now.
But everybody read it then, and though the stricter
of the educated Calvinists only coldly acknowledged
Rousseau as an ally, the common people heard him
gladly. The aristocracy of Geneva had enjoyed Voltaire's theatrical evenings too much to bring themselves
to disapprove of them.

From Paris the little frail d'Alembert 'deigned to
overwhelm that fool Jean Jacques with reasons,' in a
letter full of grave and stately irony. As for Voltaire,
he waited, as he could afford to wait. He had taught
some at least of the Genevans to be as 'mad for
theatres' as he was himself; and—he had 'Candide'
up his sleeve.

Running parallel with that controversy on theatres
was another. Of course Voltaire was in it—and the
soul of it. That goes without saying. He had been
but a short time settled in Lausanne, when one Saurin,
a poet-neighbour of his there, begged him to contradict
a certain history of Joseph Saurin, his father, as given
by Voltaire in a Catalogue of French Writers, added to

his 'Century of Louis XIV.' In that catalogue Voltaire had written of Joseph what not only he, but all the world, believed to be true. Joseph had been a pastor who, hating the life of Switzerland, had allowed himself to be very easily brought back by the preaching of Bossuet to Roman Catholicism and to France. But in France he was poor, and he hated poverty. Presently came rumours of robbery—of robbery he had committed in church. In a letter to a Lausanne pastor, Gonon, Saurin practically confessed to these robberies. This letter was published in the 'Swiss Mercury' of April 1736, and Saurin did not attempt to refute it. He had since died; and now, at his son's suggestion, this energetic Voltaire must needs unearth the whole story, and with a very rash good-nature, set to work to prove that that letter to Gonon was nothing but a forgery after all. He obtained a certificate from three of the Lausanne ministers who had been principally concerned in the affair, declaring that they had never seen the original. This certificate Voltaire put into the second edition of his 'Essay on the Manners and Mind of Nations.'

But in this October of 1758, some impertinent anonymous person reproduces the whole letter from Saurin to Gonon in another Swiss newspaper, and positively dares to doubt the authenticity of Voltaire's certificate from the three pastors.

On November 15 M. de Voltaire sits down and writes 'A Refutation of an Anonymous Article,' wherein he dwells on the useless danger and cruelty to an innocent family of attempting to convict their dead father of heinous crime.

The impertinent unknown (who turns out to be a pastor, Lervèche, who had long objected to Voltaire's theatricals at Mon Repos) writes a 'Reply' to the refutation.

Then who should appear on the scene but Grasset, the publisher, and Voltaire's enemy in the latest 'Pucelle' fracas. Grasset reprints the whole correspondence, and adds thereto Voltaire's 'Defence of Lord Bolingbroke,' and other little *brochures* from his pen most likely to give offence. The whole he calls 'The Literary War or Selected Pieces of M. de V——.'

Literary War indeed! says M. de V——; a literary libel! And do you know who this Grasset is? A scoundrel, a cheat, a common criminal! M. de V——, in short, not only loses his temper, but seems for the moment to lose sight of the Saurin cause, and to devote all his energies to getting Grasset punished. He appeals to all the local authorities. He 'knocks at every door,' and continues to knock till all are opened. He is once more his own angry, spry, busy little fighting self. Peaceful landowner and householder—all that is forgotten. Behold again the restless and terrible little enemy who fought Desfontaines.

Most people listened to him—and sympathised, if not for his rage with Grasset, at least for his zeal for the Saurins. There was but one man who threw on his enthusiasm the cold water of irony: and that was Haller, the great Swiss genius, *savant*, philosopher, linguist, botanist, poet, philologist. Until Voltaire settled at Délices, Haller had been *the* lion of the neighbourhood. Now he was only *a* lion. The situation hardly needs further explanation. Suffice it to say that Haller was as firm a Christian as Voltaire was a Deist: and that Haller had been a rather sarcastic spectator of M. de Voltaire's theatricals. All generous admiration was on the side of Voltaire, who always had plenty to spare for real talent such as Haller's.

When Haller returned a very cool answer to Voltaire's warm pleadings for the Saurins and suggested that to concern himself in so small a matter was beneath a great man's greatness, Voltaire waited a judicious ten days, and returned a mild and pleading answer.

To be beneath one's greatness to put wrong, right, and to clear a dead man's honour! Haller could have known the Voltaire who was to avenge Calas, very little. The correspondence continued. Haller was not a little stiff-necked and difficult : and Voltaire at once persistent and impulsive. Then Haller published the letters—in which he fancied he himself played a *beau rôle*—and made an enemy, though a very generous enemy, of Voltaire, for ever.

Grimm records how Voltaire one day asked an English visitor at Ferney, from whence he had come.

' From Mr. Haller's.'

' He is a great man,' cried Voltaire, ' a great poet, a great naturalist, a great philosopher—almost a universal genius in fact.'

' What you say, Sir, is the more admirable,' replied the Englishman, ' because Mr. Haller does not do you the same justice.'

' Ah ! ' said Voltaire, ' perhaps we are both mistaken.'

A like interview is also described as taking place between Voltaire and Casanova in 1760. Casanova stayed with Haller before he went to visit Voltaire ; and on leaving his first host observed how much he was looking forward to becoming acquainted with his second.

'Ah!' replied Haller, 'many persons, contrary to physical laws, have found M. de Voltaire greater when seen at a distance.'

Voltaire had presently the satisfaction of hearing that the sale of ' The Literary War ' was prohibited, and of seeing Grasset severely censured ; though he would have liked better to see him banished.

The Saurin-Grasset-Haller affair had one important influence upon Voltaire. It disgusted him with Lausanne.

In this autumn of 1758 Voltaire wrote to a very old friend, King Stanislas, saying that he had fifty thousand francs which he should like to invest in an estate in Lorraine—that he might not die on the borders of Lake Leman. Cautious Stanislas consulted the French Government. Would this meet its views ? Choiseul, representing it, as Babet's successor, replied, ' You know Voltaire well enough to decide for yourself.'

So on some date, not before November 20, 1758, Bettinelli—Italian, Jesuit, poet, and literary man— arrived at Délices as the envoy of Stanislas, sent to accept the proposed investment and tell Voltaire how delighted Stanislas would be to have him as a neighbour.

Voltaire was in the garden, gardening, when Bettinelli came, and presented an extraordinary appearance in a long pelisse, a black velvet cap, and a peruke which covered almost all his face except the nose and chin, which by now nearly met. He had a stick in his hand which had a weeding fork at one end and a pruning hook at the other ; and observed, when he saw Bettinelli, that his crop from his garden was much more abundant 'than from that I sow in my books for the good of mankind.'

The pair talked on all kinds of subjects. Bettinelli, who was not a little afraid of his host's cynic wit, nervously remarked the brilliant flash of the eyes and the sarcastic, mobile lips. He thought his host spoke slowly because he was preparing something caustic to say next; but the truth was the host had already lost most of his teeth and spoke slowly in order to be understood. The pair discussed all kinds of subjects— Italy, the Inquisition, slavery, Tasso, Ariosto, Tronchin, Bettinelli's poetry, and the famous book 'On the Mind,' which Voltaire sharply criticised; and whose author, Helvétius, he summed up 'as a fool who wanted to be a philosopher with courtiers and a courtier with philosophers.'

They spoke of Madame du Châtelet. In Voltaire's rooms were several pictures of the dead woman. 'Here is my immortal Émilie,' he said. Bettinelli records that she was the only person of whom he heard Voltaire speak with an unchanging admiration and enthusiasm. Before Bettinelli left he had a little interview with Dr. Tronchin, who congratulated him on having found Voltaire in a mood unusually serene and equable. In fact, the visit had been wholly a success—but for one thing. When Bettinelli handed Voltaire Stanislas's acceptance of his proposal to live in Lorraine, Voltaire took it, saying that he had just bought a little estate near Délices, where he intended to live out the rest of his life. On November 18 Voltaire had dated his first letter from Ferney. Bettinelli was too late.

Since the middle of this September 1758 Voltaire had been busy negotiating with a M. de Boisy for

the purchase of Ferney—formerly spelt Fernex—and
with a Président de Brosses for the life lease of
Tourney or Tournay.

There were reasons which made both estates
peculiarly suitable to a Voltaire. Ferney was in
France, in Burgundy, in the district of Gex; but it
was also on the frontier of Switzerland, only three and
a half miles from Geneva. Here one could laugh
at those straitlaced Genevans as freely as if the three
miles were three hundred; and if one offended France,
which was only a question of time, what more simple
than to drive into Geneva? Then, too, Ferney, lying
on the north shore of Lake Leman, almost joined
the Délices. Voltaire at first thoughtit would be a
sort of supplement to his first Swiss home. But,
as all the world knows, Ferney soon supplanted Délices
in its master's affections, and became the literary
capital of Europe.

There were equally strong reasons for buying
Tourney. It was in France, in Burgundy, as Ferney
was; and it was under the direction of a foreign prelate,
the Bishop of Annecy. It was on the very frontier
of the Swiss canton of Berne; and at the very gates
of that rich, powerful, intellectual Geneva, and yet
entirely independent of its prim Calvinistic laws.
From Tourney one could thus 'tease Geneva and
caress Paris; brave orders and *lettres de cachet*; have
one's works printed without the King's permission,
and get away in the twinkling of an eye from all
prosecutions.' Admirable for a Voltaire, this. Then,
too, if Ferney was a supplement to Délices—Tourney
was a prolongation of Ferney. Add to this, with the
life lease of Tourney went the title of Lord and Count
of Tourney. Was not this something to the man who

clung so tightly to the empty honour of Gentleman-
in-Ordinary ?   It was very much.   Voltaire took an
enormous pleasure in calling the attention of his
correspondents to his new designation ; and presently
signed himself, with a solemn pride and joy, 'Gentleman-in-Ordinary to the King of France and Count
of Tourney.' If Tourney was nothing in the world
but a tumbledown old country house with a ruined
farm attached to it—what difference did that make?
What was a Gentleman-in-Ordinary ?   An exile from
France the French King would have none of.   The
same sort of pleasure which he received from fine
clothes was conveyed to Voltaire by fine titles.   The
characteristic is not a grand or ennobling one ; but
it is delightfully human.

By September, then, he had these two estates in
view—' Tourney for the title, and Ferney for the land :
Ferney for a perpetuity, and Tourney only for life.'
There was not much trouble with M. de Boisy over
Ferney.   It was bought for 24,000 écus in the name of
Madame Denis, who was to inherit it after her uncle's
death.   The contract for the purchase was not actually
signed until February 9, 1759 ; but in the middle of
September 1758 Voltaire had made a kind of state
entrance into the parish, accompanied by Madame
Denis.   Madame Denis was in her very best clothes,
with all the diamonds the *ménage* Voltaire could produce.   As for Uncle Voltaire himself, he, in spite of
the fact that the weather was still very warm, enjoyed
himself vastly in crimson velvet trimmed with ermine.
The pair drove in the smartest carriage, and attended
High Mass—' droned out—false '—at the parish church,
during which the enthusiastic future tenants of the
proprietor of Ferney thumped on tin boxes to repre-

sent a welcome of cannon !   That little, lively, black-
eyed Frenchwoman, Madame d'Épinay, has left a
vivacious record of the day.   If she saw it as comic,
Voltaire did not.   Once more he justified Tronchin's
appellation for him, ' an old baby,' and enjoyed himself
like a schoolboy.

But if the Ferney negotiations had been simple,
not so the Tourney.

Président de Brosses and Voltaire were soon engaged
in a vast correspondence.   A whole book has been
written on their relations with each other.   There is no
doubt in fact that over Tourney Voltaire showed a
great deal of that spirit which people call business
capacity in themselves and meanness in others.

On September 9 he made an offer to de Brosses for
the life lease of the little estate.   De Brosses said the
offer was insufficient.   After a good deal of trouble
and haggling over small items on both sides, Voltaire
finally bought the life lease of Tourney (with all
seigneurial rights and that delightful title included) for
35,600 livres.   He undertook to make certain alterations and repairs.   A herd of cattle was included in
his purchase.   Although he was not to enter into his
life tenancy until February 22, 1759, the agreement is
dated December 11, 1758 ; and on December 24 he
made his state entrance into Tourney, as three months
before he had into Ferney.

The second occasion was much the more magnificent of the two.   Madame de Fontaine was with him
this time, as well as Madame Denis.   Both were in
diamonds.   Here, too, was their brother Mignot, the
abbé ; also *tout paré*.   The village girls handed the
ladies baskets of flowers and oranges.   The artillery
had come from Geneva, so there was no need to thump

upon tin boxes. There were drums, fifes, cannon : all
the music of flattery. The spectators were not only
peasants, as they had been at Ferney, but all the polite
persons of the neighbourhood. There was a splendid
banquet, given by the outgoing tenant of Tourney, and
served by the innkeeper of a neighbouring village.
The curé made M. de Voltaire a beautiful address.
M. de Voltaire was wholly delighted—'very gay and
content.' He answered quite *en grand seigneur*, and
as was expected of him, 'Ask anything you like for
the good of your parish and I will give it you.' Lord
and Count of Tourney ! This most impressionable of
men lived up to the part immediately. He wrote an
enthusiastic account of the proceedings to de Brosses
on the very same day, when he was back again at
Délices. 'I made my entrance like Sancho Panza
into his island. Only his paunch was wanting to me.'
'My subjects frightened my horses with musketry and
torpedoes.' The banquet (served by the native innkeeper) 'was a magnificent repast in the style of those
of Horace and Boileau.' In short, the Lord of Tourney
saw his new estates all *couleur de rose*, or almost all.
It is infinitely characteristic that in this very letter he
went on to plead for the restitution of certain tithes to
the poor of Ferney, which they had enjoyed for a century, and of which Ancian, the curé of the neighbouring parish of Moens, 'the most abominable pettifogger
in the district,' had deprived them, further 'putting
them to fifteen hundred francs of law expenses before
they knew it.' Voltaire had also appealed passionately
to the Bishop of Annecy ; and did at last obtain his
suit, but only after he had paid a very large sum out of
his own pocket.

He wrote also to Theriot that evening—tired, no

doubt, but too charmed to remember it. 'You are mistaken, my old friend; I have four paws instead of two. One paw in Lausanne, in a very pretty house for the winter; one paw at Délices, near Geneva, where good company comes to see me—those are the front paws. The back are at Ferney, and in the county'—a county, if you please, and not merely an estate—'of Tourney.'

He went on to point out the advantages of Ferney —how there was plenty of land and wood for the rebuilding operations he already had in hand; how he could get marble by the lake; how the extensive estates would really not be so costly after all. For himself, he would like to live on them quite simply. But my niece, you know—that victim of Frankfort— *she* merits luxury and indulgences. He had already set the peasants to work to mend the neglected roads about Ferney; so that in a month or two he was able to say truthfully that they had earned more in that time than formerly they had been able to do in a year. He had already chartered more than a hundred workmen, that his rebuilding and gardening operations might be put in hand at once.

The year closed full of the happiest expectations. Despite gala entrances to new estates, Madame Denis, indeed, complained that the winter of 1758–59 was dull. It was all spent at Délices: as being more out of the way of the troubling of Grassets and Hallers, than Monrion. True, plenty of visitors came from Lausanne; but there were not many who came to sleep and stay. True, too, the Délices troupe had privately acted ('the only pleasure I have in this country,' Madame Denis wrote dismally) 'Aménaïde,' which was to have its name changed to 'Tancred' later; and as 'Tancred' become immortal. But Madame Denis apparently was suffering from an indigestion which Tronchin could not cure, for she spoke slightingly of that good physician, and discontentedly of life in general. Uncle Voltaire was so absurdly busy! Trying to do a hundred things at once, and invincibly obstinate. 'It is the only sign of old age he has.' 'If I were not so sensitive I should be very happy.' When a lady complains she is sensitive, she always means that she is cross and offended. Uncle Voltaire had shown his invincible obstinacy by persisting in going on with that Saurin controversy when his niece thought he had very much better leave it alone.

Then, too, he was getting more and more engrossed every day with pulling down and putting up, with barns, farms, oxen, sheep, horses; and 'adored the country even in winter,' while Louise, as he said himself, was 'very difficult to reduce to the *rôle* of Ceres, of Pomona, and of Flora, and would much rather have been Thalia in Paris.' But when her uncle found Tourney and Ferney, he found a better life than he had ever known; and the dearest and crossest of nieces would not make him relinquish it. The year 1759 was still new-born when he was writing, not once but many times, that he was wonderfully well and happy, stronger and better than he had ever been; that he had only really lived since the day he chose his retreat; that he was so infinitely content 'that if I dared I should think myself wise.'

'Such is my life, Madame, tranquil and occupied, full and philosophic.' 'I love to plant, I love to build, and so satisfy the only tastes which gratify old age.'

'This kind of life makes one want to live.' 'Property in paper depends upon fortune; property in land depends only upon God.'

'To have found the secret of being independent in France is more than to have written the "Henriade."'

CHAPTER XXXII

FERNEY

FERNEY, as has been said, stood on the north shore of Lake Leman, in the district of Gex, three and a half miles from Geneva and almost joining Délices. The village to which it belonged, also called Ferney, was really nothing but a mean hamlet with forty or fifty miserable inhabitants, ' devoured by poverty, scurvy, and tax-gatherers.' A very ugly little church stood much too near the house.

That house, when Voltaire bought it, was very old, tumbledown, and totally inadequate to his requirements. The entrance was through two towers connected by a drawbridge. If it was picturesque, it was certainly not comfortable. When Voltaire had rebuilt it, it was certainly comfortable, and decidedly unpicturesque.

He had begun that rebuilding three months before the deed of purchase was signed. By December 6, 1758, he had twenty masons at work. By the 24th, what he might well have cynically called his *optimism* led him to think it ' a pretty house enough.' By June 1759 it was ' a charming château in the Italian style.'

By July it was ' of the Doric order. It will last a thousand years.'

THE CHÂTEAU OF FERNEY.

From an Engraving.

By November it was 'a piece of architecture which would have admirers even in Italy.' While by the March of 1761 it had grown—at any rate in its master's fancy—into 'a superb château.'

There have not been wanting to Voltaire enemies to argue persistently and vociferously that Ferney was not at all what he represented it; and that all his geese were swans. They were. Ferney at its best and completest was never anything but a plain, sensible, commodious country house. It had neither wings nor decoration; nor any architectural merit, except that its ugliness was simple and not elaborate. Voltaire was his own architect; and owned quite frankly that he knew nothing at all about architecture. The man who had travelled through Holland, Belgium, and Prussia without once stepping out of his postchaise to look at a famous picture, or an immortal sculpture, or the 'frozen music' of a grand cathedral, had as little feeling for art as for nature.

He thought Ferney a superb château because it was *his* château. Just as he was devoted to flowers and gardens, when they were *his* flowers and *his* gardens.

It is certainly not the best way of loving art or nature, but it is the only way of many persons besides Voltaire. And, after all, that comfortable feeling of landed-proprietorship, that honest pride in his cows and his sheep, his bees and his silkworms, sits pleasantly enough on this withered cynic of sixty-five; and makes him at once more human, more sympathetic—the same flesh and blood as the simple and ordinary.

He had, as he said, plenty of wood and stone for his building operations on the premises—'oak enough to be useful to our navy, if we had one ; ' and stone, which the architect thought very good, and which turned out to be very bad. He said gaily that when the house was finished he should write on the wall ' Voltaire fecit ' ; and that posterity would take him for a famous architect. As for that marble of which he had talked largely as being brought up by the lake, the man who declared that he preferred a good English book to a hundred thousand pillars of it, did not trouble to obtain much or to make an elaborate use of what he did obtain. He wanted the house ' agreeable and use-ful,' and he had it. There was a fine view from it ; though not so fine as it might have been, for it faced the high road. Still, as its happy master said, it was situated in the most smiling country in Europe ; at its feet the lake gleamed and sparkled ; and beyond the warm and gorgeous luxuriance of its perfect gardens could be seen, in dazzling contrast, the eternal snows of Mont Blanc.

When the rebuilding was finished the house was looked at without prejudice, the well-appointed home of a well-to-do *bourgeois gentilhomme*—with an un-usual love for literature. There was an ordinary hall with a stone staircase on the left which led up to the fourteen guest-rooms, all comfortably furnished, said one of those guests, who was an Englishman and had been used to solid English comfort at home. Here and there were some good pictures—or copies of good pictures—copies, most likely, since Voltaire, hardly knowing the difference, would be apt to reflect that a copy would do as well as an original, and be much cheaper. A Venus after Paul Veronese and a Flora after Guido Reni, some of the visitors declared genuine ; and some as hotly pronounced

spurious. Wagnière, that Genevan boy who lived to
write memoirs like the other secretaries, stated that
his master had about twenty valuable pictures in all;
and some good busts.   There were various family
portraits about the house : one of Madame Denis; one
of Voltaire's young mother; and, soon, a likeness of
Madame de Pompadour painted by herself, and by
herself given to Voltaire.   In Madame Denis's room
presently there was a portrait of Catherine, Empress
of Russia, embroidered in silk ; and a marble statue of
Voltaire.   There was a copy of this statue, or his bust
in plaster, in almost every room in the house.

The library was simple, and, for Voltaire, small.
Dr. Burney, the father of Fanny, who saw it in 1770,
describes it as ' not very large but well filled,' and says
it contained ' a whole-length figure in marble ' of its
master ' recumbent, in one of the windows.'   At
Voltaire's death it contained only 6,210 volumes.   But
almost every one had on its margin copious notes in
that fine, neat little handwriting.   Six thousand
volumes annotated by a Voltaire!   His sarcasm
should have made the dullest ones amusing; and his
relentless logic the obscurest ones clear.   There were a
great many volumes of history and theology; dictionaries in every language ; all the Italian poets ; and all
the English philosophers.   The Comte de Maistre,
who saw this library after Voltaire's death when it
had been bought by Catherine the Great, wondered at
the ' extreme mediocrity ' of the books.   By this he
explained himself to mean that there were no rare old
editions ; and no sumptuous bindings, which the Count
took as a sign that Voltaire was ' a stranger to all profound literature.'   It *was* a sign that Voltaire read to
act ; that books were his tools, not his ornaments;

that he loved literature, not as a sensuous delight, but as the lever that was to turn the world. 'A few books, very much marked.' That library was infinitely characteristic of the man who was doer, not dreamer; of the mind to which every poet, every philosopher, every scientist acted as a spur to new practical effort; of the man who was to go down the ages not as playwright, or verse-maker, but as he who 'conquered the intellect of France, for the Revolution.'

The *salle à manger* was distinguished only by a most extraordinary and very bad allegorical picture, called 'The Temple of Memory,' in which a Glory, with her hair dressed much *à la mode*, was presenting Voltaire (who was surrounded with a halo like a saint) to the God of Poetry, who was getting out of his chariot with a crown in his hand. On one side of the picture appeared busts of Euripides, Sophocles, Racine, Corneille, and other great men; on the opposite side were caricatures of Fréron and Desfontaines, who were being most satisfactorily kicked by Furies. Voltaire laughed at, and enjoyed immensely, this part of the picture while he was at meals. The artist was Alix, a native of Ferney, and soon an *habitué* at the château. It was fortunate for him that Voltaire was so much better a friend than he was a judge of art.

His bedroom and salon were both small rooms. The salon, entered by folding doors, contained the master's bust above the stove, six or seven pictures, 'more or less good,' a portrait of Madame du Châtelet, and casts of Newton and Locke. One of the pictures, after Boucher, represented a hunting scene. There were ten tapestry armchairs, and a table of very common varnished marble. French windows and a glass door led into the garden.

Voltaire's bedroom was principally distinguished by a neatness, cleanness, and simplicity natural to him, but very unusual in his day. The roughly carved deal bedstead one visitor regretfully regarded as 'almost mean.' It was the fashion then to spend the night in what looked like a large heavily curtained coffin. Voltaire—to the melancholy vexation of the fashionable—seems to have dispensed with most of the curtains, but could not escape a huge baldachino over his head. Inside it, hung a very bad pastel portrait of Lekain; and a candelabra containing three wax candles, so that he could see to read. On either side of the bed hung portraits of Frederick the Great, of Voltaire himself, and of Madame du Châtelet. Placed between the door and the only window were five or six other engraved portraits, all in very simple black frames. The bed hangings and the four armchairs were upholstered alike in pale blue damask.

The room contained five desks. On each were notes for the various subjects on which the author was working : this desk had notes for a play; this, for a treatise on philosophy ; a third for a *brochure* on science ; and so on. All were exquisitely neat and orderly : every paper in its right place. The writing-chair was of cane, with a cover on it to match the bed curtains. Later on, Voltaire had a second writing-chair made, which he used much in the last few years of his life : one of its arms formed a desk, and the other a little table with drawers; and both were revolving.

Just below the master's bedroom was Wagnière's, so that if Voltaire knocked on the floor during the night the servant could hear him. That he did so knock, pretty often, rests on the rueful testimony of Wagnière himself.

Quite close to the house stood a little marble bath-room with hot and cold water laid on. It was a very unusual luxury in those times, and considered a highly unnecessary one. It is pleasant to a century much more particular in such matters than the eighteenth to reflect that Voltaire was always personally cleanly and tidy to an extent which his contemporaries considered ridiculous. That fine and dirty age could hardly for-give his insisting on his ancient perukes and queer old gardening clothes being kept as trim and well brushed as if they were new and grand. His passion for soap and water was one of the complaints his enemies in Prussia had brought against him. Wagnière records that his master was 'scrupulously clean,' and also his love of washing his eyes in pure cold water. Doubtless the habit preserved them, in spite of the inordinate amount of work they had to do. To the day of his death they never needed spectacles.

Most of the visitors comment on the well-kept appearance of the house ; though one, Lady Craven, Margravine of Anspach, said the *salle à manger* was generally dirty and the servants' liveries soiled. It was at Ferney as it had been at Cirey. The master was particular, but the mistress was not. If Madame du Châtelet had been engrossed with science, Madame Denis was engrossed with amusement. Her extrava-gance and bad household management in that respect were often the cause of disagreements between her uncle and herself. And, that 'fat pig, who says it is too hot to write a letter,' as Voltaire once described his niece to Madame d'Épinay, was the sort of person who thought no trouble too great for pleasure, but any trouble too great for duty.

It is significant that when she went to Paris in 1768 her uncle seized the opportunity of having Ferney thoroughly cleaned from top to bottom.

It is said that when he caught sight of cob-webs by the pillars and porticoes of the house, which the servants had neglected to remove, he used to vigorously flick a whip, crying out, 'À la chasse ! à la chasse ! ' and the whole household, including the guests, had to join in the spider hunt.

He had in his daily employ sixty or seventy persons, and sometimes more. Five servants usually waited at table, of whom three were in livery. Martin Sherlock, the Englishman, says that the dinner consisted of two courses and was eaten off silver plates with the host's coat of arms on them ; while at the dessert the spoons, forks, and blades of the knives were of silver-gilt ; and adds that no strange servant was ever allowed to officiate at meals. Wagnière records how two of the household having robbed their master, the police got wind of the matter ; and Voltaire bade him go and warn the delinquents to fly immediately, 'for if they are arrested I shall not be able to save them from hanging.' He also sent them some money for the journey. It is pleasant to learn that the hearts of the culprits were touched by this generous kindness, and that, having escaped, they lived honest lives.

It was a rule at Ferney that all peasants who came to the house should have a good dinner and twenty-four sous given them before they pursued their way.

' Good to all about him,' was the Prince de Ligne's description of Voltaire. It was not an extravagant one.

If the house at Ferney was simple and comfortable rather than magnificent, the grounds were on a far more elaborate scale. There was enough land to grow wheat, hay, and straw. There were poultry yards and sheepfolds; an orchard watered by a stream; meadows, storehouses, and an immense barn which stabled fifty cows with their calves and served as a granary, and of which its master was intensely proud.

Then, too, there were farms which Voltaire managed himself, and so made lucrative. He was pleased to say, with a twinkle in his eye, that he also did everything in the garden—the gardener was '*si bête*.' That he had a field which was always called Voltaire's field, because he cultivated it entirely with his own hands, is certainly true. Before long he had four or five hundred beehives; turkeys and silkworms; and a breeding stable for horses, transferred from the Délices. He was not a little delighted when, in this May of 1759, the Marquis de Voyer, steward of King Louis' stables, made him a present of a fine stallion. As if he had not hobbies enough, he soon became an enthusiastic tree-planter—begging all his friends to follow his example—and sending wagons all the way to Lyons for loads of young trees for his park.

After a while that park stretched in three miles of circuit round the house, and included a splendid avenue of oaks, lindens, and poplars. In the garden were sunny walls for peaches; vines, lawns, and flowers. It was laid out with a charming *imprévu* and irregularity, most unfashionable in that formal day. Voltaire had always a 'tender recollection of the banks of the Thames,' and made his garden as English as he could. It is indeed melancholy to note that artificial water and prim terraces were soon introduced to spoil—though their master thought they improved—its luxuriant irregularity ; and that objects like lightning conductors, and fountains presided over by plaster nymphs, were not considered the least out of keeping with Nature by their lord and master. Near his silkworm house a thick linden tree with overhanging branches formed what was called Voltaire's study, and there he wrote verses ' for recreation.' Nature certainly never inspired any of *them*. Now and again there came, it is true, even to this most typical son of the most artificial of all centuries, as he cultivated his field, or pruned and weeded in his garden, such reflections as might have fallen from the lips of his great opposite, Rousseau : ' I have only done one sensible thing in my life—to cultivate the ground. He who clears a field renders a better service to humankind than all the scribblers in Europe.'

' You have done a great work for posterity,' a friend said to him one day.

' Yes, Madame. I have planted four thousand feet of trees in my park.'

No more incongruous picture could be painted than that of this ' withering cynic,' this world-famous hewer, hacker, and uprooter in his old grey shoes and stockings, a long vest to his knees, little black velvet cap and great drooping peruke, tranquilly directing, cultivating, sowing, ' planting walnut and chestnut trees upon which I shall never see walnuts or chestnuts,' consoling himself for the toads in his garden by the reflection that ' they do not prevent the nightingales from singing : ' and prophesying that his destiny would be ' to end between a seedlip, cows, and Genevans.'

For the time this country life was his element not

the less. He wrote that it was, to Madame du
Deffand, a dozen times. True, he had taken to it late.
But perhaps always, deep down in him, undeveloped,
stifled by Paris and by the burning needs of humanity,
had been the peaceful primæval tastes. Cirey had
roused them. Délices had nourished them : and
Ferney and Tourney confirmed them.

Tourney had given its master a title, but at first
it gave him nothing else. It was a county *pour
rire,* 'the land in a bad state,' 'a garden where
there was nothing but snails and moles, vines without
grapes, fields without corn, and sheds without cows,'
and 'a house in ruins.' Still, the land could be made
fertile ; and the house, if it *was* in ruins, boasted an
admirable view, and was but 'a quarter of a league'
from Geneva.

By February 1759 fifty workmen were putting it
to rights ; and by November the Count of Tourney
could say that he had planted hundreds of trees in the
garden, and used more powder (in rock-blasting) than
at the siege of a town. Everything needed repairing,
he added—fields, roads, granaries, wine-presses—and
everything was being repaired.

As at Ferney and Délices, the master personally
supervised every detail ; and so made his farms, his
nurseries, his bees, his silkworms, all pay.

In the house at Tourney he quickly made a theatre-
room. If some of the guests were disposed to laugh at
a stage which held nine persons in a semicircle with
difficulty, and to think the green and gold decorations
tawdry, Voltaire adored that 'theatre of Punchinello'
as a child adores a new toy. 'A little green and gold
theatre,' 'the prettiest and smallest possible '—he
alludes to it in his letters a hundred times. From

the September of 1760 he was anxious to transfer it
to Ferney. But meanwhile he loved it where and as
it was. Tourney also was useful to provide accommodation for the servants of the innumerable guests who
came to stay at Ferney.

No idea of Voltaire's life there could be given
without mention of that incessant stream of visitors
of all nations and languages which flowed through it,
almost without pause, for twenty years. Half the
genius—and but too many of the fools—of Europe
came to worship at the shrine of the prophet of this
literary Mecca.

As prim Geneva shut its gates at nightfall, everyone who came to sup with M. de Voltaire had to stay
all night in his house. Ferney had no inn. After
fourteen years of his life there, Voltaire might well say
that he had been the hotelkeeper of Europe. He told
Madame du Deffand, as early as 1763, that he had
entertained four hundred English people, of whom not
one ever after gave him a thought.

Too many of his guests, indeed, were not merely
self-invited : but remained at Ferney with such per-
sistency that their unhappy host would sometimes
retire to bed and say he was dying, to get rid of them.
One caller, who had received a message to this effect,
returned the next day. 'Tell him I am dying again.
And if he comes any more, say I am dead and
buried.'

Another visitor, when told Voltaire was ill, shrewdly
replied that he was a doctor and should like to feel
his pulse. When Voltaire sent down a message to say
he was dead, the visitor replied, 'Then I will bury
him. In my profession I am used to burying people.'
His humour appealed to Voltaire's. He was admitted.

' You seem to take me for some curious animal,' said Voltaire.

' Yes, Monsieur, for the Phœnix.'

' Very well: the charge to see me is twelve sous.'

' Here are twenty-four,' said the visitor. ' I will come again to-morrow.'

He did, and on many to-morrows: and was received as a friend.

But all the importunate were not so clever, and their fulsome flattery was odious to the man who loved it daintily dressed.

' Sir, when I see you, I see the great candle that lights the world.'

' Quick, Madame Denis,' cried Voltaire. ' A pair of snuffers ! '

One persistent woman tried to effect an entry by saying that she was the niece of Terrai, the last, and not the least corrupt, of Louis XV.'s finance ministers.

Voltaire sent out a message. ' Tell her I have only one tooth left, and I am keeping that for her uncle.'

The Abbé Coyer, on his arrival, calmly announced that he was going to stay six weeks.

' In what respect, my dear Abbé, are you unlike " Don Quixote " ?   He took the inns for châteaux, and you take the châteaux for inns.'

Coyer left early the next day.

Still, in spite of such rebuffs, the visitors were incessant.

One said that he could not recollect there being *more* than sixty to eighty people at supper after theatricals.   Voltaire himself said there were constantly fifty to a hundred.

Many visitors stayed for weeks; many for months; some for years.

Madame de Fontaine, with her lover *en train*, could come when she chose—and she often chose. Mignot came when *he* liked. Great-nephew d'Hornoy was a constant visitor.

At different times there were two adopted daughters and two Jesuit priests living in the house. One relative, as will be seen, was at Ferney for a decade—completely paralysed. And hanging about the house were generally a trio or a quartette of gentlemen ne'er-do-weels, who sometimes copied their host's manuscripts, and sometimes stole them.

In the midst of such a household Voltaire pursued his way and his life's work, wonderfully methodically and equably. It was his custom to stay in bed till eleven o'clock, or later. There he read or wrote; or dictated to his secretaries with a distressing rapidity. Sometimes he was reading to himself at the same time. About eleven, a few of his guests would come up and pay him a brief visit.

The rest of the morning he spent in the gardens and farms, superintending and giving orders. In earlier years, he dined with his house party—in an undress, for which he always apologised and which he never changed. Later on, he always dined alone. After dinner he would go into the salon and talk for a little with his guests. The whole of the rest of the afternoon and evening until supper-time he spent in study: in which he never allowed himself to be interrupted. One at least of his guests complained that his only fault was to be '*fort renfermé.*'

At supper he appeared in as lively spirits as a schoolboy set free from school. It was the time for

recreation : and a well-earned recreation too. He led
his guests to talk on such subjects as pleased them.
When a discussion grew serious, he would listen without
saying a word, with his head bent forward. Then,
when his friends had adduced their arguments, he advanced his own, in perfect order and clearness, and yet
with an extraordinary force and vehemence. He was
seldom his best before a large company, especially of the
kind that had come, as he said, ' to see the rhinoceros.'
But with a few kindred spirits he was as brilliant
as he had been twenty years before over the supper
table at Cirey. At Ferney he must have missed indeed
that woman who, having flung off her mantle of science
and erudition, became socially what socially all women
should be—an inspirer, a sympathiser, a magnet to
draw out men's wit—a sorceress who talked so well that
she made her companions feel not how clever she was,
but how clever they were.

Niece Denis was certainly the most goodnatured of
hostesses—if she was *gaupe*, as Madame du Deffand
said—and was grateful to her uncle's guests for miti-
gating the ennui of a country life. She was useful too.
When Voltaire was tired or bored, he could retire
directly after supper to that invariable refuge, bed ;
and leave his niece to act with his visitors. When
he was not bored and there were no theatricals, he
sometimes read aloud a canto of the ' Pucelle ' as
in old times ; or quoted poetry—any but his own,
which he never could recollect ; or talked theatres,
or played chess. It was the only game in which he
indulged, and he was a little ashamed of it. Games
are so idle !

When he went to bed he started work afresh. It
was his only intemperance. If he kept an abundant

table for his guests, he was still infinitely frugal himself. His *déjeuner* consisted only of coffee, with cream ; his supper, of eggs, although there was always a chicken ready for him in case he fancied it. He drank a little burgundy, and owned to a weakness for lentils. Of coffee, in which he had indulged freely in youth, he now took only a few cups a day. He had a habit of ignoring meals altogether when he was busy— a little idiosyncrasy somewhat trying to his secretaries. Wagnière also complained that his master was too sparing in sleep ; and called him up from that room below, several times in the night, to assist him in his literary work. When he had a play on hand he was ' in a fever.'

Many of the visitors who stayed at Ferney have left an account of their life there. Though the accounts always graphically portray the character of the writers, they sketch much less vividly the portrait of Voltaire. But from such accounts—all taken together, and corrected by each other from Voltaire's own descriptions, from Wagnière's and from Madame Denis's—Ferney, and the life there, were as nearly as possible what has been depicted. Changes in habits are inevitable in twenty years. Differing accounts may all be true—at different times. Feverishly busy for Voltaire, idle and sociable for Madame Denis ; she carried along by that unceasing stream of guests, and he watching it, half amused and half bored, from his own firm mooring of a great life's work—that was Ferney for its master and mistress from 1758 until 1778. They did not regularly take up their abode there until 1760. They did not give up Délices altogether until 1765. But from the autumn of 1758 Ferney was their real home, the home of Voltaire's heart ; inextricably associated with him by his friends and his enemies ; the subject of a thousand scandals, and of most beautiful imaginative descriptions. Nearly all great men have had one place dedicated to them—Florence to Dante ; Corsica to Napoleon ; Stratford to Shakespeare ; Weimar to Goethe ; and Ferney to Voltaire.

CHAPTER XXXIII

'CANDIDE,' AND 'ÉCRASEZ L'INFÂME'

On February 10, 1759, Voltaire's 'Natural Law,'
Helvétius's book 'On the Mind,' and six others were
publicly burnt in Paris by the hangman.

In March the 'Encyclopædia' was suspended.

'Natural Law,' it will be remembered, was nothing
but a seeking for an answer to that everlasting question
'What is truth?'

'On the Mind' was the naïve expression of the
materialism of the wittiest freethinker in Paris, Helvétius, *maître d'hôtel* to the Queen and Farmer-General.
But the Dauphin showed it to his mother, and it
received the compliment of burning. 'What a fuss
about an omelette!' said Voltaire contemptuously.
The destruction of his own 'Natural Law' disturbed
him as little. 'Burn a good book, and the cinders will
spring up and strike your face' was one of his own
axioms. From the flames of its funeral pyre, the thing
would rise a phœnix gifted with immortal life and
fame.

But the suspension of the 'Encyclopædia' hit him
hard.

Since the attempted assassination of the King by
Damiens the laws against the freedom of the press had
been growing daily more severe. True, the poor creature

had had a Bible in his pocket, but the churchmen argued somehow that it was the New Learning which had guided the dagger.   Then France had had reverses in war.   Suppose these misfortunes all came from these cursed philosophers and their 'Encyclopædia'!   As, later, whole nations attributed the rot in the crops and the ague in the bones of their children to the withering influence of that great little Corporal, hundreds of miles away from them, so in the eighteenth century in France a great party in the state attributed to the extension of learning every disaster which their own folly or foolhardiness brought upon them.

They turned, and brought all their power, influence, and money against the Encyclopædists.   D'Alembert was no fighter.   Student, recluse, and gentle friend— he was not one of those who could write with a pen in one hand and a sword in the other.   'I do not know if the "Encyclopædia" will be continued,' he wrote to Voltaire as early as the January of 1758, 'but I am sure it will not be continued by me;' and though the pugnacious little warrior of Délices wrote and passionately urged his peaceful friend not to do what his absurd enemies wished—not to let them enjoy 'that insolent victory'—still, d'Alembert withdrew.   On February 9, 1759, Voltaire wrote that he seemed to see the Inquisition condemning Galileo.

But it was as he said.   The cinders from the burning sprang up and burnt the burners.   They could mutilate the 'Encyclopædia,' but they could not kill it.   Its very mutilations attracted interest, and 'Natural Law' and 'On the Mind' continued to be sold—in open secrecy—a hundred times more than ever.

It will not have been forgotten that with 'Natural Law' had originally been published 'The Disaster of

Lisbon '; and that the doctrines of 'Lisbon' had been refuted, by the request of the Genevans, in a long, wild, rambling letter by Jean Jacques Rousseau, wherein that absurd person had pointed out that if we lived in deserts, not towns, the houses would not fall upon us, because there would not be houses to fall.

Answer a fool according to his folly! A few gay bantering lines were all Voltaire's reply at the moment. To strike quickly—or wait long—this man could do both. He loved best to strike at once; but if he could have patience and wait to gather his weapons, to barb his arrows, to poison his darts, why, he was of nature the more deadly. This time he had waited long. The bantering note was but a sop thrown to his impatience. Rousseau's Letter on Optimism bears the date of August 1756. It was not till the early part of 1759 that there crept out stealthily, secretly, quietly, the gayest little volatile laughing romance called 'Candide.'

Written in some keen moment of inspiration— perhaps at the Elector Palatine's, perhaps at Délices, where, it matters not—in that great masterpiece of literature Voltaire brought out all his batteries at once and confronted the foe with that ghoulish mockery, that bantering jest, and that deadly levity which no man could face and live.

If the optimists had talked down the passionate reasonings of the 'Poem on the Disaster of Lisbon' with that reiterated 'All is well,' 'All chance, direction which thou canst not see—all partial evil, universal good,' 'Candide's' laugh drowned those affirmations —so loudly and so often affirmed that the affirmers had come to mistake them for argument. In this novel of two hundred pages Voltaire withered by a grin the

cheap, current, convenient optimism of the leisured
classes of his day, and confounded Pope as well as
Rousseau. This time he did not argue with their theories. He only exposed them. In that searching light, in
that burning sunshine, the comfortable dogmas of the
neat couplets of the 'Essay on Man' blackened and
died, and Rousseau was shown forth the laughing-stock
of the nations.

One of the few literary classics which is not only
still talked about but still sometimes read, is 'Candide.'
Nothing grows old-fashioned sooner than humour. The
jests which amuse one age bore and depress the next.
But it is part of Voltaire's genius in general, and of
'Candide' in particular, that its wit is almost as witty
to-day as when it was written. It still trips and dances
on feet which never age or tire. Nothing is more
astounding in it than what one critic has called its
'fresh and unflagging spontaneity'—its 'surpassing
invention.' Its vigour is such as no time can touch.
It reads like the work of a superabundant youth. Yet
Voltaire was actually sixty-four when he wrote it; and
if indeed 'we live in deeds, not years : in thoughts,
not breaths : in feelings, not in figures on a dial,' he
was a thousand.

The story is, briefly, that of a young man brought
up in implicit belief in the everything-for-the-best
doctrine, who goes out into a world where he meets
with a hundred adventures which give it the lie. Life
is a bad bargain, but one can make the best of it.
That is the moral of 'Candide.' 'What I know,' says
Candide, 'is that we must cultivate our garden.' 'Let
us work without reasoning : that is the only way to
render life supportable.'

As children read the 'Gulliver's Travels' of that

past master of irony, Jonathan Swift, as the most innocent and amusing of fairy tales, so can 'Candide' be read as a rollicking farce and as nothing else in the world.

Who knows, indeed, when he puts down that marvellous novelette, whether to laugh at those inimitable traits of the immortal Dr. Pangloss—'noses have been made to carry spectacles, therefore we have spectacles; legs have been made for stockings, therefore we have stockings; pigs were made to be eaten, and therefore we have pork all the year round'—or to weep over the wretchedness of a humanity which perforce consoles itself with lies, and, too miserable to face its misery, pretends that all is well?

One woman, with her heart wrung by that cruel mockery, speaks of 'Candide's' 'diabolical gaiety.' 'It seems to be written by a being of another nature than our own, indifferent to our fate, pleased with our sufferings, and laughing like a demon or a monkey at the miseries of that humankind with which he has nothing in common.' Some have found in it the blasphemies of a devil against the tender and ennobling Christianity which has been the faith and the hope of sorrowing millions; and others discover in it only one of the most potent of arguments for embracing that Christianity—the confession that no other system so consolatory can be found. To one reader it is the supreme expression of a genius who, wherever he stands, stands alone—' as high as mere wit can go;' to another, shorn of its indecency, it is, like 'Gulliver,' but a *bizarre* absurdity for youth; while a third finds it 'most useful as a philosophical work, because it is read by a people who would never read philosophy.'

Perhaps the genius of 'Candide' lies partly in the

fact that it is both serious and frivolous, ghoulish and
gay, tragedy and comedy; and equally perfect as the
one or the other.

Voltaire assigned 'this little sort of romance' to
that convenient person, the Chevalier de Mouhy, on
whom, in 1738, had been fathered the 'Préservatif.'
The real author declared that the thing was much too
frivolous for him to have written. He had read it, to
be sure. 'The more it makes me laugh the more sorry
I am it is assigned to me.' Almost every letter of this
spring of 1759 contains a mocking allusion to *optimism*.
'Candide' was much to the fore in its writer's mind.

On March 2 the Council of Geneva condemned
the book to be burnt; and once more, as in the case
of the 'Pucelle,' Voltaire watched a bonfire with a
very twisted smile. He revenged himself by flooding
Geneva with anonymous irreligious pamphlets with
such religious names—'Christian Dialogues' and
'The Gospel of the Day'—as to deceive the very elect.

But it was not only his suspected paternity in the
case of 'Candide,' but a suspected paternity of an even
more dangerous child, that prevented Voltaire in this
spring giving up his whole soul peacefully to rebuilding
Ferney and laying out gardens. Frederick was in the
midst of a disastrous campaign; but, unfortunately, no
disaster stopped him writing to Voltaire or composing
verses. Wilhelmina's death had only healed the old
wounds for a while. They broke out afresh. In March
this strange Damon and Pythias were again squabbling
over that ancient bone of contention, Maupertuis; and
then, as inconsistently as if they had been a couple
of schoolgirls, passionately regretting their old amity.
'I shall soon die without having seen you,' wrote
Voltaire on March 25. 'You do not care, and I shall

try not to care either. . . . I can live neither with you nor without you. I do not speak to the King or the hero : that is the affair of sovereigns. I speak to him who has fascinated me, whom I have loved, and with whom I am always angry.' Then they remembered Frankfort and Freytag, and began snarling and growling again.

And then—then—a book of Frederick's poems which abused Louis XV. and the Pompadour was opened in the post on its way from Frederick to Voltaire. And in a trice Voltaire is quaking lest he should be thought to have inspired, or positively written, verse so dangerous and disrespectful.

No emergency had ever yet robbed him of his cleverness. He took the packet to the French envoy at Geneva and showed him the broken seal ; and then, by the envoy's advice, sent the whole thing to Choiseul, the head of the French Ministry. Choiseul was himself a verse-maker : he wrote a virulent versified satire upon Frederick and sent it to Voltaire. 'Tell your King, if he publishes his poems I shall publish mine.'

Voltaire says that if he had wished to amuse himself he might have seen the Kings of France and Prussia engaged in a war of verses. But he was the friend of peace as well as the friend of Frederick. He begged Frederick not to shut every door of reconciliation with the King of France by publishing that ode ; and added, that in mortal fear of its being attributed to Uncle Voltaire, niece Denis had burnt it. Frederick would not have been human had he not immediately felt convinced that those ashes contained the finest lines he had ever written. But they *were* ashes. The episode closed.

On July 27, 1759, Maupertuis died at Bâle, 'of a repletion of pride' said Voltaire. Akakia, busy with his history of 'Peter the Great,' and with touching up 'Tancred,' or his 'Chevaliers' as he called it sometimes, must needs push them aside and shoot an arrow or two of his barbed wit at that poor enemy's dead body. 'Enjoy your hermitage,' Frederick wrote back to him gravely. 'Do not trouble the ashes of those who are at peace in the grave. . . . Sacrifice your vengeance on the shrine of your own reputation . . . and let the greatest genius in France be also the most generous of his nation.' The counsel was just and noble. Alas! it was even more needed than Frederick guessed. At this very time Voltaire was writing his secret 'Memoirs for the Life of M. de Voltaire.' They were not published till after his death. They were never meant to be published at all. They contain what Morley has well called 'a prose lampoon' on the King's private life, 'which is one of the bitterest libels that malice ever prompted.'

Its incomprehensible author was still actually compiling it when, for the third time, he took up his *rôle* of peacemaker between France and Frederick.

This time, Tencin and Richelieu having been tried in vain, the medium was to be Choiseul, Choiseul being approached by Voltaire's angel, d'Argental. The moment was favourable. The campaign of 1759 was wholly disastrous to Frederick : and on August 12 he was beaten by the united armies at Kunersdorf. Chased from his states, 'surrounded by enemies, beaten by the Russians, unable to replenish an exhausted treasury,' 'Luc,' as Voltaire phrased it, 'was still Luc.' He still kept his head above the foaming waters that would have engulfed any other swimmer. 'Very

embarrassed, and not less embarrassing to other
people; astonishing and impoverishing Europe, and
writing verses,' Frederick, as if to give himself time—
as if, though he never meant to yield to such advances,
he yet did not dare to openly refuse them—coquetted
with the peace offers of M. de Choiseul, sent through
that 'Bureau d'adresse,' Voltaire. It is not a little
wonderful that Voltaire, with his itching fingers for
action, could suffer himself to be a 'Bureau d'adresse,'
a passive medium, even for a while. But he did. An
immense correspondence passed between himself and
Frederick—for the benefit of Choiseul. Frederick
was alluded to as Mademoiselle Pestris or Pertris:
and very coy was Mademoiselle over the matter.
Shall it be peace? shall it not? It was a delicate
negotiation, said that 'Bureau d'adresse,' very truly.
It was like the play of two cats—each with velvet
paws to hide its claws.

It came to nothing. Though, perhaps, when in
December there appeared in Paris a book entitled
'The Works of the Philosopher of Sans-Souci,' containing those free-thinking effusions a Most Christian
King had written under the rose, and which he would
not at all wish to see daylight, Choiseul's claw had been
active in the matter. Fortunately, Voltaire could not
be suspected. Had not Freytag taken from him at
Frankfort that 'Œuvre de Poëshie du Roi Mon
Maître,' which was none other than the 'Works of
the Philosopher of Sans-Souci' under a different
name? Still, the year 1760 opened as 1759 had done,
with Damon and Pythias still sparring at each other.
'You have embroiled me for ever with the King of
France, you have lost me my posts and pensions,
you have ill-treated me at Frankfort, me and an

innocent woman,' writes Voltaire to Frederick from peaceful Tourney in April 1760.

And in May Frederick wrote back, If you were not dealing with a fool in love with your genius,' what might I not do and say? As it is—' Once for all, let me hear no more of that niece who bores me, and has nothing but her uncle to cover her defects.'

The niece who bored Frederick must have been very nearly as bored herself throughout the remainder of this year 1759 as she confessed to have been at the beginning. Uncle Voltaire was always so engrossed with writing, or with those stupid farms and gardens. ' The more you work on your land, the more you will love it,' he had written to Madame de Fontaine in the summer. ' The corn one has sown oneself is worth far more than what one gets from other people's granaries.' And then, there were so few visitors.

Valette, a needy, clever, unsatisfactory acquaintance of d'Alembert's, was at Délices in December; and during the year one d'Aumard had arrived on a visit. But that was all.

D'Aumard was a young soldier cousin of Voltaire's mother. Of very ordinary abilities, and morals rather below the very low average of his day, that distant cousinship was the only claim he had upon Voltaire's notice. But it was more than sufficient. Voltaire had already sent him presents of money through Madame Denis, and made him a promise of a pension for life. Directly he arrived at Délices he was attacked by what was at first taken to be rheumatism. Tronchin was called in. Voltaire sent d'Aumard to Aix for the waters. But neither the first physician nor the most fashionable cure in Europe was of any avail. D'Aumard became a helpless and hopeless cripple. In

1761 Voltaire said that it required four persons to
move him from one bed to another. In this condition
he lived in Voltaire's house for at least ten years, and
finally died there. His host engaged in a long correspondence about his case with the surgeon of the Royal
Footguards, and entered into every detail with infinite
pains and minuteness. To a busy and active Voltaire
the fate of this young man, shut out of all work and
interest—hearing, as he lay on the bed from which he
was never to rise, the stir and movement of a life in
which he could never join—seemed peculiarly pitiable.
He makes a hundred sympathetic allusions to him.
That his own conduct was infinitely generous he seems
to have wholly lost sight of in the fact that d'Aumard's
fate was infinitely sad. Yet Voltaire had a reward if
he wanted one. To Madame du Deffand's question
if life were worth living he could reply 'Yes. I know
a man completely paralysed who loves it, to folly.'
The man was d'Aumard.

In this year Voltaire obtained, after the exercise of
even more than his usual persistence, and after working
himself and his friends to death to attain his aim, the
grant of two letters-patent for his lands of Tourney
and Ferney. He set great value on these letters as
declaring him a French subject.

Also in this year he heard of the loss of that very
old English friend of his, Falkener. In 1774 Falkener's
two sons came to stay with him at Ferney.

He still kept himself well *au courant* of English
affairs and English literature.

It was in 1759 he wrote to Madame du Deffand
that there was nothing passable in 'Tom Jones' but
the character of the barber; and of 'A Tale of a
Tub' as 'a treasure-house of wit.' He also read—and

yawned over—' Clarissa Harlowe ' and ' Pamela ' ; and
in 1760 he was criticising ' Tristram Shandy.' No
other great Frenchman of his day got into the heart of
English literature and English character as Voltaire
did. ' An Englishman who knows France well and a
Frenchman who knows England well are both the
better for it,' is one of the shrewdest of his sayings,
and he said many shrewd things, on the two races.
' The English know how to think ; the French know
how to please.' ' We are the whipped cream of Europe.
There are not twenty Frenchmen who understand
Newton.'

But there was another foreign country besides
England which was engaging his attention now—
Russia.

In this 1759 he produced the first volume of that
' History of Peter the Great ' which he had undertaken
to write two years earlier, in 1757, at the request of
Peter's daughter, Elizabeth.

In the spring of 1717, when Arouet was an imprudent
young Paris wit of three-and-twenty, awaiting his first
introduction to the Bastille, he had seen the great Peter
in the flesh, being shown the shops of the capital, the
lion of its season—' neither of us thinking then that
I should become his historian.'

But directly Elizabeth made the suggestion, a
Voltaire of sixty-three had embraced it with an enthusiasm which would not have been astonishing in
an Arouet of three-and-twenty, and set to work at
once.

The subject bristled with difficulties. First it involved an enormous correspondence with Schouvaloff,
the Russian minister. Schouvaloff was ready and
eager to shower maps, medals, and documents upon the

historian. But the medals, as the historian pointed
out, were not of the slightest use ; the maps were
inadequate ; and the documents had too often been
tampered with.

Then, too, there was an immeasurable difficulty, for
a writer who wanted to tell the truth, in the fact that
his hero's own daughter was not only living, but had
commissioned him to write the work. When Frederick
wanted to know what in the world made Voltaire think
of writing the history of the wolves and bears of
Siberia, he represented the point of view from which
most people then regarded Russia. A great, cold, ugly,
barbarous, uninteresting place—what in the world can
you have to say about it ?   The veil of tragedy and
romance which now hangs before that huge canvas
did not give it the potent charm of mystery in the
eighteenth century.   Only Voltaire would then have
dared to write ' Russia under Peter the Great,' and
only Voltaire could have made it readable.

He took a flying leap into that sea of difficulties,
and came up to the top safely as usual. He gave
Schouvaloff a plan of the work in advance.   First,
there are to be no unnecessary details of battles ;
secondly, the thing will be called not ' The History of
Peter the Great,' but ' Russia under Peter I.,' as giving
me greater liberty, and explaining to my readers in
advance the real aim of the book ; thirdly, Peter's
little weaknesses are not to be concealed when necessary to expose them.

The rough sketch was bold, and so was the finished
picture. But to its boldness were united that grace
and charm by which Voltaire could make disagreeable
truths sound like compliments. If to the world
generally Peter was, and should be, but the ' wisest

and greatest of savages,' 'only a king,' and a badly
brought up one at that—to Russia he was, and ought
to be, a great man and a hero ; and, Peter apart altogether—and there is a good deal of the work from
which Peter *is* entirely apart—the book 'revealed
Russia to Europe and herself,' and brought that
great country to the knowledge and the interest of
other nations.

The style sometimes bears trace of the difficulties
its author had to overcome—the fact that the subject
was chosen for him, not *by* him. 'I doubt,' he wrote
to Madame du Deffand, 'if it will be as amusing as the
" Life of Charles XII.," for Peter was only extraordinarily wise, while Charles was extraordinarily foolish.'
All the time he was writing it, 'Tancred,' Ferney,
'Candide,' Frederick, were calling his attention away
from it.

Not the less, the History was a very successfully
executed order, with which the orderer was so pleased
that in 1761 she sent the author her portrait set in
diamonds.

To the end of 1759 also belongs a very different
work of Voltaire's—one of those spontaneous, impulsive, rollicking, daring things which must have been
no little relief to his *méchanceté* to turn to from those
grave ploddings through Schouvaloff's documents.
Encouraged by that burning of 'Natural Law' and
its companion volumes, and by the suppression of the
'Encyclopædia' in the early part of the year, in November
a weekly Jesuit organ called the 'Journal de Trévoux,'
edited by one Berthier, furiously assailed not only
'Natural Law,' which fires could not destroy, but the
'Encyclopædia,' which prohibitions could not suppress,
and all the works of enlightenment in France. Vol-

taire had always an inconsistent *tendresse* for the
Jesuits. They had been good to him in his schooldays:
and among them he still numbered some of his friends.
But this thing was too monstrous! Voltaire attacked
it with sharpest ridicule, and wrote anonymously that
scathing pamphlet called 'The Narrative of the Sickness, Confession, Death, and Re-appearance of the
Jesuit Berthier.' This he followed by another pamphlet, 'The Narrative of Brother Grasse.' Both were
but burlesques. True, there was a hit in every line ;
and then, if not now, every arrow went home. But
the real significance of the pamphlets is in the fact that
they were a declaration of war. Gardens and architecture, farms and beehives—in these things is to be
found happiness perhaps. But there has been no
great man in the world who ever thought happiness
enough. That hatred of intolerance, that passion for
freedom which had been the motive power of a young
and struggling Arouet, was still the motive power of
this affluent, comfortable Voltaire of sixty-five. To be
sure, it is easier to feel sympathy with the oppressed
and the needy when one is oneself downtrodden and
poor : and something more difficult when one is oneself
prosperous and independent. It must be accounted to
Voltaire for righteousness that when he no longer
suffered himself, the sufferings of others appealed to
him only with a double force. It was in those smiling
days of Délices and Ferney that he framed his battle-
cry and formulated the creed of all the philosophers,
and the aim and the conviction of his own life, into one
brief phrase—*Écrasez l'infâme.*

Friend and foe still remember him by that motto.
The one has idly forgotten, and the other carefully
misunderstands, what it means and meant. To many

Christians, ' *Écrasez l'infâme* ' is but the blasphemous outcry against the dearest and most sacred mysteries of their religion ; and *l'infâme* means Christ.

But to Voltaire, if it meant Christianity at all, it meant that which was taught in Rome in the eighteenth century, and not by the Sea of Galilee in the first. If it *was* Christianity at all, it was not the Christianity of Christ. *L'infâme did* mean religion, but it meant the religion which lit the fires of Smithfield and prompted the tortures of the Inquisition ; which terrified feeble brains to madness with the burning flames of a material hell, and flung to the barren uselessness of the cloister hundreds of unwilling victims, quick and meet for the life for which they had been created.

L'infâme was the religion which enforced its doc-trines by the sword, the fire, and the prison ; which massacred on the Night of St. Bartholomew ; and, glossing lightly over royal sins, refused its last con-solations to dying Jansenists who would not accept the Bull Unigenitus. It was the religion which thrust itself between wife and husband in the person of the con-fessor—himself condemned to an unnatural life which not one in a thousand can live honestly and aright ; it was the religion of Indulgences, and the rich : for those who could pay for the remission of their sins and for large impunity to sin afresh ; it was the religion which served as a cloak for tyranny and oppression, ground down the face of the poor, and kept wretched-ness wretched for ever.

And above all, *l'infâme* was that spirit which was the natural enemy of all learning and advancement ; which loved darkness and hated light because its deeds were evil ; which found the better knowledge of His works, treason to God ; and an exercise of the reason and the judgment He had given, an insult to the Giver.

If there was ever a chance for the foolish to become learned, *l'infâme* deprived them of it. If the light fought its way through the gross darkness of super-stition, *l'infâme* quenched it. It prohibited Newton ; burnt Bayle ; and cursed the Encyclopædia. If men were once enlightened, *l'infâme* would be cast down from the high places where it sat—as Pope or as King, as Calvinist or as Cardinal ; but always as the enemy of that Justice which drives out oppression, as the sun drives out the night.

L'infâme cannot be translated by any single word. But if it must be, the best rendering of it is Intoler-ance.

No one can have any knowledge of the career or of the character of Voltaire without seeing that this Thing, to which in the year 1759 was first given the name of *Infâme*, was his one, great, lifelong enemy. Loathing of it coursed in his *bourgeois* blood and was bred in his bones. The boy who had seen France starve to pay for the Sun King's wars, and Paris persecuted to please his mistress and his confessor, had felt surge in him the first waves of that tireless indignation which was to turn a courtier into a reformer, and make a light soul, deep. By the time he himself became the Voice crying in the wilderness of men's sorrows, the utterer of hard truths, *l'infâme* had imprisoned, persecuted, and exiled him. And who is there who does not better hate wrongdoing when he has himself been wronged ? He had revealed God to sages through Newton ; and the hangman burnt the ' English Letters.' He had studied history, especi-ally the history of the religious wars, and he knew what *l'infâme* had done in the past as well as in the present. He declared, with that extraordinary mixture of levity and passion which is his alone, that he always had an access of fever on St. Bartholomew's Day. He had seen the works of Boyer—fanatic and tyrant—the product of a shameful system, and not the less harmful in fact because he was honest in intention. He had seen *l'infâme* prompt Damiens' knife ; and then, in its besotted inconsequence, avenge the crime of its own scholar by prohibiting all the works of enlightenment in France.

In 1757, in writing to d'Alembert, Voltaire had first given *l'infâme* a name—the Phantom. A few days later he called it the Colossus. Under any name a d'Alembert would recognise it. On May 18, 1759, Frederick the Great spoke of it by that title it was to bear for ever, in one of those bitter yearning letters he wrote to his old friend. ' You will still caress *l'infâme* with one hand and scratch it with the other; you will treat it as you have treated me and all the world.' And in June Voltaire replied : ' Your Majesty reproaches me with sometimes caressing *l'infâme*. My God, no ! I only work to extirpate it.' And the next year—June 3, 1760—' I want you to crush *l'infâme* ; that is the great point. It must be reduced to the same condition as it is in England. You can do it if you will. It is the greatest service one can render to humankind.'

Henceforward, his allusions to it in his letters became more and more frequent. Sometimes he abbreviated it to *Écr. l'Inf*. Sometimes he wrote in one corner ' *É. l'I*.' ' The first of duties is to annihilate *l'inf*. ; confound *l'inf*. as much as you can.'

' This Mr. *Écrlinf* does not write badly, said these worthy people.' One of his theories was that truths cannot be too often insisted on. 'Rub it in! rub it in!' he would cry. He rubbed in his *infâme*. Now in passionate earnest, now in jest, now cynically, now bitterly, he alluded to it at all times and seasons and to all kinds of persons. To Damilaville, who was to take Theriot's place as his correspondent and who himself loathed *l'infâme* with a deadly intensity, Voltaire hardly wrote a letter without that 'Crush the monster!' It was a catchword at last. 'I end all my letters by saying *Écr. l'inf.*, as Cato always said, That is my opinion and Carthage must be destroyed.' By it, he heated the zeal of his fellow-workers in the cause; quickened the 'phlegmatic perseverance' of d'Alembert; and rallied to new effort Helvétius, Marmontel, Holbach, and a dozen lesser men.

It has been seen that he had loathed the Thing, a nameless monster, for fifty years. The insults of the 'Journal de Trévoux' were the final spur to action. If Berthier had not pushed him to extremities, no doubt some other of 'those serpents called Jesuits' would have done it equally effectually. The time was ripe; and Voltaire was ripe for the time. He flung down the glove at last and declared upon *l'Infâme* an open war, which was to be war to the knife till he had no longer breath in his body, and the sword—his pen—fell from a dead hand.

CHAPTER XXXIV

THE BATTLE OF PARTICLES,
AND THE BATTLE OF COMEDIES

ON March 10, 1760, M. le Franc de Pompignan took the seat in the French Academy left vacant by the death of Maupertuis, and delivered an opening address which was nothing but an attack on the philosophic party.

Marquis and county magnate was Pompignan, rather a good minor poet, a native of Montauban, and, in his own province and his own estimation, a very great man indeed. In 1736 he had written a play with which he had tried, vainly, to supplant Voltaire's 'Alzire.' He and Voltaire met afterwards, in amicable fashion enough, at the house of a mutual friend. And then Voltaire retired to Cirey and Madame du Châtelet : and Le Franc to his magisterial duties in Montauban.

But by the year 1758 Montauban, and his own vanity, had so impressed the noble Marquis with the idea that his genius was wasted in a province, that he came up to Paris : stood for a vacant chair in the Academy ; failed to gain it ; stood again for another chair in 1760, and, as has been seen, won it, in succession to Maupertuis. When it is added that Le Franc was also Historiographer of France in place of Voltaire, and that he was practically the only noble-man in the kingdom who was at once clever, educated, and orthodox, his design to use that Academical chair as a stepping-stone to the tutorship of the Dauphin's sons—always one of the most influential posts in the kingdom—was not at all a wild ambition. He began his speech by praising his predecessor, Maupertuis, as in duty bound, and also as being sure to raise the ire of that arch-fiend of philosophers, Voltaire ; and then abused those philosophers and their works roundly, soundly, and at length.

The chairman of the Academy made reply in a very fulsome speech, in which he compared Le Franc to Moses, and his younger brother, the Bishop of Puy, a not illiberal churchman, to Aaron. ' The two brothers are consecrated to work miracles, the one as judge, the other as pontiff, in Israel.'

Moses was then granted an interview with the King, in which his Majesty highly praised that Academical discourse as little likely to be applauded by the impious, ' or by strong minds '—which he took to be the finest compliment he could pay it.

On March 28 one of those ' esprits forts ' was writing comfortably from Délices that he saw all storms, but saw them from the port. The port ! Of course someone sent him that Academical discourse. He applied the remarks on the philosophers particularly to himself (to be sure, the cap fitted), and took upon himself to avenge them all.

One fine day there appeared in Paris, without date, without any indication as to the place in which it had been printed, a little *brochure* of seven deadly pages entitled the ' Whens : or Useful Notes on a Discourse pronounced before the French Academy on March 10, 1760.' They were the little skiff in which Voltaire sailed into the teeth of the storm.

All his works are characteristic in a high degree, but hardly any are so characteristic as those he wielded in this Battle of the Particles.

Exquisitely dainty and gay; as fine and as sharp as needles from my lady's work-basket, and yet as ' biting and incisive as a poignard : ' such are the hall-marks of those little instruments of torture of which the ' Whens ' was the first.

' *When* one has the honour to be admitted into a respectable company of literary men, one need not make one's opening speech a satire against them.'

' *When* one is hardly a man of letters and not at all a philosopher, it is not becoming to say that our nation has only a false literature and a vain philosophy.'

' *When* one is admitted into an honourable body, one ought, in one's address, to hide under a veil of modesty that insolent pride which is the prerogative of hot heads and mean talents.'

Voltaire would not have been Voltaire, nor of his century, if he had not gone on to remind this highly correct Marquis that in a free youth he had himself coquetted with Deism and translated and circulated ' The Universal Prayer '—then commonly called ' The Deists' Prayer '—of Mr. Pope.   He also added that for his Deistic opinions this proper Le Franc had been deprived of the charge of his province ; which was not true, but made the story much better.

It is hardly necessary to say that Voltaire denied the ' Whens.'   ' I did not write them,' he told Theriot on May 20, ' but I wish I had.'

They had roused his party very effectively.   If ' the shepherd, the labourer, the rat retired from the world in a Swiss cheese,' was pushed, as the rat said, into the ' deluge of monosyllables,' how should the philosophers in Paris escape it? The famous Morellet, abbé, writer, free-thinker, one of the 'four theologians of the Encyclopædia,' whom Voltaire called *Mords-les* (Bite them) from the caustic nature of his wit, rushed into the fray with the 'Ifs' and the 'Wherefores'; and a reproduction of the luckless Le Franc's translation of 'The Universal Prayer.' Délices followed up at once with the 'Yeses' and the 'Noes,' the 'Whats,' the 'Whys,' and the 'Whos.' Délices said that chuckling sustained old age: no wonder *his* old age was so vigorous. There was not a vulnerable inch in the body or soul of that unhappy Marquis which one of those particles did not wound. A riddle ran through Paris, 'Why did Jeremiah weep so much during his life?' 'Because, as a prophet, he foresaw that after death he would be translated by Le Franc'—Le Franc having compensated for that 'Universal Prayer' by writing the most devout works ever since. Later were to come the 'Fors' and the 'Ahs.' Some were by other hands than Voltaire's. But his was the spirit that inspired them all. Some were in verse. All were brief. Then he published extracts from an early tragedy of Le Franc's, making them as absurd as he alone knew how. The affair was the talk of Paris: the most delicious farce in the world. Madame du Deffand spoke of Le Franc as buried under 'mountains of ridicule.' Wherever he was recognised he excited shouts of laughter. He solemnly and prosily defended his translation of 'The Universal Prayer' as a mere exercise in English, which it very likely was. And Paris laughed afresh. Voltaire declared that Tronchin had ordered him to hunt Pompignan for two hours every morning for the good of his health. Poor Pompignan, goaded to madness, presented a petition to

the King in which he asked the assistance of their
Majesties and recalled to them the splendid welcome
they had accorded to himself and his Academical
discourse.

But Louis XV. could not prevent Paris laughing
nor Voltaire answering by what purported to be an
extract from a newspaper of Le Franc's native
Montauban, wherein the natives of that place were
represented as appointing a committee to go to Paris
and inquire into the mental condition of the unfortunate Marquis.   But this thing was a *brochure*—a
nothing.

Délices had not done with Montauban yet.   There
was a pause.   And then Voltaire produced one of the
most scathing and trenchant satires of which even
he was capable.   It was in verse, and it was called
' Vanity.'   It began :

> Well, what's the matter, little bourgeois of a little town ?

and contains many lines which still form part of the
common talk of France.

Gay, fluent, contemptuous—written scornfully in a
colloquialism which, in that day of set and formal
phrases, was in itself an insult—Pompignan, like
Maupertuis, was stifled with badinage, and laughed—
to death.

Though all the wit of the thing, and more than
half its significance, are lost in a translation, even in a
translation some idea of the sufferings of that wretched
provincial Marquis may be gained still.

> The Universe, my friend, thinks of you not at all :
> The future less.   Look to your house and diet:
> Drink : sleep : amuse yourself: be wise : be quiet.
>   *   *   *   *   *   *

> Oh, but my beautiful Discourse, they laugh at it!
> The malice of their vulgar gibes hurts so,
> That, sure of justice, to the King I'll go.
>   *   *   *   *   *   *
> He'll make it law to find my writing good.
> I'll tell him of it all without delay
> And get the laugher's licence ta'en away.

The poem ends with lines which, as Voltaire wrote them, stabbed straight to the enemy's heart :

> Ruined great Alexander's tomb and town:
> And for great Cæsar's shade no home there be,
> Yet Pompignan thinks a great man is he.

He thought so no longer. 'Vanity' was his death-blow. The very Dauphin laughed at it. The Marquis went home to his province, and never again dared to appear at the Academy.

In 1769, when his play, 'Dido,' was acted in Paris, the Comédie Française announced quite innocently that it would be followed by 'The Coxcomb Punished' of Pont-de-Veyle. Everything was against poor Pompignan. He died in 1784. The turn of his priestly brother, Aaron, was yet to come.

If Pompignan had been nothing but a self-satisfied nobleman who over-estimated his own talents and under-estimated those of the philosophers and the Academicians, he would certainly not have deserved the fury of ridicule with which he was assailed, and the laugh would have turned against the laughers.

But this was no harmless fool. It may have been a small thing that, as Voltaire wrote, 'if Le Franc had not been covered with ridicule, the custom of declaiming against the philosophers in the opening discourse of the Academy would have become a rule.' But it would have been no small thing that a Pompignan should be tutor to the Dauphin's sons; should teach the boy who was to rule France a narrow hatred for the light and learning which alone could save it; and preach the principles of *l'infâme* to the susceptible youth who would one day practise them to the ruin of a great kingdom.

Écrasez l'infâme! Pompignan was but a victim to that purpose. Voltaire kicked him aside with his foot, and looked out for other foes to vanquish.

There were always plenty of them. He had on hand at the moment a satire called 'The Poor Devil,' which set out to be an account of the adventures of that Valette, the friend of d'Alembert and the guest of Délices, but which ended as a fiercer 'Dunciad,' ' more than a satire, more than a *chef-d'œuvre* of incomparable verve and malignity,' and which reveals to our own day many an ugly secret of the literary life and men of that strange epoch.

But the general satisfaction of whipping a multitude is nothing to the personal satisfaction of whipping a unit.

While the Pompignan affair was still running high, news came one morning—on April 25, 1760—that a comedy by a certain Charles Palissot, entitled 'The Philosophers' and bitterly ridiculing that party, was about to be played in Paris. 'Very well,' says Délices; ' I cannot prevent that. But what I can and will do is to withdraw "Tancred," already in rehearsal.' So 'Tancred' is withdrawn.

On May 2 Palissot's 'Philosophers' was performed for the first time.

A clever journalist was Charles Palissot, who, in 1755, had been Voltaire's guest at Délices with Patu

the poet.   His play was clever too, a rollicking comedy
in three acts, which not only laughed at the philosophic
party but represented them as dangerous to society and
the state.   Helvétius, Diderot, Duclos, Madame Geoffrin, and Mademoiselle Clairon were openly satirised.
J. J. Rousseau was represented on all-fours, with a
lettuce in his pocket for provender.

The 'Encyclopædia' was mentioned by name.   Two
noble ladies openly gave the play their patronage.   One
was the Princess de Robecq, the mistress of Choiseul
the minister, and so a force to be reckoned with.

'The Philosophers' had carefully omitted to attack
the two greatest of the philosophers, d'Alembert and
Voltaire.   But the one wrote an account of the thing
to the other, and that Other began to inspect his
weapons.

True, he tried mild measures at first.   Palissot
sent him a copy of the play.   And Voltaire wrote
back trying to win its author over to the right side,
or at least to an impartial attitude of mind.   But
Palissot did not mean to be convinced.   Then Abbé
Morellet-Mords-Les-Bite-Them was flung into the
Bastille, at the instigation of the Princess de Robecq
and the command of Choiseul, for having returned
a comic answer to Palissot's comedy, called 'The
Preface to The Philosophers.'   These things were
not precisely soothing.   To meet ridicule with reason
had failed.   Gibe for gibe, then ; foolery for foolery !
If Voltaire was one of the two who could play at that
game, he was always the winner when he played.

He had another, older, deadlier foe than Palissot,
who would also be the better for a beating.   The older
foe was Fréron.   And the beating he received with
Palissot was called 'The Scotch Girl.'

Fréron was still a very cool, clever, opulent, successful Parisian journalist : still the bitterest and shrewdest
foe of the philosophers, and the sharpest tool of the
Court. Voltaire, it will be remembered, had no reason to
love this ' worm from the carcase of Desfontaines,' the
defender of Crébillon, the supporter of d'Arnaud, the
founder of 'The Literary Year,' that review which,
appearing every ten days, had been for twenty-three
years 'a long polemic against the Encyclopædia in
general and Voltaire in particular.' But Voltaire seldom
made the mistake of under-rating his enemy's powers.
He spoke of Fréron as the only man of his party who
had literary taste. He acknowledged him to be of an
amazing energy and courage, of great self-command,
and an excellent critic.

But when it came to sharply criticising ' Candide '
in that 'Literary Year ' and scornfully twitting ' Candide's ' author with his dear title of Count of Tourney,
the Count was foolish enough not only to lose his
temper but to enumerate his grievances against Fréron
in a letter to ' The Encyclopædic Journal,' the rival
organ of ' The Literary Year.'

There was certainly a fine air of coolness and
indifference in the letter. But the *vif*, warm genius of
a Voltaire only assumed these qualities. Fréron really
had them. Hence, Fréron was a powerful foe.

Athirst for revenge, then, alike on Palissot and on
Fréron, Voltaire wrote ' The Scotch Girl ' in eight days.
An English play, if you please, by Mr. Hume, brother
of the historian ; translated into French by Jérôme
Carré ; and before it appears, to be read, discussed,
laughed over, and recognised in every boudoir in Paris
as a satire on Fréron and on Palissot's ' Philosophers.'
Everything fell out as the author had desired and

laboured that it should. If he *was* buried at Délices and hundreds of miles of vile roads from Paris, he had friends there only something less active and angry than himself. He had in himself the vigour and genius which can span space and move mountains.

On July 25, the day before the play was to appear, he caused to be circulated in Paris a letter in which Carré, the translator, complained of the immense efforts Fréron had made to damn ' The Scotch Girl ' in advance. These advertisements were perfectly successful. On the first night—Saturday, July 26—crowds besieged the door of the theatre before it opened ; some, the friends of Fréron, some of Palissot, some of Voltaire ; and all knowing enough of the piece to be quite sure they should be amused. In a prominent place in the auditorium shrewd Fréron had placed his pretty wife, to excite compassion for himself, and anger against his foes. He himself sat among the orchestra. Malesherbes, the minister, had a place hard by him. Palissot was in a box. Many neutral persons, piqued only by curiosity, found seats in the house. It was upon their pulse Fréron kept his finger. It was their displeasure or approval which would give the real verdict of the piece.

' The Scotch Girl ' is not at all a good play. But it is witty, topical, and infinitely audacious. ' It is not sufficient to write well : one must write to the taste of the public,' said Voltaire. He had not written well : but he had written for the psychological moment. His audience had expected him to take a bold spring from the footboard : and he jumped from the roof. His old experience of England enabled him to give one of the first sketches of a comic Englishman ever seen on the French stage. The character of Freeport is the best in the piece : and the saving of it. The scene is laid in a London coffee-house—the sub-title of the play being ' Le Café.' Fréron appeared as Frélon : which, being translated, is wasp or hornet. Wasp is a Grub Street hack ' always ready to manufacture infamy at a pistole the paragraph.' ' When I discover a trifle, I add something to it : and something added to something makes much.' The tactics of scandalous journalism are unaltered to this day. ' The Philosophers ' was broadly burlesqued : and to philosophy were gravely ascribed all the evils under the sun.

The play was received with delight. Foe as well as friend laughed aloud. Pretty Madame Fréron nearly fainted when she saw her husband thus travestied ; and did not make matters better by naïvely replying to a friend, who assured her that Wasp did not in the least resemble her husband who was neither slanderer nor informer, ' Oh ! Monsieur, it is too well done ! He will always be recognised.'

The performance took place at five o'clock in the afternoon. The next day, July 27, was a Sunday, and the day for the appearance of a number of ' The Literary Year.' It contained an account of that first night under the title of ' The Account of a Great Battle,' written in that cool and easy style, principally remarkable for its moderation and self-restraint, which was the finest weapon in Fréron's armoury. It ended with a ' Te Voltairium,' a sort of parody of the Te Deum, which was licensed by the censor, to the great indignation of the philosophers who had so often been profane—and unlicensed.

Meanwhile, at his Délices, Voltaire wrote *his* account of that first night—' An Advertisement to the Scotch Girl.' The little, pricking, red-hot needles of his style

were much less effective for his purpose now than the
judicial calm of M. Fréron. But, after all, Voltaire
was the winner. 'The Scotch Girl' had what d'Alembert called 'a prodigious success.' The provinces
received it with rapture. It was played three times a
week in Paris. Its last performance there took place
on September 2.

And on September 3 it was replaced by 'Tancred.'

No man in the world better understood the force
of contrast, and the infinite value of the striking and
the *bizarre* upon the minds of his countrymen, than
Voltaire. In France, if anywhere, he who strikes must
strike at once; must appeal immediately to emotions
which are sooner at boiling point and sooner cooled
than the emotions of any other nation in Europe.
'The Scotch Girl' had made Paris laugh; and Paris
loved laughter. It had quite forgotten for the moment
that it had also loved Fréron, its dear, clever, sociable,
amusing journalist, who was pleasantly renowned for
giving charming little suppers, and being well patro-
nised by the great. Here, then, was the moment for
this Swiss exile, who belonged to the wrong party, who
persistently thought—and said—the wrong things, and
was infinitely able and dangerous, to strike in with
his 'Tancred.' To ensure its success a hearing was all
that it wanted. Its genius could be trusted to do
the rest. Voltaire took at the tide that flood which
leads on to fortune, and sailed straight into harbour.

He began 'Tancred,' it is said, in his joy on learning
of that decree which, in April 1759, forbade spectators
henceforth to sit on the stage. On the 19th of the next
month, May, he wrote that this day an old fool finished
a tragedy begun on April 22. At first he called it
'Aménaïde,' or 'my Knights,' or 'The Knighthood,'

and designed to have it played by Lekain or Lauraguais as the work of ' a young unknown.' ' I have changed the metre,' he wrote on May 29, 1759, ' so that that cursed public shall not recognise me by my style.'

In the October of 1759 he and his amateur company had acted it at Tourney. It moved the author and Madame Denis to tears ; but as he very justly observed, they were too near relations to the piece for their emotion to count for much. When Marmontel had stayed at Délices in the summer of 1760 he, too, had wept over it—had returned the manuscript with his face bathed in tears, which told the author, he said, all he wanted to know.

Every omen was good. For several weeks during the summer of 1760 the d'Argentals had the manuscript in their charge in Paris. They had seen it put into rehearsal. Then Voltaire had withdrawn it to punish a company which dared to produce ' The Philosophers.' But that brave ' Scotch Girl ' had effectually killed ' The Philosophers.' The time was ripe indeed.

The theatre was crowded to the full. No more piquant contrast could be imagined than between the rough English burlesque of last night and the polished, romantic Sicilian tragedy of this. Yesterday there had not been a grave face in the house, and to-day every eye was wet. Madame d'Épinay was there, in the most fascinating grief. ' Satan, in the guise of Fréron,' who was in the amphitheatre, spoke of the thing as having ' the simplicity and natural beauty of the classic, above all of the Odyssey.' When d'Alembert saw it for the third time, the whole audience was in tears. Mademoiselle Clairon surpassed herself as the heroine : so that the author, always largely generous in such appreciations, said that the piece owed to her all its success ;

and d'Olivet, Voltaire's old schoolmaster, declared there had been no such acting since the days of Roscius. As for Lekain—'nothing is comparable to Lekain, not even himself.' The truth was, luckily for Voltaire, that the play was so moving that few were sufficiently masters of themselves to criticise coolly, and did not even carp at the author for writing in a metre with which they were wholly unfamiliar. Marmontel, who wept over it, had declared very justly not the less, that the style was not equal to that of Voltaire's earlier tragedies ; that it was sometimes tedious, and a little wanting in vigour. But, after all, he had wept. Marmontel's attitude describes 'Tancred' exhaustively.

Satan in the amphitheatre criticised the piece with the only criticism that need never really hurt—a just one. He had mingled praise with his blame. Voltaire was sensible enough to recognise the weight of censure so tempered.

Fréron continued to conduct his 'Literary Year' until his death in 1776. When he gave any of the actors—such as Lekain or Clairon—a bad notice, they simply revived 'The Scotch Girl.' And M. Wasp mended his manners at once.

In September Voltaire dedicated his 'Tancred' to Madame de Pompadour. But that 'chicken-hearted fellow,' as he called her, made, at the time, no acknowledgment of the compliment. The truth was, as twice before in their history, some jealous scandalmonger about the Court had read an evil meaning into his flatteries.

Meanwhile the hermit of Délices, if ever in his life, was independent of her favours. Délices was charming : Ferney nearly finished : and Tourney the most histrionic place in Europe.

In the June of 1760 Marmontel had come to stay
at Délices. Marmontel was a great man now : a successful playwright ; and the author of that once much
read and now wholly forgotten novel, ' Bélisaire.' He
was not ungrateful to the benefactor who fourteen
years earlier had launched him on the literary sea of
Paris ; while Voltaire on his side had always a fellow-
feeling for that brave heart which at eighteen had
begun the world on a capital of six louis, hope, cleverness, and a translation. Marmontel brought with him
one Gaulard ; and found at Délices a M. Lécluse, the
King of Poland's dentist, who, when he was not
mending Madame Denis's teeth, acted and sang most
agreeably.

Of course, Marmontel found Voltaire in bed, dying.
And of course the moribund read aloud the ' Pucelle '
in the most lively and delightful manner in the world ;
took the visitors to see the view from Tourney, and
discussed with them theatres, Frederick the Great,
J. J. Rousseau—everything under heaven. He also
played chess with Gaulard, and listened to Marmontel's
poetry. And after a three days' visit, hereafter recorded
in minutest detail by Marmontel, the visitors left.

Another burst of gaiety marked the autumn. ' To
get rid of public misfortunes and my own,' the arch-foe
of Fréron conducted another theatrical season, and
asked so many people as actors or audience that,
one night at least, Délices, Tourney, and Ferney all
together would not hold them, and they had to be
drafted into neighbouring houses. Ferney was neither
finished nor furnished, but there were attics ready
which accommodated a few guests and their servants. Sometimes the plan was to dine at Délices,
see a play at Tourney, and sleep at Ferney—' on the

VOLTAIRE.

From the Bust by Houdon.

top of each other,' as the host said. The theatrical troupe would stroll about the gardens of Tourney in the moonlight in the intervals of their labours; and as they were young, and of both sexes, they no doubt took advantage of so excellent an opportunity for a little love-making. Corrupter of youth! cried Geneva, who was by no means best pleased just now with a Voltaire who a little earlier had fought Dr. Tronchin tooth and nail to establish a troupe of comedians of doubtful morals, only a quarter of a league from Geneva, though on French soil. Dr. Tronchin won—for the time; the comedians were ordered away, and Voltaire and his good doctor were excellent friends again; but it is not in the Calvinistic temperament in general to forget or to forgive easily.

And then this autumn season was marked by the presence of a most dissipated *roué* of a duke, the Duke of Villars, who was a patient of Tronchin's, and considerably madder upon theatricals than his host himself. He had acted from his earliest youth at Vaux Villars, where a Voltaire of five-and-twenty had fallen in love with that gracious Maréchale, Villars' mother. But her son, though he thought great things of himself and *would* coach the company in general, was a poor performer. He casually asked Voltaire one day how he thought he acted. 'Why, Sir, like a duke and a peer,' answers Voltaire. Poor Cramer, the actor-publisher, was so misinstructed by his noble friend, that it took him a fortnight to unlearn the lesson of this bad master. When he had done so, Voltaire cried out to Madame Denis, 'Niece, thank God! Cramer has disgorged his Duke!'

Also of the company was Mademoiselle de Bazincourt, Madame Denis's pretty, poor companion, who was destined to a convent from which Voltaire could not save her, and who meantime played the parts of ' Julia, her friend,' to perfection.

On September 29 a house-warming took place at Ferney, in the shape of the marriage there of M. de Montpéroux, the envoy of France. Voltaire gave a great dinner in his new house to celebrate the event, and from henceforth lived there—at first generally, and at last entirely.

On October 20 he and his theatrical company were sharply reminded by the Council of Geneva that ' Sieur de Voltaire had yesterday a piece played at Saint Jean, the territory of the republic, in distinct violation of a promise he had made in August 1755.' They went on acting as gaily and continuously as ever. It is to be feared that to this wicked Voltaire prohibitions were only sauce to the *plat*, and made it a hundred times the more irresistible.

In the December of this 1760, which was one of the most full, varied, and active years of one of the most energetic lives ever lived by man, Voltaire appeared in a new *rôle*. He adopted a daughter.

In estimating his character no trait in it has been more lost sight of than that which, for want of a better word, may be called his affectionateness. Yet the man who was the lifelong friend of false Theriot, as well as of faithful d'Argental, who kept a warm corner in his heart for ungrateful servants and ne'er-do-weel relatives, who supported tiresome nephews and at least one trying niece, to say nothing of that crippled profligate d'Aumard, had that quality in a very high degree. Satire and cynicism were in his every lively utterance. But in his acts were a tenderness, a generosity, and a charity, to which better men than he have not attained.

Mademoiselle Marie Corneille was the great-niece of the great Corneille. Poor and provincial, her father came up one fine day to Paris and claimed his cousinship with the great Fontenelle. But Fontenelle had so long lost sight of this branch of the Corneille family that he thought the man an impostor, and left his money elsewhere. Then, who but Fréron must needs take compassion on this hapless little family of three persons—father, mother, and daughter—and have a play of their uncle's performed for their benefit? But even five thousand five hundred francs do not go far, when out of the sum debts have to be paid, three persons to live, and one to be educated. Marie, of nearly eighteen, had to be removed from her convent. A friend took charge of her for a while. And then Le Brun, secretary to the Prince of Conti and a second-rate poet, conceived the happy idea of enlisting Voltaire's sympathy for her in an ode.

It is not an exaggeration to say that Voltaire adopted her on the spot. His only feeling seems to have been one of complete delight at having the opportunity of doing good in such a charming way : and he considered it, he said, an honour for an old soldier to serve the granddaughter of his general.

On November 5 he was arranging details for her journey and her education, with Le Brun.

He wrote to her direct to assure her she should have every facility for the practice of her religion, for reading, and for music ; that Madame Denis would supply her with a wardrobe ; that she should have masters for accomplishment ; and learn to act so that in six months she would be playing *Chimène*.

In the second week in December Mademoiselle arrived. Quiet, gentle, and good, as naïvely ignorant as she was ingenuously ready to learn, tenderly and faithfully attached to the father she had left as she was to grow girlishly fond of the father she had found, Marie Corneille comes like a fresh and virgin air across the tainted and heated atmosphere of that eighteenth century, like some human angel to the Voltaire who hardly ever, perhaps never before, had intimately known a good woman.

He began at once to give her lessons in reading and writing, and in grammar. Mademoiselle had not much aptitude for that 'sublime science,' or for any science. She had come out of her convent as widely and profoundly ignorant as even those good nuns could leave a girl. And the cleverest man of his age taught her to write, and made her send him little notes, which he returned to her with her very doubtful orthography corrected ; made history as amusing as a novel, and all the teaching go gaily ' without the least appearance of a lesson.' She was to have a tutor presently, when one good enough could be found. Meanwhile Voltaire taught her by word of mouth, while she looked up into his lean face with her clear candid eyes, and he looked back and delighted in her round girlish prettiness—' a plump face like a puppy's ' —and her adorable *naïveté*. Madame Denis forgot her comforts and her flirtations to nurse her when she was ' a little ill,' and to teach her needlework when she was well. All the servants adored her, and vied with each other to serve her. Presently she had her own *femme de chambre*. Every Sunday Voltaire and his niece took her to mass. Voltaire did not only preach tolerance. He did more even than leave her, when she prayed, ' her early Heaven, her happy views.' He made every careful provision, as he had said he

would, for her to follow the faith of her fathers.   The
sneer on his lips and the scorn in his soul died as he
looked at Marie Corneille.   Trust, simplicity, innocence
appealed not in vain to Voltaire, as they have appealed
not in vain to far worse men.   There is a noble touch
in that confession of his that, though he loved her well
enough to set a very high value on her love for him, he
liked nothing more in her than her unforgetting attach-
ment to her father.   To that father (who was, it may
be added, a very cavilling and trying person) he wrote
himself, thanking him with the finest tact and delicacy
for a loan so delightful, and repeatedly congratulating
himself on being the host of so charming a visitor.
Voltaire certainly knew how to confer a favour.

It was not unnatural that, when the news of
this adoption reached them, the devout should call
out loudly at a lamb being entrusted to such a wolf.
But it is noticeable that none of the devout offered to
support the lamb in their own sheepfold.   They only
demanded a *lettre de cachet* to get her away from
Voltaire.

There was another trouble too.   Fréron, though
he had helped her himself, was bitterly angry and
jealous at Voltaire's adoption.   In his 'Literary Year'
he inserted, with a very venomous pen, calumnies on
her father, and on the mode of education Voltaire
was providing for her.   Without the smallest ground
for such a charge he declared that her tutor was to be
Lécluse, the dentist and amateur actor, whom Fréron
represented as a kind of disreputable mountebank.

Voltaire instantly rose to the provocation.   He
always rose.   But when its subject was an innocent
girl, he may be forgiven that he was more furious
than wise.   He demanded justice from the minister

Malesherbes, and a formal apology from Fréron : and failed to get either.   So there appeared first a cutting epigram, and then an exceedingly scurrilous publication called 'Anecdotes of Fréron,' which Voltaire vehemently denied, but which that very best and most trustworthy of all possible editors, Beuchot, has included, not the less, in his Works.

Fréron's calumnies were not without effect.   They lost Marie Corneille a husband : who must have been well lost, since the sting of a Wasp frightened him away.

Meanwhile the life at Ferney and Délices went a busy and tranquil way ; and Papa Voltaire began to cast about in his mind the means for providing a *dot* for his daughter.

CHAPTER XXXV

BUILDING A CHURCH, AND ENDOWING A DAUGHTER

THE novel of the winter season of 1760–61 was ' The New Eloïsa,' by Jean Jacques Rousseau.

It is hardly possible to write a life of Rousseau or of Voltaire without comparing them. Voltaire, all sharp sense : and Rousseau all hot sensibility ; Rousseau, visionary, dreamer, sensualist, sentimentalist, madman : and Voltaire, the sanest genius who ever lived, practical, businesslike, brilliant, easy, sardonic. The one's name stands as a synonym for a biting wit, the other's for a wild passion.

Yet they had much in common. Both belonged to the great philosophic party. In the burning zeal of their mutual hatred of *l'infâme* Voltaire sometimes lost his head ; and Rousseau lost his heart. Both fought tooth and nail all their lives for Tolerance and for Liberty. Both foresaw that stupendous change called the French Revolution, and both foresaw it bloodless, serene, and glorious.

By January 21, 1761, ' Eloïsa,' which had been written in the little cottage Madame d'Épinay had lent Rousseau in the Montmorency forest, had been read at Ferney.

Rousseau had already been in opposition to Voltaire both on the subject of a theatre in Geneva, and on optimism.

But still, though they had greatly disagreed, they had not been (' Candide ' notwithstanding) exactly enemies.

And then, in the October of 1760 Voltaire had written gaily on the theatre subject—' Jean Jacques showed that a theatre was unsuitable to Geneva : and I, I built one.' Jean Jacques was at once too womanish, too impulsive, and too vain to keep long on good terms with a cynical person who could airily agree to differ in that way. He admired his rival's ' *beaux talents*,' but he was jealous of them. He was jealous, too, of his power and influence in Geneva. By the June of 1760 he had worked himself into something like hating this Voltaire ; and, Rousseau-like, he sat down and wrote a letter to tell him so. Voltaire, still perfectly cool, observed to Theriot on June 26 that Jean Jacques had become quite mad. ' It is a great pity.'

And then came ' The New Eloïsa.'

That tissue of absurdities and genius, of fine, false sentiments and highly ridiculous social views—set forth with the warmth, the energy, and the passion which are Rousseau's alone—would in any case have aroused Voltaire's contempt.

But when he added to it their present differences on the theatre topic, and their past differences on optimism, and the childish rancour of Rousseau's last letter—above all, when he saw that those owls, the public, opened their stupid eyes and were quite dazzled and delighted with the sham glitter of this false romance about the highly improper Julie and her no more respectable tutor—his ire was roused.

He dubbed 'Eloïsa' 'foolish, *bourgeois*, impudent, and wearisome.' It was 'one of the infamies of the century' to have admired it. And he wrote to Theriot: ' No novel of Jean Jacques, if you please. I have read him for my misfortune ; and it would have been for his if I had the time to say what I thought of it.'

The last words were only the blind which hood-winked nobody. ' There is time for everything if one likes to use it.' Staying at Ferney at the moment was the Marquis de Ximenès, ex-admirer of Madame Denis and now forgiven that unpleasant little business of the stolen manuscript of a few years back.

There quickly appeared four letters on (or rather against) ' The New Eloïsa,' the first of which bore the signature of the Marquis, and all of which bore un-mistakable traits of a famous style.

Voltaire denied them, according to custom.

But it was the denial *pour rire*.

The wise d'Alembert wrote and remonstrated with his friend for ' declaiming openly' against Jean Jacques, who, after all, was of their party and with a warmth and ardour which might serve it well.

But Rousseau had begun to sting and irritate the sensitive skin of his great rival, and would by no means be shaken off. In the October of 1761 Voltaire said that Jean Jacques wrote about once a fortnight to incite the Genevan ministers against theatres.

In the meantime, fortunately for them both, Voltaire had interests which eclipsed even that ex-cited by a sentimental rival's annoying Puritanism or longwinded romance.

He was fighting the Jesuits and building a church.

On January 1, 1761, he wrote to tell Helvétius that he had reclaimed from the Jesuits of Ornex, his neighbours, with whom he had hitherto been on good terms, the estate belonging to six poor brothers, of which the Jesuits had robbed them during their minority.

To compass this act the Jesuits had allied themselves with a Calvinistic Councillor of State of Geneva. There is no doubt at all that Voltaire delighted, as he said, in thus triumphing over both Ignatius and Calvin ; or that the defeat of the Jesuits gave him as much pleasure as the victory of the brothers. But when it is added that he had lent those brothers, without interest, all the money necessary to reclaim their heritage ; that he spent on them an incalculable amount of that time which was more valuable to him than any money, it must be allowed that if his motives were mixed, good preponderated in the mixture.

And then he turned his extraordinary mind towards building a church.

The church scheme had been on the *tapis* as far back as the August of 1760. The truth was that the old church at Ferney was not only very hideous and tumbledown, but spoilt a very good view from the château. If churches there must be to enslave men's souls, thinks Voltaire, why, they need not offend their eyes as well. I will build a new one !

Every Sunday it was now his habit not only to attend mass with Marie Corneille and Madame Denis, but to be duly incensed thereat as lord of the manor. He also looked after his poor, and behaved very much as a conscientious country landowner ought to behave, but as, in the eighteenth century, he very seldom did.

But still this sceptic, this free-thinker, this wicked

person who had just successfully brought home to the
good Jesuits an accusation of robbery, was certainly a
character whose every act the devout might well eye
suspiciously.

Voltaire cautiously obtained the permission of the
Bishop of Annecy to change the site of the church,
and then began pulling down with a will. He was to
bear all the expenses himself. If the deed was not
strictly right in law, it was so excellent in morals that
it had been done with impunity hundreds of times
before.

In the rasing operations, part of the churchyard
wall had to be taken down, and a large cross, which
dominated the churchyard, removed.

All would have been well, however, if this unlucky
Voltaire had not had, as usual, an enemy on the spot.
When he first came to Ferney, it will be remembered
that he had successfully fought Ancian, the curé of the
neighbouring parish of Moens, for a tithe of which
Ancian had long deprived the poor of the neighbourhood. Ancian, whom Voltaire vigorously described as
'brutal as a horse, cross-grained as a mule, and
cunning as a fox,' had not forgiven that affront easily.
But worse was to come.

On December 28, 1760, a young man, wounded and
nearly bleeding to death, had been brought to the
doors of Ferney. Voltaire did not only take him in
and care for his body. With that passionate love of
fair-play which was so fatal to the ease and comfort of
his life, he determined to ferret out the rights of the
case and get justice done.

It appeared that three young men had been supping,
after a day's hunting, at the house of a woman of
whom Ancian was commonly reported the lover.

Ancian, and 'some peasants his accomplices,' rushed
in and violently attacked the three men, nearly
killing Decroze, the one who had been brought to
Ferney.

Here is a pretty state of things! says Voltaire. A
priest who is not only thief but murderer as well! He
set to work at once. He moved heaven, earth, and the
authorities to get M. Ancian 'employment in the
galleys.' He found out Decroze's father and sister.
He tried to rouse the father's timidity and apathy to
action. The sister told him, on her oath, that her
confessor had refused her absolution if she did not force
that father to renounce his son's cause.

By January 3, 1761, Voltaire was passionately
complaining that a 'feeble procedure' against the
criminal had hardly been begun. The province was
divided on the subject. All Voltaire's letters of the
time are full of it. But Ancian was protected by his
order. It was thought, as it has been often thought
before and since, that the scandal of punishing the
crime would be greater than the scandal of leaving it
unpunished.

Ancian had to pay Decroze a sum down; but he
kept his living, and nursed his revenge.

When he saw M. de Voltaire pulling down the
churchyard wall and removing the cross, he knew that
the time had come. He assured his brother curé of
Ferney and the simple people of the place that this
atheist of a Voltaire had profaned their church; that
he had not only moved the cross without first fulfilling
the usual formalities, but had cried out, 'Take away
that gibbet!' Ancian, therefore, on the biblical principle of an eye for an eye and a tooth for a tooth,
denounced Voltaire to the ecclesiastical judge of Gex

as guilty of sacrilege and impiety, and involved him in a 'criminal suit of the most violent character.'

But Ancian did not know, though he ought to have known, the sort of man with whom he had to deal. Voltaire's blood was up. A criminal lawsuit, forsooth, for ' a foot and a half of churchyard and two mutton cutlets which had been mistaken for disinterred bones ' ! There was an angry note in that laugh which meant fight. Further, his enemies were saying publicly that they hoped to see him burned, or at least hanged, for the glory of God and the edification of the faithful; and meanwhile his church building operations were stopped.

It was an old principle of his always to turn their own weapons against his foes. He had not forgotten it. He put himself into correspondence with an able ecclesiastical lawyer of Lyons. He read up ecclesiastical histories, and ancient volumes of Church law; and then suddenly flung at the head of the enemy such a mass of rules and precedents, of dreary old parallel cases, of mouldering decrees which councils had forgotten to revoke, of longwinded formulas and bylaws whose existence and orthodoxy were as indisputable as they had been unheeded, and of authorities who were infinitely sound, obscure, and confusing— that the priestly party put its hands to its ears, cried ' Peccavi ! ' and confessed itself beaten on its own ground.

In the meanwhile its surprising little foe, who ' passionately loved to be master,' had rased the whole church at Ferney to the ground, ' in reply to the complaints of having taken down half of it,' had removed the altars, the confessional boxes, and the fonts, and sent his parishioners to attend mass elsewhere.

To crown all, and to leave nothing undone that could be done, by June 21 he had forwarded the plan of his church to the Pope, and applied to his Holiness for a bull granting him absolute power over his church-yard, permission for his labourers to work on *fête* days, instead ' of getting drunk in honour of the Saints' according to custom, and for sacred relics to place in the church.

The letters to Rome are, very unfortunately, lost. But, through Choiseul, they reached there; and the requests were granted in part. On October 26, 1761, the Holy Father sent a piece of the hair shirt of St. Francis of Assisi—the patron saint of François Marie Arouet. On the same day, in tardy recognition for the dedication of ' Tancred,' came a present of the portrait of Madame de Pompadour. ' So you see,' wrote Voltaire, ' I am all right both for this world and the next.'

When his church was finished he inscribed on it *Deo Solo* (sic), which by September 14, 1761, he had altered to *Deo erexit Voltaire*. He was fond of saying that it was the only church in the universe which was dedicated to God alone, and not to a saint. ' For my part I had rather build for the Master than for the servants.'

He had designed his own tomb jutting out from the wall of the church. ' The wicked will say that I am neither inside nor out.'

In March a public event distracted his thoughts for a moment from ' Eloïsa,' Ancian, and the church building. The Dauphin's eldest son died; and Pom-pignan, as Historiographer of France, lifted his diminished head from Montauban and from those ' mountains of ridicule' which covered him, and wrote a eulogium of the little boy, which alas! for foolish

Pompignan, was also another attack on the philosophers. Voltaire waited a little. Then he wrote two
pieces of 'murderous brevity'—the 'Ah! Ahs!' and
the 'Fors.'

Down went the head of Pompignan again. If it
even peeped up for a moment, which it still did now
and then, Ferney shot an arrow at it from the richest
quiver and with the deadliest aim in the world.

But he had better things to do now than hitting an
enemy who was down.

That dear spoilt daughter of the house, who might
interrupt even the chess or the verse reading of *vif*
Papa Voltaire with impunity—who was pretty and
naïve enough to do anything in the world she liked
with him—still had no *dot*.

On April 10, 1761, Voltaire wrote to Duclos, secretary of the Academy, and proposed that he (Voltaire)
should edit and annotate Corneille's works, in an
edition of the classics then appearing under the
patronage of the Academy, for the benefit of the great
Peter's great-niece.

To say that Voltaire put his whole heart, soul, and
body into the thing and worked at it like a galley slave,
and worked till he made all Europe work too, is no
exaggeration. He began by getting up a subscription,
which remains one of the best managed, if not *the* best
managed, and certainly the most successful thing of its
kind ever undertaken. He advanced all money for preliminary expenses himself. The King of France, the
Empress of Russia, the Emperor and Empress of
Austria, Choiseul, and Madame de Pompadour figured
imposingly and attractively on his list. The nobles
and notables of France, courtiers, farmers-general, and
literary men quickly followed suit. In England the

givers included good Queen Charlotte, Lords Chesterfield, Lyttelton, Palmer, Spencer, and the great Mr.
Pitt.   To Pitt, Voltaire wrote, in the English he was
always clever enough to remember, when expedient ;
and Pitt replied favourably.

By May, only a month after the subscription was
started, and before a single copy of the work was ready,
enough money had come in to afford Marie Corneille
a yearly income of fifteen hundred francs.

Voltaire was far from finding the labour congenial.
To the vigour of his creative genius work that was
so largely mechanical soon became irritating and
tiresome.   Still, it consoled him, as he said, for those
public disasters in the Seven Years' War which were
fast making France the fable of the nations and the
laughing-stock of Europe ; and presently for that
crushing defeat of the French by Frederick the Great
at Villinghausen on July 15.

That he was an excellent commentator is proved by
the fact that his Commentary remains unrivalled, and
is still *the* text-book on Corneille.   With an ear as exquisitely delicate for a harmony as a discord, with that
single-minded love of good literature which equally
prevented him being flatterer or caviller, Voltaire was
the critic who, like the poet, is born, not made.   He
admired warmly ; but he blamed candidly.   'It is true
that Corneille is a sacred authority ; but I am like
Father Simon, who, when the Archbishop of Paris
asked him what he was doing to prepare himself for
the priesthood, replied, "Monseigneur, I am criticising the Bible." '

When Martin Sherlock was at Ferney in 1776 he
observed that the English preferred Corneille to Racine.
'That,' said Voltaire, ' is because the English do not

know enough of the French language to feel the beauties of Racine's style or the harmony of his versification. Corneille pleases them better because he is more striking ; but Racine for the French because he has more delicacy and tenderness.'

When the Commentary was finished it numbered many volumes, and 'served to marry two girls, which never before happened to a Commentary,' said the Commentator, 'and never will again.'

By a peculiarly delicate thought, *poor* literary men received copies as gifts.

The autumn of 1761 was not dull at Ferney. Among the visitors were Abbé Coyer and Lauraguais, wit and playwright, and one of those highly unsatisfactory clever people who *can* do everything, and do nothing.

Besides the visitors, the autumn was marked by the progress of the quarrel with de Brosses, from whom Voltaire had bought Tourney, and with whom he was still deeply engaged in a lawsuit for 'fourteen cords of firewood.'

The man who gave a home to d'Aumard, to Marie Corneille, and to Father Adam, and who pensioned his poor relations without in the least accounting it to himself for righteousness, was incredibly sharp and mean over this firewood with de Brosses, and wasted his time and his talents in the fight. The details of the quarrel are long, uninteresting, and profitless. But it must in justice be said that it shows Voltaire 'at his very worst : insolent, undignified, low-minded, and untruthful.' Besides quarrelling with de Brosses, with Ancian, and Rousseau, editing Corneille, writing 'Peter the Great,' revising the 'Essay on the Manners and Mind of Nations,' and looking after three estates, this wonderful man also found time in 1761 for his usual gigantic correspondence, and to write two plays. The correspondence alone comprises letters to a king and cardinals, prime ministers, and actresses, *savants* and *salonières*, besides letters to old friends like Panpan and Madame de Champbonin; letters in English and Italian, and in rhyme; and letters *from* people he had never seen. In this July a burgomaster of Middleton had written to inquire of him if there is a God; if, supposing there be one, He troubles about man; if Matter is eternal; if it can think; and if the soul is immortal. The burgomaster added that he would like an answer by return of post. 'I receive such letters every week,' Voltaire wrote to Madame du Deffand. 'I have a pleasant life.'

From 1760 until 1768 he was also writing constantly to that Damilaville who was so steady a foe of *l'infâme*, and who took Theriot's place as Voltaire's Parisian correspondent. Theriot had long sunk into a goodnatured parasite of any rich man who would give him a good dinner and an idle life; while Damilaville, if he *was* heavy and mannerless, as Grimm said, was a patient and tireless disciple; who ran all Voltaire's errands in Paris for him; despatched to Ferney constant packets of books, manuscripts, and news; and, in brief, loved and worked for Voltaire as sincerely as he loathed, and worked against, *l'infâme*.

On October 20, 1761, Voltaire wrote to tell his Angels that the fever took him on Sunday and did not leave him till Saturday—which, being interpreted, meant that at sixty-seven years old he had composed in six days the tragedy of ' Olympie.'

But even in a Voltaire—a Voltaire of whom Joubert justly said that ' his mind was ripe twenty years sooner

than other men's, and that he kept it, in all its powers,
thirty years later'—such quick work could not mean
his best work.

The Angels recommended revision.

'It was written in six days,' wrote Voltaire to a
friend whose opinion he desired. 'Then the author
should not have rested on the seventh,' was the answer.
'He did, and repented of his work,' replied Voltaire.
The play written in six days took six months to
correct.

In the meantime, and for fear one should get idle
and the brain rust, he flung on to paper a versified
comedy called 'Seigneurial Rights' ('Le Droit du
Seigneur'). It had been rehearsed at home by
December 17. It was to pose as the work of one
Picardet, an Academician of Dijon, until its success was
established.

But once again Voltaire had to reckon with an old
enemy. Crébillon of eighty-eight was still envious,
and now censor of plays. He recognised the style of
Picardet, Academician of Dijon, and refused to license
his play unless a scene from his (Crébillon's) hand was
added. Chafing Voltaire called this scene a carnage of
all his best points.

Early in the new year 1762 Crébillon died, at peace
with all the world, it was said, even his profligate of a
son—and M. de Voltaire. But Voltaire had too much
to forgive in return. He wrote the 'Éloge de Crébillon,' and once more peaceful d'Alembert had to
complain of his *vif* friend losing his temper—' a satire
under the name of a eulogy.' 'I am sorry you chose the
moment of his death to throw stones on his corpse.'
'He had better have been left to rot of himself : it would
not have taken long.'

D'Alembert was right, as he had been before.

Meanwhile 'Seigneurial Rights' had been produced on January 18, 1762, and had met with a success far above its slender merits.

January also saw another temporary resurrection of poor Pompignan. It was Voltaire himself who had provoked the poor man to turn in his grave this time, by writing to a popular tune and in a catching metre 'A Hymn Sung at the Village of Pompignan.'

This he sent round to his friends with a guitar accompaniment. It became *the* air of Paris ; and the street boys, it is said, sang it *at* the Pompignans as they passed. A little later Voltaire wrote a burlesque 'Journey of M. le Franc de Pompignan from Pompignan to Fontainebleau,' and replied to an attack Brother Aaron de Pompignan, Bishop of Puy, had been foolhardy enough to make upon the philosophers, with such a running fire of pamphlets, epigrams, and irony as might have slain a far abler foe.

And so *exeunt* the Pompignans for ever.

In January, too, Voltaire published a pamphlet called 'The Extract of the Opinions of Jean Meslier,' Meslier having been a curé who left at his death papers seeking to prove the falsehood of the religion which he had professed. Voltaire put it into shape. It was a curious and a very human document. He was not a little disgusted that 'tepid' Paris did not receive it with more enthusiasm.

But if Paris was tepid, that cold King seemed to be getting a little warmer. Voltaire wrote to tell Duclos on January 20 that his Majesty had restored to him an old pension.

'What will Fréron say to *that* ? What will Pompignan?' wrote the delighted pensioner naïvely. There was also a rumour that his Majesty has been pleased to recall M. de Voltaire. That was false. And Voltaire, since he could not reach the grapes, took the very sensible *rôle* of declaring that they were sour. No doubt they really were. The fruit of his own labours was at least far sweeter. To work in the Ferney garden with Lambert, his stupid gardener—'my privateer'—was safer too. 'Love like a fool when you are young—work like a devil when you are old,' was one of Voltaire's rules of life. He had to his hand now work, beside which even gardening at Ferney was dull and useless, and waiting in a king's antechamber a shame and a contempt.

On March 10, 1762, Jean Calas was broken on the wheel.

CHAPTER XXXVI

THE AFFAIR OF CALAS

IN 1761 and 1762 Toulouse, the capital of Languèdoc and the seventh city of France, was one of the most priest-ridden in the kingdom. The anniversary of that supreme crime of history, the Massacre of St. Bartholomew, was always legally celebrated as a two days' festival. The Revocation of the Edict of Nantes had been commemorated by two frescoes erected at the public expense. In Toulouse no Protestant could be a lawyer, a physician, a surgeon, an apothecary, a bookseller, a grocer, or a printer; he could not keep either a Protestant clerk or a Protestant servant; and in 1748 an unhappy woman had been fined three thousand francs for acting as a midwife without having first become a Roman Catholic.

The city was further celebrated for its monastic orders, the White, the Black, and the Grey Penitents; and for a collection of relics which included bones of the children massacred by Herod and a piece of the robe of the Virgin.

In such a place, not the less, Jean Calas, a Protestant shopkeeper, had lived honoured and respected for forty years.

On the evening of October 13, 1761, he, his family,

and a young friend sat at supper in his house over his shop, at No. 16 Rue des Filatiers.

Jean Calas, the father, was sixty-three years old, and rather infirm ; kind, benevolent, and serene ; anything but a bigot, in that Louis, one of his sons, who was a Toulouse apprentice, had embraced the Roman faith with the full consent of his father, who supposed the matter to be one in which each must judge for himself.

Madame Calas, though of English extraction, was an excellent type of the best kind of French *bourgeoise*—practical, vigorous, alert—aged about forty-five.

Peter, the second son, was an amiable but rather weak youth of about five-and-twenty. There were two daughters, Rose and Nanette, who were away from home upon this particular evening, as was also Louis (who was still in receipt of a money allowance from his father) ; and Donat, the youngest boy, who was living at Nîmes.

Mark Anthony, the eldest son of the family, was the only unsatisfactory person in it. Only twenty-eight years old, he was one of those gloomy and discontented characters who, the world being ' a looking-glass which gives back to every man the reflection of his own face,' saw all life *en noir*.

His character had been further soured by the discovery that the profession he had set his heart on was not open to a Protestant ; and that he could not be admitted to the Bar without producing a certificate from his curé declaring him a Catholic.

Mark Anthony endeavoured to gain this certificate by simply suppressing his Protestantism. But he failed. Change his religion he would not. If there was a bigot among the Calas, he was the one. He alone of the family had bitterly opposed the conversion of Louis.

Another situation he desired he had to give up through his father's lack of capital. He grew more and more morose. He hung about the cafés and the billiard saloons, bitter and idle. In a theatrical company he had joined he would declaim, it is said, Hamlet's monologue on death, and other pieces dealing with suicide, with an 'inspired warmth.'

The establishment at the Rue des Filatiers was completed by Jeannette Viguière, the *bonne à tout faire*, an ardent Roman Catholic and the faithful friend and servant of the family for thirty years.

On the evening of this October 13, 1761, a friend of the Calas, Gaubert Lavaysse, a youth about twenty, came in unexpectedly just as the Calas were going to sit down to supper.

Hospitable Madame bade Mark Anthony, who was sitting in the shop, 'plunged in thought,' go and buy some Roquefort cheese to add to their simple meal. He did as he was asked. He joined the party at supper in the parlour, next to the kitchen. They talked on indifferent topics. It was remembered afterwards that the conversation, among other things, fell upon some antiquities to be seen at the City Hall, and that Mark Anthony spoke of them too. At the dessert, about eight o'clock, he got up, *as was his custom*, from the table and went into the adjoining kitchen.

'Are you cold, *M. l'Aîné*?' said Jeannette, thinking he had come to warm himself.

'On the contrary—burning hot,' he answered. And he went out.

The little supper party meantime had gone into the salon, where, except Peter, who went to sleep, they talked until a quarter to ten, when Lavaysse left. Peter was roused to light him out.

When the two got downstairs into the shop a sharp cry of alarm reached the salon. Jean Calas hurried down. Madame stood at the top of the stairs for a moment, wondering and trembling. Then she went down. Lavaysse came out of the shop and gently forced her upstairs, saying she should be told all.

In the shop Lavaysse and Peter had found the dead body of the unhappy Mark Anthony suspended from a wooden instrument used in binding bales of cloth, which the poor boy had placed between two doorposts, and on which he had hanged himself. On the counter lay his coat and vest, neatly folded.

Jean Calas cut the cord, lifted the body down, put it on the ground, and used all possible means to restore life. Impelled by that awful sense of unknown disaster, Madame and Jeannette came down too, and with tears, and calling the boy's name, tried all remedies— unavailingly.

Meanwhile, Calas had bidden Peter go for the doctor. He came, by name one Gorse, but he could do nothing. Then Peter, beside himself, would have rushed into the street to tell their misfortune abroad. His father caught hold of him : ' Do not spread a report that he has killed himself ; at least save our honour.'

The feeling was in any case a perfectly natural one. But how much more natural in that dreadful day when, as Calas knew well, the body of a man proven a suicide was placed naked on a hurdle with the face turned to the ground, drawn thus through the streets, and then hanged on a gibbet.

Lavaysse had also run out of the house. Peter, finding him at a neighbour's, told him to deny that

Mark Anthony had committed suicide. Lavaysse agreed. Voltaire spoke hereafter of that decision as ' a natural and equitable ' one. It was. But it was one of the most fatal ever uttered.

The neighbours were roused by now. Many rushed in to give assistance. Among others was an old friend of the family's, Cazeing by name. Clausade, a lawyer, said the police ought to be fetched. Lavaysse ran to fetch them.

Meanwhile a crowd had gathered outside the house. It had the characteristics of most crowds—perhaps of all French crowds—it was intensely excited; it was exceedingly inventive; and it would follow a leader like sheep. What *had* happened in that house ? In 1835 there still stood over the door a signboard with the inscription, ' Jean Calas, *Marchand d'Indiennes.*' It stood there then. Calas ? Calas ? Why, Calas was a Huguenot. From among the people came a word— one of those idle words for which men shall give account in the Day of Judgment—' These Huguenots have killed their son to prevent him turning Catholic ! ' The idea was dramatic and pleased. The crowd caught it up. It was the match to the faggot, and the whole bonfire was ablaze at once.

But there was one man there at least, David de Beaudrigue, one of the chief magistrates of the city, whom, from his position, it should have been impossible to move a hair's breadth by an irresponsible word, and who is eternally infamous that, hearing such a cry, he believed it. But, for the doom of Calas, Beaudrigue was both bigot and fanatic. It has been well said by Parton, one of Voltaire's biographers, that ' if the words had blazed . . . across the midnight sky in letters of miraculous fire,' Beaudrigue ' could not have

believed them with more complete and instantaneous
faith.'

He hastened into the house with his officers and
arrested every person in it, including young Lavaysse,
who had fought his way back there through the crowd,
and Cazeing the friend. Through the ill-lit streets,
thronged with an excited mob, the little party were
taken to the Hôtel de Ville. Mark Anthony's body
was borne on a bier before them. The Calas and their
friends thought, as they might well think, that they
were only going to give testimony of what had occurred.
Grief, not fear, was in their hearts. So little did they
anticipate not returning to their house that evening
that Peter had put a lighted candle in one of the
windows to light them when they came back. 'Blow
it out,' said David. 'You will not return so soon.'

On every step of that dreadful journey to the Hôtel
de Ville the ardent imagination of that southern crowd
grew hotter. From saying that Calas had murdered
his son to prevent him turning Catholic, it was only a
step to the assertion that among the Huguenots such
an act was common, encouraged, and esteemed a virtue.
Before that town hall was reached Mark Anthony had
become a martyr to the true faith; and Jean, his
father, was already condemned to the most horrible of
all deaths, on the most horrible of all accusations.

When the prisoners reached the place they still
persisted in that most natural but most fatal falsehood,
that Mark had not committed suicide. It still did not
occur to their simplicity and their innocence that they
could ever be accused of murdering one so dear to them.
They were soon to be enlightened. They were separated, locked, with irons on their feet, into separate
cells. Jean Calas and Peter were left in complete

darkness. Cazeing was soon released. But Lavaysse, the unhappy young visitor, was imprisoned too. On the days following they were each separately examined on oath. All then confessed that the boy had committed suicide, and all told stories which tallied with each other. Their depositions were such that if clear evidence, reason, and justice ever appealed to bigots, they would have been liberated at once.

But David had been occupying his time in still further infuriating the people. The priests seconded him. One of his own colleagues warned him not to go so fast.

' I take all the responsibility,' he answered. ' It is in the cause of religion.'

It is noticeable that, in his bloody haste, and though he assumed the case to be one of murder, he had never examined the shop at the Rue des Filatiers to see if it bore marks of a struggle, or the clothes of the supposed murderers. Yet how could it be thought that ' the most vigorous man in the province,' eight-and-twenty years old, would allow his feeble father of sixty-three to strangle and hang him without making any resistance ? And if resistance was made, where were the rents and the blood stains ?

If, too, the boy had been killed because he was about to change his religion, should not his room have been searched for some objects of Catholic piety, some signs of the dreadful struggle of the soul ? His person *was* searched. On it were found a few papers of ribald songs.

For three weeks the body of this strange martyr was kept embalmed, lying in the torture chamber of the Hôtel de Ville. As it had been assumed without a shred of evidence that Mark Anthony had been about

to join the Roman Church, it was equally easy to
assume that he had also been about to enter one of the
monastic orders. Popular fancy chose the White Penitents as the order of Mark's intentions. He was buried
on a Sunday afternoon, 'with more than royal pomp,'
in the great cathedral, and with the full and splendid
rites of the Roman Church. Thousands of persons
were present, and a few days after a solemn service for
the repose of the soul of their Brother was held by the
White Penitents.

For three successive Sundays from the pulpits
in all the churches was read an admonition to give
testimony, 'by hearsay or otherwise,' against Jean
Calas.

To be sure, such testimony would never be difficult
to obtain in any case or in any place, but in priest-
ridden Toulouse, against Jean Calas, it might well have
been on all lips.

After the five prisoners had spent five months in
separate dungeons, chained by the feet, the trial began.
It must be remembered that of the accused one was
Jeannette, an ardent Roman Catholic, who had not
only helped to convert Louis, but who had given no
offence to his Protestant relatives by so doing.

On March 9, 1762, Jean Calas was tried first, and
alone, for the murder of his son on the previous
October 13. He was tried by thirteen members of the
Toulouse Parliament, who held ten sessions. The
witnesses against him were of this kind: a painter
named Mattei said that his wife had told him that a
person named Mandrille had told her that some person
unnamed had told *her* that he had heard Mark
Anthony's cries at the other end of the town. Some
of the witnesses against Calas disappeared before the

trial came on, feeling the strain on their inventive powers too great.

It was assumed by the prosecution that Mark Anthony *could* not have hanged himself in the place where the Calas swore they had found him ; but, as has been noted, the prosecution never went to see the place.

For the prisoner, on the other hand, was the most overwhelming evidence.

First, it was the most unnatural of crimes. Secondly, it was impossible at the father's age and weakness that he should have murdered his strong son alone.   If he had not murdered him alone, it must have been with the assistance of the family party, of whom one was Jeannette, the ardent Catholic, and another was Lavaysse, the casual visitor.

The testimony of all these people *for* Calas agreed absolutely—except on one or two minor and wholly immaterial points.

But, in the case of this prisoner, it was not merely that the law of his day declared him guilty until he was proved innocent.   Calas was declared guilty without being allowed a chance of proving himself innocent.   The accused was never then permitted a counsel.   But with Calas, the people sat on the judgment seat with Pilate ; assumed the prisoner's guilt, not without evidence, but in the teeth of it ; and had condemned him before he was tried.   Some of the magistrates themselves belonged to the confraternity of the White Penitents.

One of them only—M. de Lasalle—had the courage to object to the mockery of the proceedings.   ' You are all Calas,' said a brother judge.   ' And you,' answered Lasalle, ' are all People.'

By eight votes to five, then, ' a weak old man was
to be condemned to the most awful of all deaths '
(first the torture, and then to be broken on the wheel)
' for having strangled and hanged with his feeble
hands, in hatred of the Catholic religion, his robust
and vigorous son who had no more inclination towards
that religion than the father himself.'   The words are
the words of him who, said Madame du Deffand,
became all men's *avocat*, Voltaire.

Out of those thirteen judges three voted for torture
only, and two suggested that it might be better to
examine the shop at the Rue des Filatiers and see if
a suicide *were* impossible.   One hero alone voted for
complete acquittal.

The terms of the sentence display a savage ferocity,
of which only a religious hatred is capable.   To the
exquisite tortures to which Calas was condemned, even
the brutes who, drunk with blood and believing in
neither God nor devil, committed the worst excesses
of the French Revolution never fell.

This mock trial had taken place on March 9.   On
March 10 that sentence of ghoulish and delighted
cruelty was read to the victim.   He was taken straight
to the torture room, the oath was administered, and
with the rack in front to remind him of the fate
awaiting him, he was cross-examined.   He answered
as he had always answered—He was innocent.   When
asked who were his accomplices, he replied that as
there had been no crime there could be no accomplices.
One witness speaks of his ' calmness and serenity.'
Yet he was a feeble man, not young, who for five
months had been chained in a dark dungeon, accused
of the most awful of crimes, and knowing that in his

downfall he had dragged down with him everything he loved best in the world.

He was then put to the first torture—the *Question Ordinaire*. The very record of such horrors still makes the blood run cold. But what man could bear, man can bear to hear. First bound by the wrists to an iron ring in the wall, four feet above the ground, ' and his feet to another ring in the floor of the room,' with an ample length of rope between, ' the body was stretched till every limb was drawn from its socket.' The agony was then ' increased tenfold by sliding a wooden horse under the lower rope.' Thus, in mortal torment, Calas was questioned again. He maintained his innocence, and ' neither wavered nor cried out.'

After a rest—a rest!—of half an hour, during which the magistrates and a priest questioned him again, he was put to the *Question Extraordinaire*. Water was poured into his mouth by force until ' he suffered the anguish of a hundred drownings.'

He was then questioned again ; and again maintained his innocence. Then more water was poured into him, until his body was swollen to twice its natural size. He was again questioned ; with the same results.

Then the devils called Christians, who persecuted him in the name of Christ, saw that their aim would be defeated. Calas would not confess. But he could die.

He was taken on a tumbril in his shirt only—how many were to go thus to doom after him !—to the place of execution. From time to time he said ' I am innocent.' The crowd—in temper and intent the crowd who eighteen hundred years before had cried ' Crucify Him ! '—reviled him as he went, as they

had reviled his Master. At the scaffold a priest, whom
he knew personally, once more exhorted him to confess.
' What, Father ! ' he said. ' Do you too believe that a
man could kill his own son ? ' Then, again like the
Truth for Whom he suffered, he was bound on a cross.
The executioner broke each of his limbs in two places
with an iron bar. He lived thus for two hours,
praying for his judges.

A few moments before his death a priest again
exhorted him to confess. ' I have said it,' he answered.
' I die innocent.' At that supreme moment he
mentioned Lavaysse—the boy upon whom he had
brought so unwittingly ruin and disgrace. Then
David de Beaudrigue, who felt that he was in some
sort cheated of his prey without a confession, bade him
turn and look at the fire which was to burn him, and
confess all. He turned and looked. The executioner
strangled him ; and he died without a word.

His noble courage at least saved the lives of his
family. Peter was condemned to perpetual banishment, ' which if he was guilty was too little ; and if
he was innocent was too much.' He was forced into
a monastery ; and, being a weak character and told
that if he did not abjure his religion he should die
as his father had died, he recanted in a terror not
unnatural.

His mother was liberated. She crept away with
Jeannette into the country near Toulouse, to hide her
broken heart. Her two daughters were flung each
into a separate convent. Young Lavaysse was sent
back to his family, ruined alike in health and in
prospects.

Donat Calas, the youngest of the family, the
apprentice at Nîmes, had had to leave France when

the trial came on, for fear of being indicted as an accomplice. He went to Geneva.

On March 22, 1762, only twelve days after the death of Jean Calas, Voltaire mentioned the case in writing to Le Bault. He was not at once moved to take any side. The affair was not his. But if he did take any, it was the side of Catholicism. 'We are not worth much,' he said airily, ' but the Huguenots are worse than we are. *They* declaim against comedy.'

But the affair made him think. Two days later he wrote that it ' took him by the heart.' Then he learnt that Donat was near him—at Geneva; that the boy had fled there on hearing of the trial. *That* seemed like guilt. ' I am interested as a man, and a little as a philosopher. I want to know *on which side* is this horror of fanaticism.' At the end of March, Audibert, a merchant of Marseilles, who had happened to be in Toulouse when the Calas tragedy was enacted, called on Voltaire and told him the facts of the case as they had appeared to him. Foul play somewhere, thinks Alain's pupil and Arouet's son, putting those facts together. But where? ' I told him (Audibert) that the crime of Calas was not probable; but it was still more improbable that disinterested judges should condemn an innocent man to be broken on the wheel.'

Disinterested? There lay the crux. Voltaire's feelings were roused; but they had not run away with him. On March 27 he wrote to d'Argental: ' You will ask me, perhaps, why I interest myself so strongly in this Calas who was broken on the wheel? It is because I am a man. . . . Could you not induce M. de Choiseul to have this fearful case investigated?'

Every day, nay every hour, a mind far keener and

shrewder than any Choiseul's was investigating it
then : collecting evidence ; writing innumerable letters ;
working, working ; tempering with cool discretion a
zeal that burnt hotter every moment as the innocence
of Calas forced itself upon his soul ; labouring with that
' fiery patience,' that critical judiciousness, which in such
a case alone could win.

At the end of April he went from Ferney to Délices,
that he might be nearer Donat Calas ; study him ; hear
an account of his family from his own lips. The boy
was only fifteen ; cried when he told that piteous story ;
and spoke of both his father and mother as infinitely
kind and indulgent to all their children.

Lest he should be moved by those emotions which
grew stronger every day, or by a moral conviction in
the innocence of Calas not fully borne out by physical
facts, Voltaire sought the opinion of wise and capable
friends. He employed Végobre, an able (and notably
unimaginative) lawyer of Geneva, to investigate legal
points ; and for hours and hours would remain closeted
with him. Ribotte-Charon, a merchant of Toulouse,
himself warmly interested in the case, Voltaire induced to examine the site of the supposed murder and
to study local details. One Chazel, solicitor of Mont-
pellier, he engaged to interview the leading magistrates of the Languedoc district and to procure
documents.

But to obtain a formal investigation of the affair
it was necessary to get the ear of the Chancellor of
France, the Count of Saint-Florentin. Voltaire incited
every powerful friend he had in the world to assail
this person. Villars and Richelieu were made to
bombard him. What was the use of Dr. Tronchin's
famous and influential patients if they could not be

induced to attack M. Florentin too ?   Tronchin roused
them, and they did as they were told.   At Geneva was
the Duchesse d'Enville, also a Tronchin patient, clever,
powerful, and enlightened.   Voltaire fired her with his
own   enthusiasm,   and   she   wrote   direct   to   Saint-
Florentin.   As for Pompadour and Choiseul, Voltaire
undertook them himself.   The Pompadour was always
'one of us' in her heart; and while she hated the
Jesuits, Choiseul did not love them.

By the end of June, Voltaire had brought Madame
Calas up to Paris and begged his Angels, 'in the name
of humankind,' to take her broken life under their
wings.   She had not been easy to persuade to come.
She was crushed to the earth, as she might well be.
Hope for the future, or hope for vengeance for the
past, she had none.   Only one passionate desire seems
to have been left her—to get back her daughters from
the convents into which they had been forced.   The
property of criminals was then confiscated to the King,
and she had not a farthing in the world.   But Voltaire
paid all her expenses—content to wait until the
generosity of Europe should refund him.   For counsel
he gave her d'Alembert and the famous *avocat*,
Mariette.   On June 11 he appointed Élie de Beaumont as Mariette's colleague.   It is always a part of
cleverness to discover the cleverness of others.   Beaumont was young and unknown ; but he was a most
able choice.

On July 4 Peter Calas escaped from his monastery,
and joined Donat at Geneva.   Voltaire had thus the
two brothers under observation.   He put them through
searching inquiries.   Peter was naturally a most important witness.

On July 5 Voltaire first spoke to d'Argental of

the ' Original Documents concerning the Calas ' which
in this month he gave to the world.   They are for
all time a model of editorial genius.   They consist
only of an extract from a letter from Madame Calas,
and of a letter from Donat Calas to his mother.
Voltaire's name did not appear at all.   They contain
that most damning of all evidence—a perfectly clear
and simple statement of plain facts.   If the editor contributed order and brevity, he left the quiet pathos of
the woman and the passionate eagerness of the boy to
speak for themselves.

The ' Original Documents ' he quickly followed up
by a ' Memoir and Declaration ' : the ' Memoir ' purporting to be by Donat Calas, the ' Declaration ' by
Peter.

Once again he wholly obliterated himself.   Only a
Voltaire's genius could have curbed a Voltaire's passion
and made him rein in, even for a while, his own fiery
eloquence, speak as those poor Calas would have
spoken, and wait.

He knew now, by every proof which can carry conviction to the mind, that they were innocent; and he
had given those proofs to the world.

But that was not enough.   In August he published
' The History of Elizabeth Canning and of the Calas.'
Nothing he ever wrote shows more clearly how perfectly he understood that April nation, his countrymen.   ' Documents ' and ' Declarations '!   Why, they
at least *sounded* dull ; and eighteenth-century Paris
was not even going to run the risk of a yawn.   ' One
might break half a dozen innocent people on the wheel,
and in Paris people would only talk of the new comedy
and think of a good supper.'   But Paris loved to be
made to laugh one moment and to weep the next;

to have its quick pity touched and its quick humour tickled—in a breath.

'The History of Elizabeth Canning' is sarcastically amusing—an account of that enterprising young Englishwoman who nearly had another woman hanged on the strength of a story invented by herself and her relatives.

'It is in vain that the law wishes that two witnesses should be able to hang an accused. If the Lord Chancellor and the Archbishop of Canterbury depose that they have seen me assassinate my father and my mother, and eat them whole for breakfast in a quarter of an hour, the Chancellor and the Archbishop must be sent to Bedlam, instead of burning me on their fine testimony. Put on one hand a thing absurd and impossible, and on the other a thousand witnesses and reasoners, and the impossibility ought to give the lie to all testimonies and reasonings.'

'The History of the Calas' was that sombre and terrible story told by a master mind : passionate, and yet cool ; moving, and yet cautious in argument ; the work at once of the ablest, keenest, shrewdest lawyer in the case, and of the man who said of himself, almost without exaggeration, that for three years, until Calas was vindicated, a smile never escaped him for which he did not reproach himself as for a crime.

He did not appeal to ' that great and supreme judge of all suits and causes, public opinion,' in vain. The Calas case became the talk of Europe. Men felt, as Donat had been made to say in his Memoir, that 'the cause was the cause of all families ; of nature ; of religion ; of the state ; and of foreign countries.'

Voltaire had his Calas pamphlets translated and published in Germany and England. Generous England

came forward with a subscription list for the unhappy
family, headed by the young Queen of George III., and
to which the Empress of Russia and the King of Poland
became contributors.

But still, to rouse men's interest was but a means
to an end. The end was to obtain first from the
Council of Paris a decree ordering that the case should
be re-tried, and then that fresh trial itself. The obstacles were not few or trifling. Louis XV. and Saint-
Florentin, in spite of the influence brought to bear
upon them, were both opposed to such a course. A too
strict and searching justice did not suit the monarchy
of France. Louis XV. was always wise enough to let
sleeping dogs lie if he could, instead of convening
States-General and dismissing and recalling ministers
to please the people they governed, like that weak fool,
his successor. 'Why can't you leave it alone?' was
the motto of both King and Chancellor over the Calas
case. And they would have lived up to it, but that the
public opinion which had a Voltaire as its mouthpiece
was too strong for them.

Another difficulty lay in the fact that Lavaysse *père*
was so terrified by the Parliament of Toulouse that he
took much persuading before he would appear openly
on the side of Voltaire and as a witness for his own
son. Then, too, the natural passionate eagerness of
Madame Calas to get back her daughters, immediately
and before the time was ripe, had to be curbed ; and,
far worse than all, that miserable Toulouse Parliament
had so far entirely declined to furnish any of the papers
concerning the trial, or even the decree of arrest.

In September Élie de Beaumont was ready with
an able 'Memoir' on the case, signed by fifteen of his
brother barristers. He showed that there were 'three

impossibilities' in the way of Calas having murdered his son. 'The fourth,' said Voltaire, 'is that of resisting your arguments.' The 'Memoir' was naturally more technical than Voltaire's, but it was not more clever, nor half so moving.

Another friend of the case, the brave Lasalle, who had become 'the public *avocat* for Calas in all the houses of Toulouse,' and had been challenged to a duel on the subject by a brother magistrate, was also in Paris in November. In December, through the untiring exertions of the Duchesse d'Enville, herself a mother, Nanette and Rose, the daughters, were restored to Madame Calas.

On December 29 Voltaire wrote that this restoration was an infallible test of the progress of the case. But, he added, 'it is shameful that the affair drags so long.'

Drags so long! Through the kindly veil that hides the future, even a Voltaire's keen eyes could not penetrate. For nine months he had now dreamt Calas, worked Calas, lived Calas. Every letter he wrote is full of him. For that one man whom he had never seen, and who died as, after all, thousands of others had died, the victim of religious hatred, Voltaire forgot the drama which his soul loved, and that aggravating Jean Jacques' latest novel, 'Émile,' which his soul scorned. Calas! Calas! For those nine months the thing beat upon his brain as regularly and unremittingly as the sea breaks on the shore. For Calas was more than a case : he was a type.

Voltaire had first thought that he saw in that dreadful story *l'infâme* in the garb of a cold and cruel Calvinism, changing the tenderest instincts of the human heart into a ferocity which made a father the

murderer of his own son.   And then he had discovered
that it was that old *l'infâme* he knew better—*l'infâme*
who in the person of priest and magistrate kept the
people ignorant, and then inflamed that ignorance for
their own shameful ends.

What Calas had suffered, others might suffer.   While
he was unavenged, while that criminal law and procedure which condemned him went unreformed, while
his judges were not rendered execrable to other men
and hateful to themselves, who was safe ?

To Voltaire the cause of Calas was the cause of
Tolerance ; that Tolerance which was the principle
and the passion of his life.

CHAPTER XXXVII

THE 'TREATISE ON TOLERANCE'

ONE of the disadvantages of biography as compared with fiction is, that in real life many events occur simultaneously, and the dramatic effect of a crisis is often spoilt by that crisis being extended over a long period of time and being interrupted by trivialities.

The Calas case, at whose 'dragging' Voltaire had cried out at the end of nine months, lasted for three years—a period which is certainly a severe test of enthusiasm.   Voltaire's triumphantly survived that test.   At the end of those three years he was only more eager, passionate, and laborious than he had been at the beginning.

But in the meantime there were Ferney, Tourney, and Délices to manage ; Madame Denis always needing amusement, and Marie Corneille always needing instruction ; that busy, hot-headed rival, Rousseau, to be taken into account, to say nothing of friends and enemies, visitors and plays.

On March 25, 1762—just about the time when the first rumours of the Calas story reached Voltaire— 'Olympie' took what may be called its trial trip at Ferney.   Two or three hundred people sobbed all through it in the most satisfactory manner, and all felt cheerful enough to enjoy a ball and a supper afterwards.

In April, these enthusiastic amateurs were once
more delighted by a visit from the great actor Lekain.
He had been at Délices in 1755 ; but there was a beautiful new little theatre at Ferney now, where ' Olympie '
was played again. Lekain looked on as a critic ; and
Voltaire did the same, being debarred from his dear
acting by a cold in the head.   ' Tancred ' was played
too, and when there came that line :

> Oh cursed judges ! in whose feeble hands—

the whole house got upon its feet and howled itself
hoarse. It would not have been like Voltaire to hide
from his friends, even if he could have done so, a
subject that so possessed him as the subject of Calas.
' It is the only reparation,' he said, writing of the scene,
' that has yet been made to the memory of the most
unhappy of fathers.'

Charming the audience with her soft voice and
round girlish freshness, Marie Corneille was now
always one of the actresses. She had by this time a
pretty *dot* as well as a pretty face ; and Papa Voltaire,
in addition to the proceeds of the Corneille Commentary,
had settled a little estate upon her. A suitor naturally
appeared soon upon the *tapis*. But though he was
warmly recommended by the d'Argentals, M. Vaugre-
nant de Cormont seems to have been chiefly remarkable
for large debts, a very mean father, and the delusion
that he was conferring a very great honour on Mademoiselle by marrying her. He had taken up his abode
at Ferney, and when he had received his *congé* was
not to be dislodged without difficulty. Mademoiselle
was serenely indifferent to him ; so no harm was
done.

Marrying and giving in marriage was to the fore in

the Voltaire *ménage* just then.   In May Madame de
Fontaine became the wife of that Marquis de Florian
who had stayed with her at Ferney and long been her
lover.   Voltaire was delighted—not in the least on the
score of morality—but because he thought the pair
would suit each other, which they did.

On June 11, 1762, 'Émile, or Education,' Jean
Jacques' new novel, was publicly burnt in Paris.   Nine
days after, it was condemned to the same fate in Geneva.
'Émile' expresses in nervous and inspired language
some of those theories which Voltaire's friend, Dr.
Tronchin, had worked so hard to bring into practice.   It
was not so much the education of children that 'Émile'
dealt with, as the education of parents.   To abolish the
fatal system of foster-motherhood, instituted that the
real mothers might have more time for their lovers,
their toilettes, and their pleasures, to portray a child
brought up in natural and virtuous surroundings—even
an eighteenth-century censor could not have found
matter meet for burning in this.   But 'Émile' was only
a scapegoat.   'The Social Contract,' published a little
earlier, was what the authorities really attacked.

Neither the publication of 'Émile,' nor its burning,
particularly attracted Voltaire's notice at first.   Like
Lasalle, he was all Calas.   On July 21 he wrote in-
differently to Cideville that Rousseau had been banished
from Berne and is now at Neufchâtel, 'thinking he is
always right, and regarding other people with pity.'   For
the 'Profession of Faith of a Savoyard Vicar' which was
'imbedded in "Émile,"' Voltaire indeed not only felt,
but expressed, a very sincere admiration.   But your
'Eloïsa' and your 'Émile,' and your hysterics generally,
why, they bore me, my dear Jean Jacques!   And you
are so dreadfully longwinded, you know!   However,

the 'Savoyard Vicar ' had shown that Rousseau had the
courage of his unbelief.   It was the kind of heroism in
which Voltaire was not going to be behindhand.   In
July 1762 appeared his 'Sermon of Fifty,' whose
excellent brevity was a reproach and a corrective to the
four immense volumes of 'Émile,' and whose virulent
attack upon the Jewish faith was at least as outspoken
and unmistakable as the Vicar's 'Profession.'

This fifty-paged pamphlet is noticeable as the first
of Voltaire's works which is openly anti-Christian.
Goethe declared that for it, in his youthful fanaticism,
he would have strangled the author if he could have
got hold of him.

Rousseau, of course, took 'The Sermon of Fifty'
amiss, as he was fast coming to take amiss everything
Voltaire did.   Jean Jacques was quite persuaded, for
instance, that it was Voltaire who had incited the
Council of Geneva to burn 'Émile'; and, presently,
that it was Voltaire's hand which guided the pen of
Robert Tronchin's 'Letters from the Country,' which
favoured the burning of 'Émile,' and to which Rousseau
was to make reply in the brilliant and splendid inspiration of his famous 'Letters from the Mountain.'

The truth seems to have been that Voltaire laughed
at Jean Jacques instead of losing his temper with him ;
or, rather, that he lost his temper with him for an occa-
sional five minutes, and then laughed and forgave
him.   Végobre, the lawyer, who is described as having
'no imagination' to invent such stories, was once
breakfasting at Ferney when some letters came detailing
the persecution inflicted on Rousseau for his 'Vicar.'
'Let him come here ! ' cried Voltaire.   'Let him come
here !   I would receive him like my own son.'

The Prince de Ligne also records how, after Voltaire

had vehemently declared that Jean Jacques was a monster and a scoundrel for whom no law ever invented was sufficiently severe, he added, ' Where is he, poor wretch ? Hunted out of Neufchâtel, I dare say. Let him come here ! Bring him here : he is welcome to everything *I* have.'

All the sentiments were genuine, no doubt. It would have been perfectly in Voltaire's character to abuse Rousseau by every epithet in a peculiarly rich vituperative vocabulary, and to have received him with all generous hospitality and thoughtful kindness as a guest in his house for months ; to have quarrelled with him and abused him again, and once more to have received him as a brother.

After all, Voltaire was not a perfect hater.

That sodden, worthless Theriot came to Délices for a three months' visit in July, with all *his* treachery and ingratitude amply forgotten ; and in October that very showy hero, Richelieu, who was always in money debt to Voltaire, descended upon his creditor with a suite of no fewer than forty persons. They had to be accommodated at Tourney, and *fêtes* and theatricals devised for their master's benefit. The Duchesse d'Enville and the Duke of Villars were also staying with Voltaire, who was quite delighted to discover that a Richelieu of sixty-six still kept up his character for gallantry, and to surprise him at the feet of a charming Madame Ménage, a Tronchin patient. The pretty face and wit of Madame Cramer also quite vanquished the susceptible elderly heart of the conqueror. Voltaire offered to get rid—temporarily—of her husband. But Richelieu had reckoned, not without his host indeed, but without his hostess. Sprightly Madame Cramer laughed in his face.

The first authorised publication of a work which had been suggested at Richelieu's supper table thirty-two years earlier belongs, by some *bizarrerie* of destiny, to this 1762, which also saw the noblest work of Voltaire's life—the defence of Calas and the preaching of the Gospel of Tolerance.

Whoso has followed its author's history has also followed the ' Pucelle's.'

Alternately delight and torment, danger and refuge ; now being read in the Cirey bathroom to the ecstatic bliss of Madame de Graffigny, now passed from hand to hand and from salon to salon in Paris, now being copied in Prussia, and then burnt in Geneva, hidden in Collini's breeches at Frankfort, and stolen from Émilie's effects by Mademoiselle du Thil—the adventures of the ' Pucelle ' would form a volume.

Considered intrinsically, it is at once Voltaire's shame and fame. It is to be feared that there are still many people who are only interested in him as the author of the ' Pucelle ' ; while there are others to whom the fact that he wrote it blots out his noble work for humanity, and the bold part he played in the advancement of that civilisation which they, and all men, enjoy to-day.

That Voltaire took in vain the name of that purest of heroines, Joan of Arc, is at least partially forgivable. He did not know, and could not have known, the facts of her life as everybody knows them to-day. His offences against decency may be judged in that well-worn couplet :

> Immodest words admit of no defence,
> And want of decency is want of sense.

Only one excuse need even be offered. Voltaire wrote to the taste of his age. As the coarse horseplay and boisterous mirth of the novels of Fielding perfectly portrayed humour as understood by eighteenth-century England, so the gay indelicacies of the 'Pucelle' represent humour as understood by eighteenth-century France.

The fact that women, and even women who were at least nominally respectable, were not ashamed to listen and laugh at those airy, shameful *doubles ententes*, proves that the thing was to the taste of the time ; as the fact that 'Tom Jones' and 'Joseph Andrews' were read aloud to select circles of admiring English ladies proves that Fielding likewise had not mistaken the taste of his public.

The 'Pucelle' is infinitely bright, rollicking, and amusing. Voltaire's indecency was never that of a diseased mind like Swift. He flung not a little philosophy into his licence, and through sparkling banter whispered his message to his age. Those ten thousand lines of burlesque terminated, it has been said, the domination of legends over the human mind. Condorcet goes so far as to declare that readers need only see in the author of the 'Pucelle' the enemy of hypocrisy and superstition.

But the fact seems to be that though Voltaire was constantly hitting out, as he always was hitting, at hypocrisy and superstition, the blows this time were only incidental ; and that he wrote first to amuse himself, and then to amuse his world.

That he succeeded in both cases, condemns both it and him.

If Voltaire's connection with Madame du Châtelet was a blot on his moral character, the 'Pucelle' was a darker blot. It spread wider to do harm. His passionate and tireless work for the liberation of men's souls and bodies, for light and for right, make such blots infinitely to be regretted.   That the best work in the world is not done by morally the best men is a hard truth, but it is a truth.

Of the 'Pucelle' it can only be said,

> But yet the pity of it, Iago!—O Iago, the pity of it!

On February 12 of 1763 the man who had not only written the most scandalous of epics, but had tended Marie Corneille with as honest a respect and affection as if she had been his own innocent daughter, married her to M. Dupuits, cornet of dragoons, handsome, delightful, three-and-twenty, and head over ears in love with Mademoiselle.   M. Dupuits united to his other charms the fact that his estates joined Ferney, and that he was quite sufficiently well off.   One little trouble there had been.   Père Corneille disapproved not only of this marriage, but of any marriage, for his daughter. Voltaire sent him a handsome present of money to assuage his wounded feelings, but did not invite him to the ceremony lest young Dupuits should have cause to be ashamed of his father-in-law, and that graceless Duke of Villars, who was also at Ferney, should laugh at him.   The ceremony took place at midnight on February 12, and the wedding dinner was at least magnificent enough to give Mama Denis, as Marie called her, an indigestion.   There were no partings. The young couple took up their abode at Ferney, where their love-making gave the keenest delight to a large element of romance still left in Voltaire's old heart, and where presently their children were born.

It was not wonderful that the good fortunes of Marie Corneille should have incited many other off-shoots of that family to 'come pecking about,' as

Voltaire said, to see if there was anything for them. Only a month after she was married, a certain Claude Etienne Corneille, who was in the direct line of descent from the great Corneille, and not in the indirect, like lucky Marie, appeared at Ferney. But Voltaire, though he thought Claude an honest man and was sorry for him, could not adopt the whole clan. His mood was still adoptive, however.

In this very year he took to live with him Mademoiselle Dupuits, Marie's sister-in-law; and Father Adam, a Jesuit priest. Mademoiselle Dupuits was not less pretty than Marie, and very much more intelligent. Several of the noble Ferney visitors amused themselves by falling in love with her.

On March 2 Voltaire had written, 'We are free of the Jesuits, but I do not know that it is such a great good.'

The suppression of the Order of Ignatius (it was not confirmed by royal edict until 1764) first occurred to him as a splendid tilt at *l'infâme*—as the happiest omen for the future that those who had been so intolerant should themselves be tolerated no more. But reflection cooled him. What is the good of being rid of Jesuit foxes if one falls to Jansenist wolves? 'We expel the Jesuits,' he wrote to that good old friend of his, the Duchess of Saxe-Gotha, in July, 'and remain the prey of the convulsionists. It is only Protestant princes who behave sensibly. They keep priests in their right place.'

None of these reflections taken singly, nor all of them taken together, prevented Voltaire from receiving into his house—'as chaplain,' he said sardonically—a Jesuit priest called Father Adam, whom he had known at Colmar in 1754, and whose acquaintance he had

since renewed at neighbouring Ornex. To be sure,
Voltaire had no need to be afraid of any priestly influence, especially from one of whom he was fond of
saying, that though Father Adam, he was not the first
of men.

Like the Protestant princes, Voltaire knew very
well how to keep *his* priest in his proper place. The
Father was an indolent man, with a little fortune of
his own and a rather quarrelsome disposition. But
he made himself useful at Ferney for thirteen years by
entertaining the visitors and playing chess with his lord
and master. One of the visitors declared that Adam
was Jesuit enough to let himself be beaten at the game
—his opponent so dearly loved to win ! But another,
La Harpe, who was at Ferney a whole year, denies this,
and declares that Voltaire frequently lost the game,
and his temper, and when he saw things were going
badly with him told anecdotes to distract his adversary's
attention. A third authority states that when the
game was practically lost to him, M. de Voltaire would
begin gently humming a tune. If Adam did not take
the hint and retire at once, Voltaire flung the chessmen
one after another at the Father's head. Prudent
Adam, however, usually left at once. When Voltaire
had become calmer, he would call out profanely,
' Adam, where art thou ? ' The Father came back ;
and the game was resumed as if nothing had happened.

Another member of a colony, which, as Voltaire
said, was enough to make one die of laughter, was the
fat Swiss servant, Barbara or Bonne-Baba, who showed
her contempt for her illustrious master quite plainly
and to his great enjoyment, and assured him she could
not understand how anybody could be silly enough to
think he had an ounce of common-sense.

If it was a laughable household, it was, as its master also said, a household that laughed from morning till night, and could be, that lively cripple d'Aumard included, as lighthearted as childhood.

But through all, never forgotten for a moment or put aside for a day, was the affair of Calas.

On March 7, 1763, that affair had its first triumph. On that day the Council of Paris met at Versailles, the Chancellor presiding, and all the councillors and ministers, religious and civil, attending, and decreed that there should be a new trial and that the Toulouse Parliament should produce the records of the old. Madame Calas and her two girls were present. All through the winter it had been considered an honour to call upon them, or to meet them at the d'Argentals' house. Councillors and officials vied with each other in thoughtful attentions to them all. During the sitting of the court one of the girls fainted, and was nearly killed with kindness. Some person, thought to be young Lavaysse, with a style charmingly candid and simple, has written an account of the day. Not only was the court 'all Calas'—its eighty-four members unanimously voted for the case to be retried—but her Catholic Majesty, Marie Leczinska herself, who had by no means forgotten to hate their great *avocat*, Voltaire, received Madame Calas and her daughters with kindness. The King himself had 'formally approved' that the papers of the procedure at Toulouse should be sent to the Council of Paris. The hostile influence of Saint-Florentin had been more than counteracted by the favourable, though secret, influence of Choiseul.

When Voltaire, waiting feverishly at Ferney, heard the long hoped-for decree, his heart gave one great leap of joy. 'Then there *is* justice on the earth ; there *is* humanity,' he wrote. 'Men are not all rogues, as people say ; . . . it seems to me that the day of the Council of State is a great day for philosophy.'

He eagerly concluded that this at last was the beginning of the end. But there was still infinite room for that slow courage called patience.

Now being passed from hand to hand in Paris, and having been so passed since the beginning of the year 1763, was what may be called the fruit of the Calas case : fruit of which men to-day may still eat and live : the pamphlet of two hundred pages which advanced by many years the reign of justice, of mercy, and of humanity—the 'Treatise on Tolerance.'

That sermon, of which the text is Calas, is one of the most powerful indictments ever written against the religious who have enough religion to hate and persecute, but not enough to love and succour. Voltaire was no Protestant, but that 'Treatise' helped the 'definite affranchisement' of the Protestant in Catholic countries as no party tract ever did. It gave the fatal blow to that 'Gothic legislation' which, if it was dying, still showed now and then a superhuman strength in acts of fiendish barbarism. Sooner or later, said Choiseul, such seed as is sown in Voltaire's Gospel of Tolerance *must* bear fruit. What if the author of it had thrown decency to the winds in the 'Pucelle' ? What if, basing his attack on seemingly irreconcilable statements and incorrect dates, he had in keen mockery attacked the Scripture and Christianity ? Not the less 'the true Christian, like the true philosopher, will agree that in making tolerance and humanity prevail, Voltaire, whether he wished it or no, served the religion of the God of peace and mercy : and, instead of anger,

will feel a reverent admiration for the ways of a Provi-
dence which, for such a work, chose such a workman.'

Voltaire did not avow his little Treatise. What
censor would or could have licensed such a thing ?
For a long time it was not even printed. By Voltaire ?
What could make you think so ? The old owl of
Ferney screwed up his brilliant eyes and chuckled.
'Mind you do not impute to me the little book on
Tolerance. . . . It will not be by me. It could not
be. It is by some good soul who loves persecution as
he loves the colic.'

That he foresaw it would be one of his best passports
to posterity, did not make him in the least degree more
anxious to own it to his contemporaries. Abundant
experience had proved to him that if it is 'an ill lot to
be a man of letters at all, there is something still more
dangerous in loving the truth.'

So through the year 1763 the 'Treatise on Tolerance'
was passed from hand to hand in Paris : by a good
priest, you understand ; by nobody in particular. And
at Ferney, Voltaire, having preached tolerance, practised it.

At the convent into which Nanette Calas had
been thrown was a good Superior who had loved and
pitied the girl and poured out upon her the thwarted
maternal instincts of her woman's heart. It is very
pleasant to see how a hot partisan like Voltaire not only
gave the Sister her due, but dwelt tenderly on her
tenderness ; sent on to his brethren, the philosophers,
her kind little letters to Nanette ; and warmed his old
heart at the pure flame of the affection of this 'good
nun of the Visitation.'

Then, too, when in June the liberal-minded citizens
of Geneva appealed against the condemnation of rival

Rousseau's 'Émile,' and when on August 8 that condemnation was revoked at their request, Voltaire was quite as delighted as if Jean Jacques had always been his dearest friend, and as if he had thought anything about that hysterical 'Émile,' except the 'Profession of the Savoyard Vicar,' worth the paper it was written on.   Tolerance !   Tolerance !

About the same time he produced the 'Catechism of an Honest Man,' which had a like burden ; and before the year 1763 was out he was deeply engaged in helping other unfortunates whom the case of Calas and that 'Treatise' threw at his feet.

In 1740 a daring Protestant gentleman of that fatal Languedoc, called Espinas, or Espinasse, gave supper and a bed to a minister of his faith.   For this heinous crime he was condemned to the galleys for life, and had been there three-and-twenty years when his story reached Ferney.   Through Voltaire's exertions he was released in 1763, and came to Switzerland, where his wife and children were living as paupers, on public charity.   After interceding passionately for them for not less than three years, Voltaire succeeded in getting back a small part of the property which Espinas had forfeited on his imprisonment.

After Espinas came the case of Chaumont.   In February 1764 Voltaire was writing to Végobre to say that Choiseul had delivered from the galleys one Chaumont, whose crime had consisted in listening to an open-air Protestant preacher—'praying to God in bad French.'   He had companions in irons whom Voltaire's power and pity could not free.   But Chaumont himself came to Ferney to thank his benefactor ; and all Voltaire's little *entourage* made him compliments, including Father Adam.

Though that 'Tolerance' was not yet tolerated in Paris; though at the beginning of 1764 it was forbidden to go through the post, as if it contained the germs of some infectious disease ; though Calas was still unexculpated, and even powerful Choiseul could not push his authority far enough to liberate the innocent companions of Chaumont, still Voltaire thought that he saw light in the sky, and in the east the beginning of a beautiful day. 'Everything I see,' he wrote in prophetic utterance on April 2, 'sows the seeds of a Revolution which must infallibly come. I shall not have the pleasure of beholding it. The French reach everything late, but they do reach it at last. Young people are lucky : they will see great things.' And again : 'I shall not cease to preach Tolerance upon the housetops . . . until persecution is no more. The progress of right is slow, the roots of prejudice deep. I shall never see the fruits of my efforts, but they are seeds which must one day germinate.'

Tolerance ! Tolerance ! Between writing it, living it, dreaming it, the thing might have become a monomania, a possession. Only its great apostle was also a Frenchman—the most versatile son of the most versatile people on earth.

At the end of 1763 he had been privately circulating in Paris a gay novelette in verse called ' Gertrude, or the Education of a Daughter ' ; and a little later he was reviewing English books for a Parisian literary paper.

Then, too, in the autumn of 1763 the young Prince de Ligne—eighteen years old, bright, shallow, amusing, ' courtier of all Courts, favourite of all kings, friend of all philosophers '—had been staying at Ferney. It is said that before his arrival Voltaire, dreadfully fearing

he should be bored, took some strong medicine, so that
he could say (truthfully this time) he was too ill to
appear.   This very self-pleased and much-admired
young Prince is now only known to the world by the
account he has given of Voltaire *intime*.

He writes vividly both of his host's greatness and
littleness; tells how he loved the English, bad puns,
and his best clothes; how his torrents of visitors
wearied him, and what artful designs he invented to get
rid of them; how good he was to the poor; how 'he
made all who were capable of it think and speak;'
was charmed to find a musical talent in his shoemaker
—'*Mon Dieu!*   Sir, I put you at *my* feet—I ought to
be at yours'—how he thought no one too obscure
and insignificant to cheer with the liveliest wit and the
most amazing vivacity ever possessed by a man of
sixty-nine.

Ligne says he was quite delighted with the 'sublime
reply' of a regimental officer to the question 'What is
your religion?'

'My parents brought me up in the Roman faith.'
'Splendid answer!' chuckles Voltaire.   'He does not
say what *he* is!'

Early in 1764 young Boufflers, the son of that
Madame de Boufflers who was the mistress of King
Stanislas, and perhaps Madame du Châtelet's predecessor in the heart of Saint-Lambert, also came to
Ferney.   Boufflers was travelling *incognito* as a young
French artist.   He did not forget to write and tell
his mother of his warm reception by her old acquaintance.   Voltaire, with that rare adaptability of his,
easily accommodated himself to his guest's youth and
treated him *en camarade*; while Boufflers, on his part,
drew with his artist's pencil a clever rough sketch of

his host when he was losing at chess with Father Adam.

A further distraction from 'Tolerance' and the Calas came in the shape of the first public performance of 'Olympie' in Paris, on March 17, 1764. It had already been named by the public 'O l'impie!'—a title the author was by no means going to apply to himself; while as for it applying to the piece— 'Nothing is more pious. I am only afraid that it will not be good for anything but to be played in a convent of nuns on the abbess's birthday.'

'Olympie' was well received. But it was feeble, in spite of those many alterations of which the indefatigable author vigorously said, 'You must correct if you are eighty. I cannot bear old men who say "I have taken my bent." Well, then, you old fools, take another!'

He also said that he had written it chiefly to put in notes at the end on suicide, the duties of priests, and other subjects in which he was interested; so it was not wonderful that even his friends had to own it a failure.

When another play of his, called 'The Triumvirate,' was performed in July—purporting to be the work of an ex-Jesuit, and having cost its dauntless master more trouble in rewriting and altering than any of his other pieces—it was confessed a disaster by everyone.

But, after all, both pieces had served as a distraction to their author; so they had their worth and use.

Another event in the spring of 1764 also changed the current of his thoughts, turned them back to his far-away youth, and to the strifes and weariness of a Court he had renounced for ever. On April 15 died Madame de Pompadour. Voltaire was not behindhand in acknowledging that he owed her much. To be sure, she had supported 'that detestable Crébillon's detestable Catilina,' and had not been always a faithful friend in other respects. But she had been as faithful as her position permitted. She had had, too, ' a just mind : ' she ' thought aright.'

Of the easy manner in which Voltaire and his century regarded her morals it need only be said that it affords an excellent insight into theirs.

' Cornélie-Chiffon ' (as Voltaire called Marie Dupuits) ' gave us a daughter ' in June. Before that date, Mademoiselle Dupuits, her sister-in-law, portioned out of the ' Corneille Commentary,' had been married. Ferney was the resort of innumerable English, who came to see M. de Voltaire's plays, and told him what they thought of them with their native candour. The first volume of ' The Philosophical Dictionary ' slipped out in July 1764 anonymously, 'smelling horribly of the fagot.' Voltaire of course swore industriously that he had nothing to do with that ' infernal Portatif,' and of course deceived nobody.

In September he smuggled it, by a very underhand trick and with the connivance of some booksellers of Geneva, into that town.

His friends, the Tronchins, were so angry at the *ruse* that through their agency the ' Dictionary ' was burnt there in the same month by the executioner.

And then that great work, the rehabilitation of the Calas, was completed at last. In June 1764 the new trial had been begun. On March 9, 1765, exactly three years since he had paid for it the extreme penalty of that savage law, Calas was declared innocent of the murder of his son. With his innocence was re-established that of his whole family, of Jeannette

Viguière, and of young Lavaysse. The accused had to constitute themselves prisoners at the Conciergerie as a matter of form. There all their friends visited them, including Damilaville, who wrote of the visit to Voltaire. Still well known is Carmontel's famous engraving of this prison scene, with Lavaysse reading to the family, including Jeannette, his ' Memoir ' on their case.

The Council who tried them had five sittings, each four hours in length, and a sixth which lasted eight hours. There were forty judges who were unanimous in their verdict—'Perfectly innocent.'

As all the money subscribed for Madame Calas by Voltaire's efforts had been swallowed up in law expenses and long journeys, these forty judges petitioned the King for a grant to her and her children. And his Majesty presented them with handsome gifts of money. The family then asked him if he would object to them suing the Toulouse magistrates for damages.

But of this course Voltaire disapproved. ' Let well alone,' he said in substance : and they did.

It must be observed that not only had the sullen Parliament of Toulouse put every obstacle in the way of the new trial taking place, but that it never ratified the judgment of the Council of Paris. But that mattered little. The worst that Toulouse could do was done.

One of the magistrates, the infamous David de Beaudrigue, ' paid dearly for the blood of the Calas.' In February 1764 he was degraded from his office. He afterwards committed suicide. That innocent blood was indeed on him and his children. His grandson fell a victim to the fury of the tigers of the Revolution, who had not forgotten the drama of the Rue des Filatiers.

When the courier came with the news of the verdict
to Ferney, young Donat Calas was with Voltaire, and
Voltaire said that his old eyes wept as many tears as
the boy's.   In a passion of delight he wrote to Cideville
that this was the most splendid fifth act ever seen on
a stage.

But he had not done with the Calas yet.   The King's
gifts of money were insufficient.   So Voltaire got up
subscriptions for engravings of Carmontel's picture, and
made all his rich friends subscribe handsomely for copies.
One hung over his own bed for the rest of his life.

Peter and Donat Calas settled in Geneva.   When
in 1770 their mother and Lavaysse visited them there,
they all came on to Ferney.   Voltaire said that he
cried like a child   He never forgot to do everything in
his power to benefit and help the two young men, and
gave at least one of them employment in his weaving
industry when he established it at Ferney.

The Calas case was not without wide results on
current literature, art, and the drama.

Coquerel, who wrote a history of the case, states that
there are not less than one hundred and thirteen publica-
tions relating to it.   It forms the subject of ten plays
and 'seven long poems.'

Besides Carmontel's engraving, there are pictures of
'Jean Calas saying Good-bye to his Family,' 'Voltaire
promising his support to the Calas Family,' and many
others.

But its most important, its one immortal result, was
the 'Treatise on Tolerance'—the work of the man
without whom Calas would have never been avenged,
and *l'infâme* been left unchecked till the Revolution.

It is hardly possible to over-estimate the nobility
of Voltaire's part in the redemption of the Calas.

A man who did not love him said justly that such
a deed would cover a multitude of sins. *'Oh mon amie !
le bel emploi du génie !'* wrote Diderot to Mademoiselle
Voland. . . . 'What are the Calas to him? Why
should he stop the work he loves to defend them? If
there were a Christ, surely Voltaire would be saved.'

When one reflects on the enormous expenditure of
time, labour, and money the case required of him, and
the fact that he thoroughly knew the value of each,
Diderot's words do not seem greatly exaggerated.

To suppose he had any thought of his own glory in
the matter is not reasonable. He persistently gave the
lion's share of the credit to Élie de Beaumont. He himself had already as much fame as man could want. If
he *had* wanted more, he knew to it a thousand avenues
quicker and safer than the long Via Dolorosa of a legal
reparation.

That kind of fame would only endanger his person
and prestige, and make his chances of being well received
by King and Court weaker than ever.

But that he *did* recognise Calas as one of the best
works of his nobler self seems likely from a trifling
incident.

Thirteen years later, on his last visit to Paris, someone, seeing the crowds that surrounded him whenever
he went out into the street, asked a poor woman who
this person was who was so much followed.

'It is the saviour of the Calas,' she replied.

No flattery, no honour, no acclamation of that
glorious time gave Voltaire, it is said, so keen a pleasure
as that simple answer.

CHAPTER XXXVIII

THE SIRVENS AND LA BARRE

DESNOIRESTERRES has well observed that this mad eighteenth century produced the extraordinary anomaly of being at once that of scepticism and intolerance, of the most degraded superstition and the most bare-faced irreligion.   It might be thought—it is generally thought —that persecution would certainly not proceed from persons who were too indifferent to their faith to make the slightest attempt to live up to it.   But if the history of religious hatred be closely followed, it will be seen that it is precisely these persons who are the cruellest persecutors.   Perhaps they act on that old principle of compensation—' Give me the desire of my soul, and the gratification of my flesh, and by the scaffold, the torture, and the wheel, I will bring souls to the faith *I* only pro- fess.'   There seems no other explanation of the fact that this ' rotten age whose armies fled without a fight before a handful of men ; this age which laughed at everything and cared for nothing but wit,' was as fiercely intolerant and besottedly bigot as the age of Ignatius Loyola and Catherine de' Medici.

The case of Calas was but one of many.   It was not finished when another, scarcely less sombre and terrible, was brought under Voltaire's notice.

In 1760 there lived near fanatic Toulouse, at a place

called Castres, a Protestant family of the name of Sirven. Sirven *père*, aged about fifty-one, was a professional *feudiste* ; that is to say, he was a person learned in feudal tenures, who kept registers and explained the obsolete terms of ancient leases, and thus was brought much in contact with the great families of the province. Thoroughly honest, honourable, and respectable, his wife shared these qualities with him.   They had three daughters—Marie Anne, who was now married, Jeanne and Elizabeth, who both lived at home.

Elizabeth, the youngest, was feeble-minded ; but on that very account—on that old, tender parental principle of making up by love for the cruelty of fortune —she was the dearest to her parents.   On March 6, 1760, the poor girl suddenly disappeared.   After vainly hunting for her all day, when Sirven reached his home at night he was told that the Bishop of Castres desired to see him.   He went.   The Bishop informed him that Elizabeth, whose deficient brain was certainly not equal to weighing the *pros* and *cons* of different religions, had ardently desired to become a Roman Catholic, and that to receive instruction on that faith she had been placed in the Convent of the Black Ladies.   The poor father received the news more calmly than might have been expected.   He said that he had no idea his daughter wished to change her religion ; but that if the change was to be for her good and happiness, he would not oppose it.

The situation was a strange one.   But it had a very common solution.   The Bishop had a strong-minded sister who had caught that 'epidemic of the time,' which the infected called religious zeal.

Meanwhile poor Elizabeth in her convent, having been first 'taught her catechism by blows,' as Voltaire

said, began, like many another weak intellect under
strong suggestion, to see visions and to dream dreams.
She became, in short, what a nun might call a saint, but
what a doctor would call a lunatic. The Black Ladies
declared that she implored them to corporally chastise
her for the good of her soul; and it was certainly a
fact that when she was returned to her parents in the
October of 1760, quite insane, her body was ' covered
with the marks of the convent whip.' If her father
complained loudly of her treatment, such complaints,
though natural, were infinitely imprudent. My Lord
Bishop and the authorities kept a very keen official eye
on M. Sirven, and harried him on the subject of his
daughter whenever a chance offered. The sheep had
gone back to the wolves, the brand to the burning.
Rome never yet sat down with folded hands, as other
Churches have done, and calmly watched her children
desert her.

In the July of 1761 the Sirvens moved to a village
called St. Alby, that Sirven might be near some business on which he was engaged.

On December 17, 1761, when he was staying at
the château of a M. d'Esperandieu, for whom he was
working, Elizabeth slipped out of her home at night,
and never returned. Her mother and sister had at
once given notice of her disappearance, and prayed
that a search might be made. Sirven, called home,
arrived on the morning of the 18th, and caused a still
further search to be prosecuted. But in vain. A fortnight passed. On January 3, 1762, the unhappy
father, who fancied, not unnaturally, that Elizabeth
might have been decoyed away by her Roman friends,
had to go in pursuit of his trade to a place called
Burlats.

That same night the body of Elizabeth was discovered in a well at St. Alby.

The authorities were at once communicated with,
and the judge of Mazamet, the David de Beaudrigue of
the case. The body was taken to the Hôtel de Ville.
There was abundant local testimony to the effect that
the poor girl had often been seen looking into the well,
muttering to herself. The case was clearly one of
suicide or misadventure. Either was possible. But
that it was one of the two was morally certain.

A lodger in the Sirvens' house at St. Alby could
swear that only the footsteps of one person had been
heard descending the stairs of the house on the night
of December 17, before Jeanne had hastened to those
lodgers and told them of Elizabeth's flight. In addition to this, while the poor girl herself had been tall
and strong, her mother was feeble and old ; her married
sister, who was staying with her parents, was also
feeble and in ill-health ; and Elizabeth could easily have
resisted Jeanne, had she attempted, unaided, to be her
murderess.

Singly, then, none of the three could have killed
Elizabeth ; and that they had done it together, apart
from the inherent improbability and the inhuman
nature of such a crime, there was not an iota of
evidence to prove. As in the case of Calas, no cries
had been heard, and there were no signs of a struggle.

As for Sirven himself, he could declare an *alibi*.
On the night in question he had supped and slept at
the château of M. d'Esperandieu.

But such evidence, or any evidence, weighed nothing
with a people who had at the moment innocent Calas
in irons in the dungeon of Toulouse. ' It passes for
fact among the Catholics of the province ' wrote Vol-

taire in irony that came very near to being the literal
truth, 'that it is one of the chief points of the Protestant religion that fathers and mothers should hang,
strangle, or drown all their children whom they suspect
of having any *penchant* for the Roman faith.'   Sirven's
public, like Calas's, had 'a need of dramatic emotion
enough to change truth into a legend.'

What use to examine the body?   No facts will alter
our conviction.   Beaudrigue, savage bigot though he
was, had known his profession; the Beaudrigue of this
case, Trinquier, the judge of Mazamet, was a little
ignorant tradesman, who through the whole affair
showed himself to be a tool in clever hands, a wire
pulled—at Rome.

At first, Sirven was mad enough to rely on his
own innocence, and the innocence of his family, to
save them all.   January 6 to 10, 1762, was spent
in examining the witnesses.   The honest Catholic
villagers of St. Alby bore testimony to a man in favour
of Sirven.   But the attitude of the doctors who
examined the body might well have alarmed him.   It
alarmed his friends; on their advice he employed an
avocat, Jalabert.

Jalabert was devoted and expert.   But the devotion
of a saint and the brilliancy of a genius would not have
helped the Sirvens.

They were charged with the murder of Elizabeth,
and instantly took their decision.   Proofs had not freed
Calas—why should they save them?   'Remembering
the fury of the people' of Toulouse, 'they fled while
there was yet time.'

They stayed at their old home, Castres, at the house
of a friend, for one night.   Under the cover of the next
they walked through rain, mire, and darkness to five-

miles distant Roquecombe.   So far, they had at least been together.

But they saw very clearly now that they could not hope to escape notice if they travelled *en famille*.

On January 21 or 22 the unhappy father tore himself from them, and for a month remained hidden among the mountains, only ten miles from Castres. Then he moved on.   Through the snows of an icy winter he crossed the frontier, arrived at Geneva, and early in the April of 1762, at Lausanne.

His family, after having endured infinite perils and hardships, arrived there in June.   On the way, among the glaciers and in the bitter cold of a mountain winter, Marie Anne had borne a dead child.

They had one consolation.   Their flight was not unnecessary.   Three Declarations had been published against them ; though it was not until March 29, 1764, that the court formally sentenced the parents to be hanged, and the daughters to witness that execution, and then to perpetual banishment, under pain of death.

On September 11 this sentence was carried out in effigy.

By that time the generous republicans of Berne had given Madame and her daughters, who were living at Lausanne, a little pension ; their property having, of course, been confiscated to the King.   Père Sirven was working at his trade at Geneva, and so was a near neighbour of Voltaire's.

Moultou, the friend and correspondent of Rousseau, brought the Sirvens one day to Ferney.   Voltaire already knew their history.   But the time was not ripe for another Quixotic knight-errantry.   Calas was not yet vindicated.   Apart from the inordinate amount of work it would entail, to take a second case in hand

might militate against the interests of the first.   Then
the affair of the Sirvens would present far greater
legal difficulties.   They had fled the kingdom.   They
would have to be acquitted, if they were to be acquitted,
not by the Parliament of Paris, but by the Parliament
of Toulouse.   And Voltaire was too much of an artist
not to be perfectly aware that this cause would not
have the *éclat* and the dramatic effects of the Calas'.
'It lacked a scaffold.'

But when the Sirvens clung with tears about his
feet and implored him, as the saviour of Calas, to save
them also—'What was I to do?   What would you
have done in my place?'   'It is impossible to picture so
much innocence and so much wretchedness.'   When
the d'Argentals reproached him as unwise, 'Here are
too many parricide lawsuits indeed,' he wrote.   'But,
my dear angels, whose fault is that?'   And, again, as
his excuse, 'I have only done in the horrible disasters of
Calas and the Sirvens what all men do : I have followed
my bent.   That of a philosopher is not to pity the unfortunate, but to serve them.'   He records himself how
a priest said to him, 'Why interfere ?   Let the dead
bury their dead ;' and how he replied, 'I have found an
Israelite by the roadside : let me give him a little oil and
wine for his wounds.   You are the Levite : let me be
the Samaritan.'

That priest's answer, if any, is not recorded.

In short, the thing was done.

On March 8, 1765, the day before the Calas suit
was triumphantly concluded, Voltaire wrote joyfully
that the generous Élie de Beaumont would also defend
the Sirvens.   After that March 9 Voltaire could throw
himself yet more thoroughly into the case.   Calas is
vindicated !   So shall the Sirvens be !

But if there had been need for patience in the first affair, there was a hundred times greater need in the second.

The Parliament of Toulouse declined to give up its papers, as it had declined before. And then that flight —'the reason of their condemnation is in their flight. They are judged by contumacy.'

In June, too, the death of Madame Sirven—' of her sorrows '—removed a most important and most valuable witness for the defence. Then the Sirvens had no money. Voltaire had to supply all—brains, wealth, influence, labour, literary talent. For seven years he worked the case with an energy that never tired, an enthusiasm that never cooled. When it had been going on for four years, he wrote that it ' agitated all his soul.' 'This ardour, this fever, this perpetual exaltation'— what worker, however hot and persevering he fancy himself, is not ashamed by it, and astounded ?

Voltaire wrote Memoirs for the Sirvens. He won over the disapproving d'Argentals to be as ' obstinate ' about it (the phrase is his own) as he was himself. He got up a subscription to which the great Frederick and the great Catherine of Russia gave generously ; and Madame Geoffrin made her *protégé*, Stanislas Augustus Poniatowski—now King of Poland—contribute too.

Finally, Voltaire succeeded in persuading Sirven to return to Mazamet, where the case was re-tried ; and on December 25, 1771, when Voltaire was seventy-seven years old, the Parliament of Toulouse met and completely exculpated the accused. As Voltaire said, it had taken them two hours to condemn innocence, and nine years to give it justice. Still, the thing was done.

In 1772 the Sirvens came to Ferney to thank their

benefactor, and afforded him one of the highest of human pleasures : ' the sight of a happiness which was his own work.'

The year 1765, in which Voltaire showed so much public spirit, was not privately uneventful. In it he gave up Délices, which he had bought in 1755, and whose place Ferney had altogether usurped in his heart. In 1829 Délices was still in possession of the Tronchin family, from whom Voltaire had rented it.   In 1881 it was a girls' school.

In 1766 he also gave up the lease of Chêne, his house in Lausanne.

In the January of 1765 Voltaire and Frederick the Great were again reconciled after a quarrel and a break in their correspondence which had lasted four years. Frederick, forsooth, had chosen to take as a personal insult the fact that Voltaire should waste his talents writing that stupid history about ' the wolves and bears of Siberia ' !   And why in the world should he want to dedicate his ' Tancred ' to that old enemy of the Prussian monarch's, the Pompadour ?   Voltaire, on his side, was minded to write any history he chose, and dedicate his plays to anybody he liked, and would thank Frederick not to interfere.

Then, at the end of 1764 he hears that Frederick is ill—and to the wind with both his heat and his coldness at once.

Frederick replied rather witheringly to the peace overtures on January 1, 1765 : ' I supposed you to be so busy crushing *l'infâme* . . . that I did not dare to presume you would think of anything else.'

But the ice was broken.   Both succumbed to the old, old, fatal, potent charm.   They wrote to each other about ' once a fortnight ; ' discussed everything in heaven and earth; and until they should be mortal enemies again, were, once more, more than friends.

Frederick was once again, too, the friend not only of Voltaire, but of Voltaire's country. The Seven Years' War had been concluded in 1763 by the Peace of Hubertsburg. Frederick kept Silesia; and France, with her feeble ministry and her doddering King, lost, to England, Canada, Saint Vincent, Grenada, Minorca.

Changes were rife elsewhere too. Voltaire's friend Elizabeth, Empress of Russia, had died in 1762, and was succeeded nominally by the miserable Peter, but really by his wife, Catherine the Great. In 1763 Peter disappeared under strong suspicions of poison, and Catherine reigned in his stead.

Many kings and potentates have been named the Great, but few so justly as Catherine.

If she was the perpetrator of great crimes, this woman of three-and-thirty was, even at her accession, of vast genius, of extraordinary capacity as a ruler, broad and liberal in her aims, and an enlightened lover of the arts. She declared that since 1746 she had been under the greatest obligations to Voltaire; that his letters had formed her mind. With the telepathy of intellect, these two master-minds had from their different corners of the world detected each other's greatness. They never met in the flesh. But from their correspondence it is easy to see their close spiritual affinity. Their earliest letters, which are preserved, date from the July of this 1765.

Voltaire shocked even Paris and Madame du Deffand by the airy way in which he took that little peccadillo of the Empress's, 'that *bagatelle* about a husband.' 'Those are family affairs,' he said, not without a wicked twinkle in his eyes, ' with which I do not mix myself.' It is certain that, whether or no he believed Catherine a murderess, he regarded her as a great woman and served her when he could.

There came an opportunity in August. Her Majesty is pleased to admire girls' education as conducted in Switzerland, and sends Count Bülow to arrange for a certain number of Swiss governesses to be brought to Moscow and Petersburg to instruct the noble *jeunes filles* of those cities.

Splendid idea ! says Voltaire. But that ' *bagatelle* about a husband ' weighs on the Puritan conscience of Geneva. It is extraordinary now to think that any civilised government could have dared so to interfere with personal liberty as to prevent women over age going to teach anyone they chose, anywhere they liked. But this is precisely what Geneva did. Voltaire was exceedingly angry. The refusal reflected on him. But he had done his best for Catherine, though in vain.

While this little affair was going on, a new friend, the young playwright La Harpe, of whom Voltaire was to see more hereafter, and an old friend, whom he had not seen for seventeen years, were both staying with him at Ferney.

On July 30 had arrived there ' the sublime Clairon.' She had been the first actress of her day when Voltaire had known her in Paris. Now she was the finest tragic actress of the eighteenth century, and in the rich maturity of her two-and-forty years a most clever and cultivated woman. She had helped Voltaire's plays· enormously ; some she had made for him. He said so, at least. Further, she was one of the philosophers. In 1761 she had protested against the excommunication of actors as a class ; and Voltaire, remembering

Adrienne Lecouvreur, had seconded her with all the force and irony of his style.

When she reached Ferney her host was so ill that she had to declaim her *rôle* in his ' Orphan of China,' which cured him on the spot. Part of her visit he hobbled about on crutches, crippled by an attack of sciatica and half blind from an affection of the eyes, but as mentally lively and alert as if he had had both of those requisites for happiness, ' the body of an athlete and the soul of a sage.'

Mademoiselle was not well herself, and under Tronchin. But she went on acting against the express orders of that good physician. It was in her blood, as it was in Voltaire's. He had entirely rebuilt his theatre for her. He went quite mad over her superb talent ; and declared that for the first time in his life he had seen perfection in any kind. Blind though his avuncular affection might be, when he beheld Clairon in the flesh he did not suggest that Madame Denis (who, with her sister, was acting too) could in any way be her rival.

Clairon was still at Ferney in August. Soon after she left, that faithful Damilaville paid a visit there ; and during the summer had come, under the chaperonage of Lord Abingdon, the famous John Wilkes. ' Voltaire is obliging to me beyond all description' was Wilkes's record of his reception ; while Voltaire, on his part, bore enthusiastic testimony to the great demagogue's inexhaustible life and wit.

On the 8th or 9th of that August, when Voltaire was acting or telling stories, nimbly gesticulating with those crutches, events of sinister importance to him, and of importance to all men who hated *l'infâme*, were taking place in Abbeville.

On one of those days, two large crucifixes in the

MADEMOISELLE CLAIRON.

From an Engraving after a Picture by Carle Van Loo.

town, one on a bridge, the other in a cemetery, were shamefully and blasphemously mutilated. The town was naturally very angry. It set itself busily to work to find the culprits. A few days later three suspected persons, all boys under one-and-twenty, were brought up before the authorities and questioned.

While their examination was proceeding, the Bishop of the diocese organised a solemn procession through the streets to the places where the sacrilege had been committed, and, kneeling there, invoked pardon for the blasphemers in ominous words, as 'men who, though not beyond the reach of God's mercy, had rendered themselves worthy of the severest penalty of this world's law.'

The mutilated crucifixes were placed in a church, to which the people flocked in crowds, and in a temper of mind very different from that of Him who hung there in effigy and in the supreme agony had prayed for His murderers.

On September 26 a formal decree of arrest was issued against the three young men, d'Étallonde de Morival, Moisnel, and the Chevalier de la Barre.

D'Étallonde had already flown to Prussia; partly, no doubt, because his conscience was ill at ease, but partly, too, because he, or his friends, knew the times and the people. In Prussia he was afterwards made, through Voltaire's influence, an officer in Frederick's army.

Moisnel was a timid and foolish boy of eighteen.

Jean François Lefebre, Chevalier de la Barre, was a young Norman, not yet twenty years old. He had been educated by a country curé. His aunt, the Abbess of Willancourt, had given him masters, and he had rooms assigned to him in her convent. It is thought, but is not certain, that La Barre was in the army. What *is* certain, is that this clerical education had been a very bad one. The Abbess, if not a wicked woman, was certainly one who loved pleasure ; who enjoyed a joke, even if it were against the religion she professed ; who gave rollicking little supper parties ; adored her good-looking lively young scapegrace of a nephew, and permitted him not only to sing roystering and indecent drinking songs with foolish companions within her sacred walls, but to keep there a library which included not only some very indecorous books—but that little volume which ' smelt of the fagot,' ' The Philosophical Dictionary.'

At her supper parties young La Barre had often met one Duval, or Belleval, who, it is said, had been in love with the Abbess, and was not a little jealous of her handsome nephew. It was Duval who had heard young La Barre chant Rabelaisian ditties, and quote ' what he could recollect ' from the ' Pucelle ' and ' The Epistle to Uranie.' It was Duval who hated him, and Duval who denounced him.

On October 1, 1765, La Barre was arrested in the Abbey of Longvilliers, near Montreuil. Moisnel was also arrested.

On October 4 the Abbess burnt her nephew's library, which would have been a prudent act if she had done it thoroughly, but she did not. On October 10 the authorities searched the boy's rooms, and found in a press some indecent literature—*and* that ' Philosophical Dictionary.'

After five cross-examinations, unhappy young Moisnel said practically what his judges told him to say, not only respecting himself, but respecting La Barre. He swore that d'Étallonde had mutilated the crucifixes, an assertion to which La Barre also swore. D'Étallonde was safe in Prussia. Moisnel, who was delicate in health and in horrible fear of death, lost in the trial the very little sense he had ever had. Young La Barre, on the other hand, kept all his pluck, wit, and coolness.

To a charge that, on the Feast of the Holy Sacrament, he and his two companions had lingered near a religious procession in the street, and neither knelt nor uncovered as reverence and custom demanded, he pleaded ' Guilty.' He was in a hurry, he said, and had no evil intentions.

To the charge that to a person who bade him take another route if he could not behave himself, he had replied that he looked upon the Host as nothing but a piece of pastry and for his part could not swallow all the apostolic assertions, he answered that he might have used some such words.

It is not unworthy of remark that, though under torture he confessed to having mutilated the crucifix in the cemetery, the judges discovered no proof, and no proof ever was discovered, that he had mutilated the crucifix on the bridge. It is very much more remarkable that in his sentence the affair of the crucifixes was not even mentioned, and that he and absent d'Étallonde were condemned for ' impiously and deliberately walking before the Host without kneeling or uncovering; uttering blasphemies against God, the Saints, and the Church; singing blasphemous songs, and rendering marks of adoration to profane books.'

Now it will be allowed by any fair-minded person— whatever be his religion or irreligion—that to thus insult a faith, dear to millions of people for hundreds of generations, merited a sharp punishment.

As Voltaire said, ' it deserved Saint Lazare.'

On February 28, 1766, d'Étallonde and La Barre were condemned to have their tongues torn out with hot irons, their right hands to be cut off, and to be burnt to death by a slow fire. In the case of La Barre this sentence was so far graciously remitted that he was to be beheaded before he was burnt ; but, on the other hand, he was further condemned to the torture Ordinary and Extraordinary, to extract from him the names of his accomplices. Even for that time the sentence was so brutal—' could they have done more if he had killed his father ? '—that no one believed it would be carried out. Against absent d'Étallonde, of course, it could not be. A public appeal was made to the King. Ten of the best *avocats* of Paris declared the sentence illegal. La Barre was taken to the capital, and his case retried there, where ' a majority of five voices condemned to the most horrible torments a young man only guilty of folly.' He was taken back to Abbeville. All through the trial he had borne himself with a high courage. It did not leave him now. He recognised many old acquaintances on the way back, and saluted them gaily. On the last evening of his life he supped with his confessor—a priest whom he had often met at his aunt's gay table. ' Let us have some coffee,' he is reported to have said ; ' it will not prevent my sleeping.' Bravado, perhaps. But *bravado* and *brave* are of the same origin. The next day, July 1, 1766, began with the torture. On his way to the scaffold the poor boy recognised among the cruel crowd of spectators not only many men whom he had called friend, but, to their everlasting shame, women too. That ' barbarism which would have made even drunken savages shudder,' the pulling out of the tongue,

was so barbarous that the five executioners only pretended to do it. On his way up to the scaffold La
Barre's shoe dropped off. He turned and put it on
again. He bound his own eyes, and talked calmly to
the executioners, and then died with 'the firmness of
Socrates'—a harder death.

It is said that the executioner who cut off the head
did it so cleverly that the spectators *applauded*. The
body was thrown to the flames—with 'The Philosophical Thoughts' of Diderot; the 'Sopha' of Crébillon; two little volumes of Bayle; and 'The Philosophical Dictionary,' which was supposed to have
inspired the indecent impiety of which the unhappy
boy had been guilty, but which certainly does inspire
a religion not so unlike the religion of Christ as the
savage hatred which killed La Barre.

The event caused a fearful sensation, even in the
eighteenth century. The victim was so young, and
had so nobly played the man. To the last moment,
popular opinion had believed in a reprieve. One of
the people who so believed was Voltaire. Vague
reports of the case had reached him at first. Some
young fools had been profaning a church, and then
declaring in cross-examination that they had been led
to do so by the books of the Encyclopædia! But then
wild boys who commit drunken frolics do not read
books of philosophy!

And when the tidings of that 1st of July had come—
'My dear brother, my heart is withered.' Grimm
wrote boldly and significantly of the event that
'humanity awaited an avenger.' But this time how
could the avenger be Voltaire? On the lips of all the
churchmen were the words—Philosophy hath done
this thing. This is where your fine free-thinking, your

mental emancipation, lead men ! Certainly, it might have been answered that La Barre was not the product of philosophy, but of the Church ; educated by a curé, finished by my Lady Abbess ; sheltered, after his sin, in the Abbey of Longvilliers ; given for his last confessor a priestly boon companion of those wild suppers at the convent. If the philosophers mocked at religion, what of the licentious priests of that wicked day ? Château-neuf, Chaulieu, Desfontaines—the names of a score of others must have come to Voltaire's lips. This boy had put the teaching of such men into action. The more fool he ; but not the greater criminal. There were a thousand excuses for him ; and 'tears come easily for the youth which has committed sins which in ripe age it would have redeemed.'

But Voltaire, with a guilty conscience one may hope, seems to have remembered that he had written not only 'The Philosophical Dictionary,' but the ribald 'Pucelle.' He might thereby have had some hand in La Barre's undoing ; and when he saw that men flung the whole responsibility for that sin on him and his brothers, the Encyclopædists, he feared.

By July 14 he had gone to Rolle in Vaud. He had been there in the spring for his health ; now he went for his safety.

But, safe or dangerous, he must write his view of the case. By the 22nd of the same month his account of 'The Death of the Chevalier de la Barre' was complete. Clear, masterly, succinct, it is perhaps one of the finest tracts in the cause of humanity ever written, even by Voltaire himself. On July 25 he was asking clever young Élie de Beaumont if there was any law, date 1681, by which those guilty of indecent impieties could be sentenced to death. He had himself looked every-

where in vain; which was not wonderful. There was
no such law. The ignorance and fanaticism of the
judges had 'supposed its existence.' 'This barbarity
occupies me day and night.' True, La Barre was past
the reach of human help. But Voltaire could hope
that his cries 'might frighten the carnivorous beasts
from others.' They did that. The popular fury to
which he gave mighty voice saved feeble Moisnel.
After La Barre's death the judges did not dare to
proceed with the suit.

In 1775, when d'Étallonde was staying with him at
Ferney, Voltaire wrote a pamphlet called 'The Cry of
Innocent Blood,' which had as its object the restitution
of his civil rights to that young officer, to whom
Frederick had accorded a long leave of absence. If he
never obtained that restitution or full justification for
the memory of La Barre, at least he never ceased to
try. He worked the case for twelve years, and his
labours were only stopped by death.

Partly for his own safety; partly in horror of a
country which could sanction a vengeance so awful;
partly in longing for an Elysium where he and his
brothers might live and speak as free men, in this
July of 1766, at Rolle, this boy Voltaire conceived the
mad and hot-headed scheme of retiring, with all the
enlightened, to Cleves, and forming there a literary
society, with a printing press.

A dream! A dream! The other philosophers would
not entertain the idea for a moment. Some of them,
at least, felt 'little suppers and the *opéra-comique*' to
be among the necessities of existence. D'Alembert,
chief of them all, who had refused the Presidency of
the Berlin Academy and to be tutor to Catherine the
Great's son for a quiet life and Mademoiselle de

Lespinasse, was not going to be tempted from either—
for Cleves !

'I see,' wrote Voltaire, 'that M. Boursier' (which
was one of his innumerable *noms de guerre*) 'will
have no workmen.'   So he went back to Ferney.

'The suit and the sacrifice of the Chevalier de la
Barre remain one of the indelible stains with which
the magistracy of the eighteenth century tarnished and
defiled its robes.'

That 'Philosophical Dictionary'—of which the thin
first volume had been burnt with La Barre ; which in
March 1765 had been publicly destroyed in Paris by
the hangman ; which Rome anathematised, and of
which liberal London had already demanded a fifth
edition—is one of the greatest of Voltaire's works, and
one which should be still popular.   It stands alone,
without rival or counterpart.   Brief articles on an
enormous variety of subjects gave infinite scope for
Voltaire's versatility.   Since he had written that first
article, 'Abraham,' which had made even sullen Frederick laugh, the thing had been its author's commonplace book.   If an article is too daring even for the
'Encyclopædia'—put it in the 'Dictionary.' If one feels
gay, write buffoonery ; or seriously, write with passion.
The 'Dictionary' had room for everything.   Mockery,
sarcasm, lightness, wit, gaiety, profundity, the most
earnest thought, the most burning zeal, banter, irony,
audacity—they are all here.   'The Philosophical Dictionary' has been well said to be 'the whole of citizen
Voltaire.'

He had smuggled it into Geneva, and then gaily
and without a pang of conscience denied that he had
anything to do with its authorship.   'If there is the
least danger about it, please warn me, and then I can

disown it in all the public papers with my usual candour
and innocence.'

He kept it by his side, and wrote, now in this mood,
now in that, first one article and then another, until it
numbered eight volumes.

Even in this age of many books there is always
room for another, if it be sufficiently piquant and
out of the common.   The astonishing variety of the
subjects, and the not less marvellous versatility of the
style, the ease, the life and the humour of those eight
volumes are qualities which may well appeal to the
most jaded of modern readers.   Its frequent profanity,
indeed, is a blot dyed too deeply into the texture of
the book to be eradicable by any editor.   But, apart
from this, to the bored person—always in search of a
new literary sensation, of something which has not
been done a thousand times before, of something that
will not be done a thousand times again—may be
well recommended a volume of 'The Philosophical
Dictionary.'

CHAPTER XXXIX

VOLTAIRE AND GENEVA : VOLTAIRE AND LA HARPE

Now Voltaire was not only genius and philanthropist, he was also a country gentleman.

He played the part to the life. He amicably exchanged seeds and bulbs with his neighbours, and admired their gardens in return for their admiration of his ; he invited them to dinner parties and theatricals ; and, like many another of his class, could not for the life of him help interfering in local politics.

Geneva was a republic. But its constitution was not to modern ideas—or to Voltaire's ideas—at all republican.

In the governing class, which consisted of the Great Council of Two Hundred, the Little Council of Twenty Five, and the Consistory of the Clergy, the people were not represented at all.

These people were divided into the shopkeepers, or Bourgeoisie, who demanded a share of political power ; and the journeymen mechanics, who were not only without any political rights, but could not even set up in business for themselves, occupy any official post, or go into the liberal professions. These (so-called) Natives, a very large class, were the descendants of foreigners who had settled in Geneva. They asked for the rights enjoyed by the Bourgeoisie ; while the Bourgeoisie, scornfully refusing the demands of the

Natives, themselves asked for some of the privileges enjoyed by the Councils.

Voltaire, now as ever, was on the side not of the governing class, but of the people who had a right to share in the government, but did not; and, now as ever, he was irresistibly tempted to interfere in what was not his business.

In the autumn of 1765, 'in spite of Espinas, Calas, and Sirven, who surround me ; of wheels, gallows, galleys, and confiscations ; and of Chevaliers de la Barre who do not precisely pour balm in the blood,' he began to take upon himself the highly unnecessary and stormy *rôle* of peacemaker between the Genevan Bourgeoisie and Magistracy.

He first tried to get up some mediatory dinner parties at Ferney, at which the heads of these two parties were to meet and amicably discuss their differences ! The Council of Twenty Five responded with a chilly dignity that it was very much obliged to M. de Voltaire, but it was not going to settle political disputes in *that* way ; while four of the Bourgeoisie joyfully accepted so pleasant an invitation, and arrived at Ferney in M. de Voltaire's carriage, graciously sent for their convenience.

These four guests showed such a sweet reasonableness on all topics under discussion, that, says Voltaire, writing to that haughty Council, there is surely hope of a reconciliation ?

The Council, in response, will be obliged if the Lord of Ferney will consider the matter closed.

Not he.

At the request of the Bourgeoisie he drew up a document stating their claims, sent it to France and begged her to step in and settle the dispute.

She selected as mediator her new envoy at Geneva, M. Hennin, who arrived on December 16, 1765, whose mediation did not prosper at all, but who was, and remained, much Voltaire's friend.

By this time the Bourgeoisie had become not a little aggressive and dictatorial, and the long mediatory dinner parties had begun to bore Voltaire.

After all, the most oppressed class were the Natives. Two of them called at Ferney, and presently brought its lord a written statement of their grievances against the Bourgeoisie, which were not few or slight. He promised help, entered into the smallest details, and dismissed them with memorable words. 'You are the largest part of a free and industrious people, and you are in slavery. . . . If you are forced to leave a country which your labours make prosperous, I shall still be able to help and protect you.'

He wrote a little introductory letter to that statement which the Natives purposed to present to M. de Beauteville, the new mediator sent by France, to succeed, if that might be, where Hennin had failed.

'What is the Third Estate?' said the Abbé Sieyès. 'Nothing.' 'What ought it to be? Everything.'

In 1766 it was nothing. In the eye of the law, said de Beauteville, it positively did not exist.

He dismissed the petition with contumacy, and sent the Natives to the Councils, who received them in the same way.

Then M. de Voltaire himself wrote a petition for them; but before they sent it to the mediators (three had now been appointed, one by France, one by Berne, one by Geneva), he warned them of their probable failure, in a prophecy which Geneva long remembered. 'You are like little flying-fish. Out of the water, you are eaten by birds of prey; in it, by larger fish. You are between two equally powerful parties: you will fall victims to the interests of one or the other, or perhaps of both together.'

When the petition was presented on April 28, 1766, the unlucky Natives were threatened with imprisonment if they did not reveal its authorship. They did. Notwithstanding, a few days later, Auzière, their leader, was thrown into prison, a result Voltaire had long foreseen. Here the affair ended, for a time at least. Voltaire summed up his own position, with his usual neatness, in writing to d'Argental on May 6. 'The Natives say that I take the part of the Bourgeois, and the Bourgeois that I take the part of the Natives. The Natives and Bourgeois both pretend I pay too much deference to the Councils, and the Councils say I am too friendly to both the Bourgeois and Natives.'

The Councils, in point of fact, were exceedingly angry with Voltaire, to whom happened precisely what happens to the foolish person who separates fighting dogs. The dogs growl at him and begin fighting again, and their master considers his interference uncommonly impertinent.

The air of Geneva was sultry with storms in this season of 1766; or Voltaire had upon him one of those pugnacious moods in which he had rent limb from limb Pompignan, Fréron, Desfontaines. To be sure, he seldom gave the first blow; but the moment he saw a chance of a fight he was as agog to join in it at seventy-two as he had been at twenty-two.

The Protestant minister called Jacob Vernet was the unlucky person who offended him now. Vernet was clever, and himself a writer. He had been friendly with Voltaire until 1757, when he sharply

criticised the 'Essay on the Manners and Mind of
Nations.' Then they further fell out on that vexed
topic, a theatre in Geneva; and when d'Alembert's
famous article appeared in the 'Encyclopædia,' Vernet
broke off all intercourse with Voltaire, telling him
the reason. Then Vernet drew a portrait of Voltaire
in his 'Critical Letters of an English Traveller.'
The likeness was not sufficiently flattering to please
the original, who thereupon attacked Vernet in a
'Dialogue between a Priest and a Protestant Minister.' Vernet complained to the Councils that he
had been libelled. And in May 1766 Voltaire wrote
against Vernet one of the most virulent of personal
satires which ever fell from his pen—'The Praise of
Hypocrisy.' It lent his hand cunning for that kind
of work. His next was the famous poem entitled
'The Civil War of Geneva.'

The excuse for this savage personal polemic was the
case of one Covelle, who in 1763 had been condemned,
for an offence against morals, to make confession of the
same to the Consistory of Geneva, to kneel to the
President of the Consistory, be reprimanded, and ask
pardon. He confessed, but more than that he declined
to do.

The mode of punishment has long been decided to
be an unwise one. Voltaire, always in advance of his
age, considered it an unwise one then. He took the
part of Covelle, who personally was a wretched creature,
as deficient in brains as in morals. But he stood for a
cause.

After having been remanded for a fortnight for
consideration, he presented to the Consistory a paper,
the substance of which had been supplied by Voltaire,
and which stated that the ecclesiastical laws did not

compel kneeling to the Consistory, being reprimanded by it, or asking pardon from it.

Covelle published this statement, or rather Voltaire did, and between my Lord of Ferney and the authorities began a battle of pamphlets. They fill three large volumes, and may still be seen in Geneva. Voltaire also wrote twelve public letters in the name of Covelle, allowed him a small pension, and then made him the hero of 'The Civil War of Geneva.'

The hatred expressed in that poem redounded, as hatred is apt to do, on the hater. Bitterness and anger are not gay. They spoilt, artistically, 'The Civil War of Geneva.'

The poem is not, unluckily for Voltaire, only a satire on parties, though it *is* a satire on that retrograde and conservative faction which he held was ruining Geneva. It is also a savage satire against individuals. It attacks with a sudden blind fury (Voltaire having hitherto been temperate in his dislike of him) 'that monster of vanity and contradictions, of pride and of meanness,' Jean Jacques Rousseau. It tore Vernet's reputation to shreds. It descended to personal insult, and, that there might be no possible mistake, its victims were spoken of by name. The malice kills the wit. More indecent than the 'Pucelle,' 'The War of Geneva' is much less clever and amusing. A picture of a travelling Englishman, that Lord Abingdon who had introduced Wilkes at Ferney and must needs put *his* spoke into the wheel of the Genevan party quarrels, is certainly happy. The young gentleman who, with his 'phlegmatic enthusiasm,' drags his dogs and his boredom all over Europe, and expects, no matter where he is, the mere fact of his being English to remove all obstacles and alter all conditions which he is pleased to dislike, will be certainly recognised as a type.

But as a whole ' The Civil War of Geneva ' contains Voltaire's vices without his virtues.   The poem, like all his writings, certainly *did* something.   In 1769 the decree to which Covelle had refused to submit was abolished.   ' The War of Geneva,' which was brought out canto by canto, appeared complete in 1768.

The strife of parties which that poem celebrated, and should have celebrated exclusively, had not been healed by the mediators sent by France.   Very well, says France—if persuasion will not do, we will try force.   By the January of 1767 French troops were quartered along the Lake of Geneva with the view of bringing the aggravating little Genevan republic to its senses by famine and blockade, and unlucky, and comparatively innocent, Ferney was almost unable to get the necessaries of life.

Voltaire was not the person to starve in silence. The soldiers were spoiling the trees in his park ; poor d'Aumard could not get his plasters ; Adam was very ill and could have neither doctor nor medicine (' so he is sure to recover ') ; and the household generally lacked everything except snow, ' and we have enough of that to stock Europe.'   Choiseul must be written to !   Voltaire wrote to him and pointed out that it was not the Genevans France was punishing, but Ferney ; and on January 30 Choiseul sent an order exempting Ferney from the general rule and giving Voltaire an unlimited passport for himself and his household.

It was a very large one by now.   Durey de Morsan, an amiable elderly ne'er-do-weel, had joined it, and lived there on Voltaire's charity, sometimes doing a little copying in return for his board and lodging.

There was also a *protégé* of Richelieu's, called Gallien, who repaid Voltaire's hospitality with the basest ingratitude ; and an ex-Capuchin monk, known to Ferney as Richard, who, when he had been generously entertained for two years, decamped with money, manuscripts, and jewels belonging to his host.

And then, besides its regular inmates, there poured through the house a continual stream of visitors.   In 1766 there had stayed there Madame Saint-Julien, a gay, goodnatured, and highly connected little lady, whom Voltaire called his ' butterfly philosopher ; ' and La Borde, playwright for himself, and first *valet de chambre* for the King.

Here, too, also in 1766, had come James Boswell, Esquire, of Auchinleck, for whose benefit M. de Voltaire is pleased to assume the manner and style of Mr. Boswell's great patron, and to speak of that patron as ' a superstitious dog.'

Voltaire would hardly have been his vain old French self if he had not modified his opinion of the great Doctor when Boswell told him that Johnson had said that Frederick the Great wrote as Voltaire's footboy, who had acted as his amanuensis, might do.

To be sure, when Boswell got home and asked the Doctor if he thought Rousseau as bad a man as Voltaire, that staunch old bigot had replied, ' Why, Sir, it is difficult to settle the proportion of iniquity between them.'

But Voltaire did not know of that answer.

Also in 1766, Grétry the musician, then only five-and-twenty, had often come over from Geneva, where he was staying, to visit Voltaire.   Madame Cramer had first introduced him. The conversation often turned on comic opera, which Voltaire had once hated, but which, as expounded by Grétry, he was soon to love, and at seventy-four to write gaily himself.

When Grétry spoke of his host's prodigious reputation, he records that Voltaire characteristically replied that he would give a hundred years of immortality for a good digestion.

Chabanon, friend of d'Alembert, musician, poet, dramatist, had also paid a first visit here in 1766. He came back again on May 1, 1767, and stayed seven months. He has left behind him a good account of that visit. He evidently guessed—what not all Voltaire's friends did guess—that one day the world would be interested in them only as having known Voltaire, and would be grateful to them for writing as little about themselves, and as much about their host, as possible.

While Chabanon was at Ferney, the leisure Voltaire's 'devouring ardour' for study allowed him was spent, of course, in play-acting. He had just written a new play, 'The Scythians,' and loved it as he always loved his latest born. He was not a little disgusted when Ferney would have none of it, and demanded an old favourite, 'Adélaïde du Guesclin,' instead.

'I cannot think what they see in that "Adélaïde,"' says its author discontentedly to Madame Denis.

Ferney and Chabanon only ratified the judgment of Paris in disliking 'The Scythians.' Played there on March 26 of this same 1767, the rude *parterre* had 'no respect for the old age which had written it,' and made such a noise that the first performances were 'regular battles.' There were only four in all.

The French officers of the blockading troops came
en masse to Ferney in this spring to witness the
theatricals.   Colonel Chabrillant, the colonel of Conti's
regiment, stayed for a long time as a guest at the
château ; and if he did, after the visit, forget to write a
single word of thanks to his host or Mama Denis, why,
that was a sort of ingratitude to which Voltaire should
have been accustomed.

Three companies of the same regiment were
quartered in the village of Ferney, and some of the
grenadiers often came as audience to the performances,
and at least once as actors.   As a reward for their
services Voltaire gave them supper and offered them
money.

' We will not take anything,' they said.   ' We have
seen M. de Voltaire.   That is our payment.'

The celebrity was as delighted as a boy.   ' My
brave grenadiers ! ' he cried, and invited them all,
whenever they wanted a meal or well-paid work, to
come to Ferney.

When his guests were tired of acting themselves,
they could, and did, now go to Geneva and see other
people act.   Through the influence of Voltaire upon
M. de Beauteville, that French envoy had so far
worked upon the prim Councils of Geneva that they
had allowed a theatre to be opened in their Puritan
town in April 1766.   ' Olympie ' was played there, and
the loveliest comic operas.   Voltaire had the whole
troupe to Ferney, where they acted four for his benefit.
The Geneva theatre had only a short life.   It was
burnt in February 1768.   The townspeople hated it
so, that when they saw it in flames they made no
attempt to save it.

In the light of subsequent events, it seems almost

certain that Voltaire received many of his visitors and
gave many of his entertainments to keep Madame Denis
in a good temper, and reconcile her to the country which
she hated ; while other festivities he arranged for the
benefit of the lighthearted young people he always
liked to have about him.

When there was a supper and a dance after
theatricals he himself appeared for a moment only, and
then retired to his room, which adjoined that where,
not the guests, but the servants were dancing, and
where he tranquilly worked or slept to the sound of the
music.   Sometimes he did not even appear to do the
honours of the house at all ; and declared of himself
that he would have been dead in four days if he
had not well known how to live quietly in the midst
of uproar, and alone in a mob.

He had the usual quarrel on hand to keep him
busy.   That conceited La Beaumelle, who had been
a thorn in his flesh in Prussia, assailed him in the
summer of 1767 with no fewer than ninety-four abusive
anonymous letters.   Voltaire put the matter into the
hands of the police.   But in 1770 La Beaumelle, who
had further complicated the situation by marrying the
sister of young Lavaysse, the Calas' unfortunate friend,
began an objectionable commentary on Voltaire's works,
and would have finished it but that he (La Beaumelle)
died in 1773.

That Voltaire spent energy and time in trying to
inspire, and that he knew no greater delight than when
he did inspire, his visitors with his own passion for hard
work in place of idle pleasure, is on the testimony of
Chabanon and of a fellow-visitor of Chabanon's, the
famous La Harpe.

La Harpe from the first came to Ferney to be a

brilliant pupil to this great past master of so many
arts ; to learn from the author of ' Zaire ' and of ' Alzire,'
of ' Mahomet ' and of ' Mérope,' of 'The Princess of
Navarre,' 'The Prodigal Son,' 'Brutus,' and 'The
Scotch Girl,' how to write every kind of play that ever
playwright has written.   It has been mentioned that
La Harpe had been at Ferney in 1765—part of the
time with that noblest exponent of the drama, Clairon.
He was here also in 1766 with Chabanon.   And now,
in the beginning of 1767, he came once again—this
time with his young wife, and for a visit which lasted
more than a year.

La Harpe was a clever, arrogant, and very self-
satisfied young man of about eight-and-twenty.   His
tragedy, ' Warwick,' produced in 1763, made him
famous in his own age.   In this, he is only celebrated
as the first writer in France who 'made criticism
eloquent.'   He had led a disreputable youth, and had
just married his landlady's daughter as a reparation
for wrong done to her.   But in that age almost everybody was disreputable ; and if virtue had been a *sine qua
non* in society, there would have been no society at all.

Voltaire took this promising youth to his warm and
sanguine old heart at once.   He was poor !   He was
clever !   He could act !   What more did one want ?
With Voltaire's help he had gained a prize at the
Academy.   And with further help he should do greater
things than that.   Nothing is pleasanter in Voltaire's
character as an old man than the enthusiastic interest
and delight he took in his young literary *protégés*.   He
worked with them, corrected them, praised them, went
into raptures over their talents to his friends, financed
them, fathered them, housed them, and in the desire
for their fame quite forgot his own.

The memorable La Harpe visit of 1767 opened
under the rosiest aspects. The little bride had the
youth in which Voltaire delighted, and she turned
out to be 'a comedian without knowing it.' If 'The
Scythians' had been hissed in Paris, Madame de la
Harpe reciting Act II. made Ferney sob. La Harpe,
too, 'declaimed verses as well as he wrote them,' and
was 'the best actor in France.'

So there were theatricals galore.

If thorns pricked on the rose stems and there were
clouds in the bluest of skies, it was not Voltaire who
spoke of them.

It is Chabanon, the fellow-guest, who sketches La
Harpe as overbearing, impatient of correction, uncommonly quarrelsome, and quite forgetful of the fact that
his host's position and seniority of nearly fifty years
demanded some sort of respect.

Old Voltaire was goodnatured enough to criticise
the young man's plays for him, and La Harpe received
the criticisms with the sulkiness of offended dignity.
Voltaire was not patient by nature, heaven knows.
But he kept his coolness and his temper with this
irritating young man to a degree quite extraordinary.
It was always 'the little La Harpe,' or 'my dear child,'
or 'Ah! the little one is angry!' with a goodnatured
laugh.

When one day the conceited visitor went so far as to
rewrite some verses in his part in Voltaire's 'Adélaïde'
—'which seemed to me feeble '—' Let us hear them, my
son,' says Voltaire. And when he had heard them, as
improved by La Harpe—

'Good,' he said. 'Yes, that is better. Go on
making such changes. I shall only gain by them.'

On another occasion, La Harpe, at a dinner party

of twenty persons, recited an ode by one old foe of
Voltaire's, Pompignan, on the death of another, J. B.
Rousseau, without stating the name of the author.

'Very good,' says Voltaire. 'Who wrote it?'

The audacious La Harpe makes him guess. And
at last tells him.

'Pompignan.'

That name, as La Harpe himself said, was a *coup
de théâtre* indeed. There was a silence. 'Repeat the
lines again,' says Voltaire. As La Harpe repeats them,
the Patriarch listens with fixed attention. 'There is
no more to be said. It *is* a beautiful stanza.'

Was this the same man whom the mere suggestion
that d'Arnaud's sun was rising and his setting, had
spurred to the folly of the Prussian visit? Was this
the man so thin-skinned that every gnat-bite of a criticism made him raw and mad? The truth seems to
be that Voltaire had a very weak spot in his heart for
La Harpe, and loved him better than his own glory.

Not many years ago, in a grocer's shop in Paris, was
discovered an autograph letter of Voltaire's in which
he begged the Controller-General for a pension for his
protégé.

'It seems to me that, M. de la Harpe having no
pension, mine (from the King) is too large by half, and
that it should be divided between us.'

If this could be arranged—'La Harpe, and everyone else, can easily be made to think that this pension
is a just recompense for the services he has rendered to
literature.'

The request was not granted. La Harpe never even
knew that it had been made. But its singular generosity and delicacy are not altered by those facts.
Well might Voltaire's bitterest enemy, Jean Jacques

Rousseau, write of him : ' I know no man on earth whose impulses have been more beautiful.'

But his treatment of La Harpe was something better even than a noble impulse.

In the beginning of 1768, after the young couple had been guests in his house for more than a year, and after one of them at least had received full measure, pressed down and running over, of help, forbearance, and kindness, Voltaire discovered that valuable manuscripts had been stolen from him.   Among others were those secret Memoirs written in 1759, which expressed the feelings of an angry, younger Voltaire, but not of a wiser and older one.   To Paris had been sent not only copies of ' The Civil War of Geneva,' but anecdotes for his Histories which Voltaire was keeping until the death of the persons concerned left him at liberty to publish them.

There was a loud domestic explosion at Ferney. The strongest and gravest suspicion fell upon La Harpe. He vehemently denied everything, and accused a certain Antoine, a sculptor, of the crime.   Antoine simply said La Harpe was a liar.

Madame Denis, who herself was suspected of a foolish elderly *tendresse* for La Harpe and of complicity in the affair with him, took his side, with, one may safely assume, a torrent of eloquence.   But eloquence, not proof, was all either she or La Harpe had to offer. From his room La Harpe, ' putting arrogance in the place of repentance,' wrote his generous old host many impertinent little notes.   He might have spared him.

Voltaire had often had manuscripts stolen from him before, and always alas ! by his own familiar friends whom he trusted.   But this time he felt the treachery

with peculiar bitterness.   He was not passionate
and furious as he generally was.   His attitude was
that of knowing La Harpe to be guilty and longing
to find him innocent.   He made as little of it as he
could.   ' This little roguery of La Harpe's is not
serious,' he wrote.   ' But it is certain and proven.'
In the November of 1767 La Harpe had been in Paris
for a time, when ' he gave the third canto of " The Civil
War of Geneva " to three persons of my acquaintance.'

' I did not reproach him,' Voltaire wrote sadly to
Hennin, ' but his own conscience did.   He never alluded
to the affair and looked me straight in the face, or spoke
of it without turning pale with a pallor not that of
innocence.'   Still, if I can help him in the future as I
have done in the past, I shall do so ; ' only, if Madame
Denis brings him back to Ferney I must lock up my
papers.'   ' His imprudence has had very disagreeable
consequences for me, but I pardon him with all my
heart ; he has not sinned from malice.'

Only to his intimate friends did he admit La Harpe
had sinned at all.   The sinner was dear to him.   He
must lie, if need be, to prove his innocence to the world.

Naturally, the La Harpes had to go away.   And
since they must go, would it not be better for their accomplice, Denis, to go too ?   It was not her first offence.
She had helped Ximenès to steal manuscripts in 1754.
Then, too, she was bored to death with Ferney ; and
her ' natural aversion to a country life,' wrote poor
Voltaire ' in confidence ' to her sister, had had very ill
effects upon her temper.   Not all the *fêtes* and the visitors could make up to her for Paris.   Voltaire said that
he had been the innkeeper of Europe for fourteen years
and was tired of the profession.   ' This tumult does not
suit my seventy-four years or my feebleness.'   ' Madame

Denis has need of Paris.' Here was one excuse for getting rid of her. And if more were wanted, there was her health which required the air of the capital and fashionable doctors ; there were business affairs there which she might see to for her uncle ; and a necessity of economising at Ferney brought about by her extra-vagance, and ' muddle, which,' said Grimm, ' is carried by Mama Denis to a degree of perfection difficult to imagine.'

To his friends Voltaire gave her health and the business to be looked after in Paris as reasons for her visit. They were that lesser part of the truth which is useful to conceal the greater. If he was loyal to La Harpe, so he was to Madame Denis. Of her share in the theft of the manuscripts he uttered not a word.

He gave her twenty thousand francs to spend in Paris, over and above the yearly income which he had settled on her.

Before March 1, 1768, the two La Harpes, Madame Denis, Marie Dupuits, and her husband, who had fallen under the ban of suspicion too and declined to utter a word or give an iota of evidence on either side, had all started for the capital.

Voltaire dismissed the servants—except a couple of lacqueys and a valet. He sold his horses. ' An old invalid recluse ' had no need of them. Seven visitors who were staying in the house at the time, seeing their host's evident need of solitude, tactfully departed. There only remained Father Adam, faithful Wagnière, a colleague of Wagnière's called Bigex—a Savoyard, who had formerly been trusted servant and copyist in the service of Grimm—and two of the usual ne'er-do-weels, de Morsan and an ex-American officer called Rieu. Both these persons seem to have suppressed themselves

with great success when they were not wanted, and to
have been regarded by their benefactor as part of the
household effects. He always spoke of himself as being
entirely alone. Ferney was cleaned and put in order,
and the stream of visitors ceased to flow.

It was certainly not because Voltaire was idle, but
because his seventy-four years did not prevent him still
being what the French call *malin*, that this Easter he
decided to do what he had done at Colmar : play once
more that ' deplorable comedy,' *faire ses Pâques*.

A priest was dining with him one night at Ferney.
' Father D——,' says Voltaire, ' I wish, for example's
sake, *faire mes Pâques* on Easter Day. I suppose you
will give me absolution ? '

' Willingly,' says the priest. ' I give it you.' No
more was said.

On Easter Day 1768, Voltaire, accompanied by
Wagnière and two gamekeepers, went solemnly to
church, preceded by a servant carrying ' a superb Blessed
Loaf ' which the Lord of Ferney was in the habit of
presenting every Easter Sunday. After the distribution
of this bread Voltaire mounted the pulpit and turned
round and preached a little sermon. Protestant Wagnière had warned him against doing this. He felt sure
it was illegal. But his master's mood was a wicked one ;
and, moreover, several thefts had been committed of late
in his parish while all the people were at church, which
gave him a text. His remonstrances were ' vigorous,
pathetic, and eloquent,' and he warmly exhorted the
people to the practice of virtue. The unhappy curé,
not knowing what to do, hurried to the altar and
proceeded with the mass. Voltaire spoke a few words
in his praise, and then got down from the pulpit and
resumed his own seat.

The story got noised abroad. Good Marie Leczinska mistook it for a conversion. The philosophers for once were at one with the orthodox, and condemned the deed. And so of course did Biort, Bishop of Annecy, who was also Prince and Bishop of Geneva, and of whose diocese Ferney was part.

In that wicked world of the eighteenth century there were few good bishops. But the Prelate of Annecy was one of them. He was also of strong character and of sound judgment and reason, with a fine capacity for irony.

On April 11, 1768, he wrote Voltaire a very excellent letter. He could not take, he said, as hypocrisy a deed which, if hypocritical, would tarnish a great man's glory and make him despicable in the eyes of all thoughtful persons. ' I hope your future life will give proof of the integrity and sincerity of your act ; ' and then, in language of great dignity and even beauty, he attempted to recall the sinner to a sense of sin, and reminded him of that hour which could not now be far distant, when the faith would be his only hope, and his fame and glory the shadows of a dream.

Voltaire replied on April 15, purposely misunderstanding the Bishop's letter and taking his remarks as compliments. He felt the act needed excuse. To d'Alembert, who was as free-thinking as any man in Paris, he wrote apologetically, that, finding himself between two fourteenth-century bishops, he was obliged to ' howl with the wolves.' He abused Biort as a fanatic and an imbecile. But he knew very well that he was neither. He was not so imbecile, at least, that he put any faith in a devout and serious letter M. de Voltaire was pleased to write to him on April 29, and replied on

May 2 in terms which showed very clearly that he knew his Voltaire—to the soul.

He had already issued a mandate to the clergy of his diocese forbidding them to give the Sacrament to this profane person. He now sent the whole correspondence to the King, and, as the only punishment adequate to the offence, he begged for a *lettre de cachet* for M. de Voltaire. Saint-Florentin was bidden to write the culprit a formal epistle, saying that the King strongly condemned 'this enterprise' on the part of his ex-Gentleman-in-Ordinary. But there was no *lettre de cachet*. The incident had amused the Court. *That* covered a multitude of sins.

For the time the affair was over. But alas ! only for the time.

Though there were few visitors in Madame Denis's absence, there were some. In the August of this 1768 two very lively young men, both about twenty years old, came over from Geneva to call upon the Patriarch of Ferney. One of them, named Price, more than forty years after, told a friend the little he recollected of the occasion. His companion was then known as the son of Lord Holland, but later and now as Charles James Fox. He had first visited Ferney in 1764 when he was sixteen.

Voltaire was delighted to see his visitors, but, as usual, declared that they had only come to bury him ; and though he walked about the garden and drank chocolate with them, did not invite them to dinner.

The only part of their conversation Price recollected after that interval of forty years was that the host gave them the names of such of his works as might open their minds and 'free them from religious prejudice,' adding, ' Here are the books with which to fortify yourselves.'

Charles paid other visits to Ferney, and Voltaire soon learnt to love him, as all the world loved that generous and brilliant youth. ' Y^r son is an English lad and j an old Frenchman,' the Patriarch wrote to Lord Holland after Charles's next visit. ' He is healthy and j sick. Yet j love him with all my heart, not only for his father but himself.' Voltaire gave the young man dinner this time, in his ' little caban ; ' and Charles became a *persona grata* at Ferney, as in all the world.

Another Englishman with whom Voltaire was brought into relation in the summer of 1768 was Horace Walpole. Voltaire had seen Horace's ' Historic Doubts on Richard III.,' and characteristically wrote that it was fifty years since *he* took a vow to doubt, and reminded Horace that he had known his father and uncle in England. Horace sent a copy of his book, and the correspondence drifted on to that favourite topic of contention between literary Englishmen and Voltaire—Shakespeare. Voltaire, who wrote in his own language—what need to write in English to ' the best Frenchman ever born on English soil ' ?—pointed out with just pride in reply that he had been the first to make Shakespeare, Locke, and Newton known to the French, and that, in spite of the persecutions of a clique of fanatics. ' I have been your apostle and your martyr : truly English people have no reason to complain of me.'

If some new friends came into Voltaire's life in this solitary 1768, more old ones went out of it.

On June 24 of this year died Marie Leczinska. Friend ? Well, once. There was that pension *sur sa cassette*, and ' my poor Voltaire.'

In the autumn died Olivet—a friend indeed—the

best of Latinists, the kindly schoolmaster at Louis-le-
Grand.

In December, that silent staunch laborious worker
for the philosophic faith, Damilaville, met death with
the resolute courage with which he had faced life, and
left the world poorer for one of those rare people who
say nothing and do much.

Voltaire mourned him as a public as well as a
personal loss. He mourned him characteristically—
that such a man should die while Frérons waxed fat!
But since they did, the less time to sit idle and weeping.

Up then, and at them with those little deadly
arrows of which the Voltairian quiver was always full—
the arrows called Pamphlets.

CHAPTER XL

THE COLONY OF WATCHMAKERS AND WEAVERS

'WHAT harm can a book do that costs a hundred
crowns?' Voltaire had written to Damilaville on
April 5, 1765. 'Twenty volumes folio will never make
a revolution; it is the little pocket pamphlets of thirty
sous that are to be feared.'

He had acted on that principle all his life. But he
had never acted upon it so much as in his hand-to-
hand battle with *l'infâme*. He never acted upon it so
often as in his eighteen months' solitude at Ferney in
1768–69.

For many years, from that 'manufactory' of his,
as Grimm called it, he poured forth a ceaseless stream
of dialogues, epistles, discourses, reflections, novelettes,
commentaries, burlesques, reviews. Hardly any of
them were more than a few pages in length. But each
dealt with some subject near to his wide heart; cried
aloud for some reform which had not been made, and
must be made; pointed out with mocking finger some
scandal in Church or State; satirised with killing
irony some gross abuse of power; turned on some mis-
carriage of civil justice the searchlight of truth; laughed
lightly, in dialogue, at the education of women by nuns
in convents to fit them to be wives and mothers in the
world; drew up damning statistics of the 9,468,800

victims 'hanged, drowned, broken on the wheel, or
burnt, for the love of God' and their religion from the
time of Constantine to Louis XIV. ; pleaded vivaciously
against the eighty-two annual holidays set apart by the
Church on which it was criminal to work but not to be
drunken and mischievous ; enumerated the 'Horrible
Dangers of Reading,' of knowing, of thinking ; and
lashed with the prettiest of stinging little whips a
corrupt ministry, a wicked priesthood, and *l'infâme*,
l'infâme.

'*Il fait le tout en badinant.*' Serious ? Why, no.
'Our French people want to learn without studying ;'
and they shall. Instruct ! Instruct ! but as one instructs
a child with a lesson in the form of a story, or the
simplest little sermon with a sugar-plum of a joke at the
end. This was such a laughing philosopher that many
persons have doubted if he really could have been a
philosopher at all. He turned so many somersaults,
as friend Frederick put it plaintively. But the somersaults gained him an audience, and once gained he
knew very well how to keep and teach it. It was one
of his own sayings that ridicule does for everything and
is the strongest of arms. He proved the truth of that
assertion himself—in the pamphlets by which he held
the attention and commanded the intellect of the
eighteenth century.

Read them now—they are the most amusing reading
in the world—and beneath the sparkling mockery, see
the burning meaning.

They are much more, considered as works of art
alone, than brilliant burlesques. Each of them is
endowed with Voltaire's 'unquenchable life,' and
'stamped with the express image' of his whole per-
sonality. Gay, crisp, and clear, expressing his ideas in

the fewest and easiest words and in the most vivacious and graceful of all literary styles, they conveyed
to his generation 'the consciousness at once of the
power and the rights of the human intelligence.'

Through these pamphlets 'the revolution works in
all minds. Light comes by a thousand holes it is
impossible to stop up.' 'Reason penetrates into the
merchants' shops as into the nobles' palaces.'

What better proof could Voltaire himself have
wanted of the growth of that liberty and tolerance
which he loved, and strove to make all men love and
have, than the fact that the government, autocratic
and all-powerful as it was, could not prevent those
pamphlets selling and working in their midst?

'Opinion rules the world,' said Voltaire himself.
At last he had made his opinion, Public Opinion.
'From 1762 to the end of Voltaire's life, it was on the
side of the philosophers.'

True, the authorities still burnt his works. In
1768 he had written 'The Man with Forty Crowns,' a
burlesque story 'on the financial chaos which fifteen
years later brought France to bankruptcy.' That must
be burnt of course. France hated unfavourable prophecies. It *was* burnt. But by now Voltaire's pamphlets were like Shadrach, Meshech, and Abednego.
Flames could not hurt them. And when they came
out of the fiery furnace it was only with an added
lustre and glory.

Well for Voltaire if those pamphlets could have
engrossed all his solitude. In Beuchot's edition of his
writings they fill ten large volumes. Here surely was
occupation enough for a lifetime! But Voltaire had
time for everything, and was for ever the spoilt boy
who loved his own way.

The Easter of 1769 reminded him of last Easter and
the fact that the Bishop of Annecy had forbidden his
priesthood to allow him to confess or communicate.
Very well then ! I will do both.

His feeble body had been ill and ailing for a year—
a condition of things which is apt to make the mind
unreasonable.   There was a recent case of a man
called Boindin, who, dying unfortified by the Sacraments, had been refused Christian burial.   There was
always the case of Adrienne Lecouvreur—' thrown into
the kennel like a dead dog.'

Voltaire declared, to persons whom he could have
no object in deceiving, that he had lately had ' twelve
accesses of fever.'   He was seventy-five years old.
And death always was and had been a far more present
reality to him than to most people.

These things taken together form, not at all a valid
excuse, but some sort of honest excuse for an act that
needs a great deal of excusing.

Voltaire was in bed one day in the March of 1769,
dictating to Wagnière, when he saw from his window
Gros, the Ferney curé, and a Capuchin monk who had
come to help him with the Easter confessions, walking
in the garden.   Voltaire sent for the Capuchin and
told him that he was too ill to leave his bed, but as a
Frenchman, an official of the King, and seigneur of the
parish, he wished there and then to make his confession.   And he put the usual fee of six francs into
the Capuchin's hand.   The poor man, with the fear
of his Bishop before his eyes, nervously temporised,
said he was very busy and would return in a few
days.

' Trust me to get even with him ! ' cries the patient
when M. le Capuchin had retired.   Burgos, ' a kind of

surgeon,' is sent for, and having felt the invalid's pulse, is fool enough to say that it is excellent.

'What, you ignorant fellow ! Excellent ? ' roars the sick man.

Burgos feels it again. It is a very different pulse this time, and M. de Voltaire is in a high fever.

'Then go and tell the priest.'

Six days elapsed and no priest appeared. So the very active-minded invalid caused the whole household to be roused in a body in the middle of the night, and to hurry off to the curé saying their master was dying and presenting a certificate signed by himself, Wagnière, Bigex, and Burgos, which declared the invalid's pious desire to die fortified with the Sacraments and in the bosom of the faith in which he was born and had lived.

Neither curé nor Capuchin appeared.

Then Voltaire sent a lawyer to the curé, saying that if he did not come, the Lord of Ferney would denounce him to the Parliament as having refused the Sacraments to a dying man.

The poor curé was in such a fright that he was attacked on the spot, says Wagnière, by the colic.

On March 31, Voltaire drew up before a notary a statement in legal form declaring himself, in spite of calumnies, to be a sincere Catholic. Among others, the complaisant Father Adam witnessed this statement.

The next day, April 1, the Capuchin appeared at Ferney. The Bishop of Annecy had been consulted, and now sent by the Capuchin a profession of faith for Voltaire to sign.

The invalid, who had already recited a hurried jumble of the Pater, the Credo, and the Confiteor, replied that the Creed was supposed to contain the whole faith ; and though the unhappy Capuchin went

on presenting to him at intervals the Bishop's paper
to sign, he would do nothing but repeat his statement
about the Creed.   After having delivered to the Capuchin a long homily on morality and tolerance (which
Wagnière found 'very touching and pathetic') the
sick man suddenly called out loudly, 'Give me absolution at once,' which the terrified confessor, who had
entirely lost his head, did.   Then Voltaire sent for the
curé, who administered the Sacrament.

The notary was also present.   'At the very instant
the priest gave the wafer to M. de Voltaire' he declared
aloud that he sincerely pardoned those who had
calumniated him to the King 'and who have not succeeded in their base design, and I demand a record of
my declaration from the notary.'   He recorded it.   No
sooner was Voltaire left to himself than this amazing
invalid jumped out of bed and went for a walk in the
garden.

Meanwhile, curé and Capuchin laid their terrified
heads together and bethought themselves of some
means to avoid the consequences of having absolved
and given the mass to the scoffer without his having
signed the declaration drawn up by the Bishop.

On April 15, they summoned seven witnesses whom
they had persuaded to declare on oath that they had
heard M. de Voltaire pronounce a complete and satisfactory confession of faith, which confession they
invented and sent to the Bishop.

The hocus-pocus was on both sides, it will be seen.
But Voltaire was responsible for it all.   Paris—even
Paris—received the news of his 'unpardonable buffoonery' 'pretty badly.'   The d'Argentals entirely disapproved of it, and Dr. Tronchin condemned it with
severity.

'Useless *méchancetés* are very foolish,' Voltaire had said.   He regarded this one as indispensable.   When he wrote to his Angels excusing himself, he declared that he had need of a buckler to withstand the mortal blows of sacerdotal calumny, and that such a duty, neglected, might at his death have had very unpleasant consequences for his family.   These were not sufficient reasons for his act.   But they at least free him from 'the reproach of erecting hypocrisy into a deliberate doctrine.'   As Condorcet says, 'such deceptions did not deceive, while they did protect.'   'Disagreeable as these temporisings are to us,' they damn deeper the time which made them a pressing expedient, than the time-server.

As the Bishop of Annecy had accused Voltaire of holding impious conversations at his dinner table, he now took advantage of Madame Denis's absence to have pious works read aloud to him at that meal.   When a President of the Parliament of Dijon was dining with him, Massillon, of whom Voltaire was a warm admirer, was the author chosen.   'What style! What harmony! What eloquence!' cries the Patriarch of Ferney as he listens to those magnificent periods, to the denunciations like a god's.   The reader continued for three or four pages.

'Off with Massillon!' cries Voltaire, and 'he gave himself up to all the folly and *verve* of his imagination.' Irreverence?   Malicious mockery?   It has been generally thought so.   May it not rather have been that both sentiments were perfectly genuine? that in one there expressed itself the passionate admiration and in the other the irresponsible liveliness, of which this extraordinary character was equally capable?

Though he had nearly harried the life out of one

poor Capuchin of Gex, though he had wantonly
insulted the faith of all the Capuchins, almost his next
act was to obtain for them, through Choiseul, an
annuity of six hundred francs for the Gex monastery,
in return for which benefit the Brothers gave him the
title of Temporal Father of the Capuchins of Gex.   He
derived a monkeyish delight from it ; used to sign his
letters with a cross, ' †, Brother Voltaire unworthy
Capuchin ; ' but then he also derived an honest delight
from the good he had been able to do the monastery.

Who can explain him ?

Presently he was writing to Cardinal Bernis to
obtain the Pope's permission for Father Adam to wear
a wig on his bald head during mass.   The climate
was cold, the poor Father rheumatic, and his Holiness
had been obliged to forbid wigs to the priesthood as
they had so often been used as a disguise for unworthy
purposes.

All through religious controversies and irreligious
acts, Voltaire was engaged in a long, constant, and
very flattering correspondence with Catherine the
Great.   Even Frederick, in the beguiling days before
the Prussian visits, had not so gratified Voltaire's self-
love.   Voltaire was the teacher, and Catherine, the
greatest of queens and the cleverest of women, his
humble pupil.   In 1768 she had taken his advice—there
is no subtler form of flattery—upon inoculation, and
herself submitted to the operation.   And in this 1769
she sent him the loveliest pelisse of Russian sable, a
snuff-box she had turned with her own royal hands,
her portrait set in diamonds, and an epitome of the
laws with which she governed her great empire.   Here
surely was balm for solitude, calumny, sickness, old
age, every mortal misfortune !   Voltaire warmed body

and soul through the snowy Swiss spring in that gorgeous pelisse. In March, he had another present, which delighted his queer old heart hardly less. Saint-Lambert—Saint-Lambert, who had robbed him of his mistress and wounded him with a wound which another man could never have forgiven or forgotten—sent him his poem, ' The Seasons.' And the poet Voltaire writes to his brother of the lyre the most charming compliments and congratulations.

Before this, he was writing the kindest letters to La Harpe again. When Madame Denis, in the latter half of this October 1769 and after an absence of a little less than eighteen months, burst into Ferney, her uncle seems to have folded her in his arms, received her with as much delight as if she had always been trustworthy, practical, sensible, and considerate, and to have let bygones be bygones as only he knew how.

The Dupuits were already home again ; and Voltaire was busy with a new business which had been in his mind since he first came to Ferney, and in practical existence at least since 1767.

From the moment he had bought his estates he had felt the full weight of his responsibilities as a landowner, and realised as keenly as Arthur Young, the philosophic farmer who rode through France prophesying her downfall, that agriculture is the true wealth of a nation.

' The best thing we have to do on earth is to cultivate it.'

At more than threescore years and ten, this old son of the pavement had set himself to learn, and did learn, the whole *technique* of agriculture. Directly he bought Ferney he began putting the barren land round it under cultivation, and so occupied all persons on his estates

who were out of work.   When he was seventy-eight
he was still hard at work with his own hands on that
field which had been called Voltaire's Field, because he
cultivated it entirely himself.

It has been seen how he planted avenues of trees.
Four times over he lined his drive with chestnut and
walnut trees, and four times they nearly all died, or
were wantonly destroyed by the peasants. ' However,
I am not daunted. The others laugh at me. Neither
my old age nor my complaints nor the severity of the
climate discourage me. To have cultivated a field and
made twenty trees grow is a good which will never be
lost.'

He entered into a long correspondence with Moreau
—that rare being, a practical Political Economist. He
delighted in Galiani's famous ' Dialogues on Corn '—
never was man in the right so wittily before—and
in this very 1769 he was thanking Abbé Mords-les-
Morellet for his ' Dictionary of Commerce.'

For, after all, the Land meant the People ; and
commerce there must be, if the work of the People on
the Land were to be remunerative.

Many terrible accounts have been given of the condition of the French poor before the Revolution. But
theirs was a misery which no passion and eloquence
can overstate.

Forbidden at certain seasons to guard their wretched
pieces of land by fences lest they should interfere with
my lord's hunt, or to manure their miserable crops lest
they should spoil the flavour of my lord's game ; forbidden, at hatching seasons, to weed those crops lest
they should disturb the partridges ; and forbidden,
without special permission, to build a shed in which
to store their grain—the fruit of their lands and their

labour, if there was any such fruit, was always lost to them.

Taxes alone deprived them of three-quarters of what they earned. On one side was the *corvée,* or the right of the lord to his peasants' labour without paying for it; and the *taille,* or the tax on property, which exacted a certain sum from each village ; so that if the rich would not pay, the poor *must.*

Add to this the toll-gates, so numerous that fish brought from Harfleur to Paris paid eleven times its value *en route* ; the fines exacted when land was bought or sold ; above all, the enormous tax upon salt, which soon was as the match to fire the gunpowder of the Revolution ; the tithes exacted by the Church ; the fees for masses for the dead, for burying, christening, and marrying, coupled with the bitter injustice that the clergy of that Church were themselves exempt from all taxation.

Add to these regular taxes the irregular ones.

On the accession of Louis XV. one was levied, called the Tax of the Joyful Accession. Joyful ! The people who paid it lived in a windowless, one-roomed hut of peat or clay; clothed in the filthiest rags ; ignorant, bestial, degraded ; creatures who never knew youth or hope ; who died in unrecorded thousands, of pestilence and famine ; or lived, to their own cruel misery, a few dark years ' on a little black bread, and not enough of that.'

Such were the fifty poor of Ferney as Voltaire found them, but not the twelve hundred he left.

Whatever his sins were—and they were many— he had one of the noblest and most difficult of virtues— a far higher conception of his duty to others than the men of his time. It was fashionable to talk philanthropy in the eighteenth century, but dangerous, as well as unmodish, to practise it.

'True philosophy . . .' wrote the great Doer in the midst of the Dreamers, 'makes the earth fertile and the people happier. The true philosopher cultivates the land, increases the number of the ploughs, and so of the inhabitants ; occupies the poor man, and thus enriches him ; encourages marriages, cares for the orphan ; does not grumble at necessary taxes, and puts the labourer in a condition to pay them promptly.'

He had begun by getting back for the Ferney poor that tithe of which Ancian had deprived them, and by making the peasants mend and make roads—at fair wages. Later, he petitioned the King for 'some privileges for my children ; ' and Gex was at last declared free from all the taxes of the farmers-general, and salt, which used to be ten sous the pound, came down to four.

His building operations at both the church and château gave occupation to many masons. Then the masons must have decent dwellings in which to live themselves ; and here was more work.

In 1767 he could write that he had formed a colony at Ferney ; that he had established there three merchants, artists, and a doctor, and was building houses for them. By 1769 he recorded with an honest pride that he had quadrupled the number of the parishioners, and that there was not a poor man among them ; that he had under his immediate supervision two hundred workers, and was the means of life to everyone round him.

Nor did he forget to provide them with pleasure as well as with work. Every Sunday the young people of the colony used to come up to the château to dance.

Their host provided them with refreshments, and was the happiest spectator of their happiness.

Then he started a school, and himself paid the schoolmaster. There had been a time when he had thought that ' it is not the labourer one must teach, it is the *bon bourgeois*, the inhabitant of towns : that enterprise is grand and great enough,' which, for his day, it certainly was. It was a hundred years in advance of his time. Even that drastic reformer, Frederick the Great, had announced superbly, ' The vulgar do not deserve enlightenment.' So what wonder that in 1763 even a clearsighted Voltaire prayed for ' ignorant brothers to follow my plough ' ?

The wonder rather is that by 1767 his views had so enormously progressed that when Linguet, the barrister, wrote to him that in his opinion all was lost if the *canaille* were shown that they too could reason, he emphatically answered, instancing the intelligent Genevans who read as a relaxation from manual labour—' No, Sir ; all is not lost when the people are put into a condition to see that they too have a mind. On the contrary, all is lost when they are treated like a herd of bulls, for sooner or later they will gore you with their horns.'

Prophetic—but if many heard that voice crying in the wilderness, none acted on his words, save himself.

But in prospering Ferney there was room not only for a school and a doctor, masons and labourers, but for special industries. From the first, Voltaire had cultivated silkworms. He was never the man for an idle hobby. Why should no use be made of the silk ? Before 1769, the Ferney theatre, which Madame Denis had lately used as a laundry, was turned into a silkworm nursery. From busy Geneva came stocking weavers, only too glad to colonise in a place where the lord and master lent them money 'on very easy terms,' built decent dwellings for them, and gave them the full benefit of his knowledge of affairs.

By September 4, 1769, Voltaire, always alive to the advantages of a good advertisement, sent to the Duchesse de Choiseul the first pair of silk stockings ever made on his looms. If she would but wear them they *must* be the mode! What stocking would not look beautiful on a foot so charming? Voltaire found time to engage his Duchess to wear them, in a gay, coquettish, and essentially French correspondence. Madame had made a mistake, it appears, and sent him, as a pattern, a shoe much too large for her. Neither his thousand schemes and labours nor his seventy-five years had spoiled his talent for flattering badinage. His Duchess accepted his stockings and his compliments, showed both to her friends, and thus put some fifty to a hundred people, including young Calas who was helping his benefactor, out of the way of want.

On February 15, 1770, the party quarrels in Geneva came to a climax—and bloodshed.

The Natives had not forgotten the promise made to them four years earlier. ' If you are forced to leave your country . . . I shall still be able to help and protect you.'

Neither had Voltaire.

On February 10, 1767, in writing to de Beauteville, the French mediator, he had suggested the scheme of a working colony—the nucleus of the idea of some enterprising person enticing the great watchmaking industry of quarrelsome Geneva to form a settlement, which should be managed by its founder and should bear his name. The scheme had appealed to Choiseul.

In 1768, with Voltaire's co-operation and approval, that minister founded the colony of Versoix—or Versoy, as Voltaire spells it—which was designed to be what Ferney actually became.

The crisis of February 15, 1770, caused great numbers of the Native watchmakers of Geneva to flee from the city and take refuge at Versoix and at Ferney. Versoix was unequal to the emergency. There were no houses for the workers. But Ferney rose to the occasion. That was always part of its old master's genius.

Only a few months after the Natives had first consulted him, this far-seeing person had begun to build workmen's dwellings in his village. The overflow from those 'pretty houses of freestone,' he now took into the château itself. So far, so good.

The next thing to do was to obtain the permission for his settlement from the authorities. The authorities were personified by M. de Choiseul. Voltaire had helped him with his Versoix. So Choiseul could not, and did not, refuse to help Voltaire with Ferney.

To start the watchmakers in their new home at their old trade, Voltaire advanced sixty thousand livres. He at once found occupation for fifty Genevan workmen, not counting the inhabitants of Gex. He himself bought gold, silver, and jewels for the work, a better bargain than the workpeople could do for themselves.

In six weeks he had watches ready for sale—of exquisite workmanship, artistic design, and to be sold at least one-third cheaper than they could be in Geneva. The Duke of Choiseul bought the first six watches ever made by Voltaire's manufactory.

By April 9 the old courtier was promising the

Duchess that she should soon have one worthy to wear even at *her* waist.

Then he began his system of personal advertisement. The handsomest commission in the world on every watch he sold could not have made the neediest agent work harder or more cunningly than did this Voltaire, who received at first no commission, never could expect a large one, and had need of neither large nor small.

On June 5, 1770, he sent round a circular to all the foreign ambassadors—'diplomacy *en masse*'—a most beautiful circular from 'The Royal Manufactory of Ferney' (in capital letters), and recommending watches —'plain silver,' from three louis, to repeaters at forty-two. That flaming document is still preserved.

The advertiser wrote a letter with it. 'I never write for the sake of writing,' he said; 'but when I have a subject I do not spare my pen, old and dying as I am.'

Catherine the Great was appealed to; and in answer to her 'vaguely magnificent order for watches' to 'the value of some thousands of roubles,' Voltaire had to apologise for his workmen having taken advantage of her goodness, and sent her watches to the value of eight thousand!

The Empress replied imperially—as she was obliged to do—that such an expense would not ruin her. And in his next letter her artful old friend warmly recommended his pendulum clocks—'which we are now making'—and asked her to assist him in promoting a watch trade between Ferney and China. She did.

Ferney was soon sending watches not only to China, but to Spain, Italy, Russia, Holland, America, Turkey, Portugal, and North Africa, besides carrying on an enormous trade with Paris.

' Give me a chance and I am the man to build a city,' said Voltaire to Richelieu. With a chance he could have done anything. Kings and commoners, cardinals, great ladies—he appealed to them all. Is not rosy-faced Bernis at Rome? Well, why should not he promote the sale of watches for me in the Imperial City?

Babet totally ignored the commission. He was almost the only person to whom Voltaire applied who behaved so badly. And Ferney wrote him such a stinging reproach for his neglect, that poor Babet must have regretted he had not been more obliging.

As for Frederick the Great, he did better even than buy watches by the cartload like the other great potentate, Catherine.

He gave for twelve years free lodging in Berlin, with exemption from all taxation, to eighteen families of refugee Genevan watchmakers. This started the watch-making industry in his capital.

To Madame Dubarry, who had succeeded to the honours and dishonour of the Pompadour, the Gentle-man-in-Ordinary-to-the-King sent presently the loveliest little watch set in diamonds.

He left no stone unturned. He supervised every detail. In 1773 Ferney sold ' four thousand watches worth half a million of francs.' All losses Voltaire bore himself. Capable and alert as he was, they were sometimes heavy.

He had had a royal order, for instance, on the occasion of the marriage of the Dauphin with Marie Antoinette, which was encouraging but expensive. He was never paid.

Nothing daunted him however. By the June of 1770 he had begun building those much-needed houses in the rival, or rather the sister, colony of Versoix. And then, as if he found weaving and watchmaking insufficient for his energy, by 1772 he had started a lacemaking industry. That butterfly Madame Saint-Julien must make this airiest of gossamer fabrics—'the beautiful blonde lace which was made in our village'—the fashion. 'The woman who màde it can make more very reasonably. She can add a dozen workers to the staff, and we shall owe to you a new manufactory.' The vigorous boy who wrote the words, originated the scheme, and carried it to successful issue, was only seventy-eight. He personally negotiated with the shop which was to buy and sell his new wares when made. Cannot one see him haggling and bargaining and enjoying himself, with a twinkle in his bright old eyes and a very humorous shrewdness in the curves of his thin lips?

But if he wanted a reward for all this trouble, he had it. The miserable hamlet had become a thriving village, and the desert place blossomed like a rose. The master's corn fed his people, and his bad wine (' which is not harmful ') gave them drink. His bees produced excellent honey and wax, and his hemp and flax, linen.

Here dwelt together, as one family, Catholics and Huguenots. 'Is not this better than St. Bartholomew?' 'When a Catholic is sick, Protestants go and take care of him;' and *vice versa*. The good Protestant women prepared with their own hands the little portable altars for the Procession of the Holy Sacrament, and the curé thanked them publicly in a sermon. Gros had died—of drink, said Voltaire—and his place had been taken by Hugenot, an excellent priest, generous and liberal-minded, the friend of all his people whatever their faith, and of M. de Voltaire, who was supposed to have none at all.

Here surely was the tree of Tolerance he had planted, bearing beautiful fruit. It might well warm his old heart to see his little colony firm on 'those two pivots of the wealth of a state, be it little or great, freedom of trade and freedom of conscience.'

The man who worked the case of Calas for three years, the case of Sirven for seven, and the cases of Lally and d'Étallonde for twelve, was not likely to grow tired of the little colony always beneath his eyes. Nor was he unmindful of the claims not only Ferney, but all Gex, had upon his bounty. When it was devastated by famine in 1771 he had corn sent him from Sicily, and sold it much under cost price to his starving children and the poor people of the province. Their sufferings and sorrows were his own. He pleaded passionately for those who were, and had been for generations, miserable with the hopeless misery that is dumb; but who, before many years were past, were to cry aloud their wrongs with a great and terrible voice which would reach to the ends of the earth.

All Voltaire's letters in his later years are full of his watchmakers and weavers, their prosperity or their poverty, what he had done for them or what he would do. Did his own glorification play no part in his schemes? It doubtless played some. But the fact that he may have been vain does not alter the fact that he set an example which Christians have nobly followed, but which, in his day at least, they certainly did not set *him*.

Voltaire, sceptic and scoffer, too often of evil life and unclean lips, was not only the High Priest of Tolerance, but the first great practical philanthropist of his century.

CHAPTER XLI

ONE spring evening of the year 1770 the idea was suggested, at the table of the Neckers in Paris, of erecting a statue to the great Voltaire.

Necker was a prosperous banker, and, to be, Controller-General.

Madame, his wife, once the beloved of Gibbon, was the daughter of a Swiss minister and one of the first *salonières* in the capital.

The plan was immediately approved and acted upon by her seventeen guests. They formed themselves into a committee to receive subscriptions, and decided that the work should be entrusted to the famous Pigalle, who was to fix his own price, which he did very modestly.

Madame Necker herself communicated the plan to Voltaire.

He was boyishly delighted at the compliment. He answered gaily that he was seventy-six and had just had a long illness which had treated both his mind and body very badly, and that if Pigalle was to come and model his face he must first have a face to model. ' You would hardly guess where it ought to be. My eyes have sunk three inches; my cheeks are like old parchment; . . . the few teeth I had are gone. . . . This is not coquetry, it is truth.'

It was. Dr. Burney, who visited Ferney in this year, spoke of his host as a living skeleton—'mere skin and bone'—but he spoke, too, like everybody else, of the gleaming eyes full of living fire; and d'Alembert wrote to the model himself: 'Genius . . . has always a countenance which genius, its brother, will easily find.'

Subscriptions had flowed in from the first with unprecedented generosity. The magnificent Richelieu contributed magnificently. Frederick, one of the first to wish to give, wrote to ask d'Alembert of what amount his gift should be.

'An écu, Sire, and your name,' says d'Alembert. But Frederick gave more than money. In noble words and a most generous eulogy, he blotted out Frankfort and the past for ever. 'The finest monument to Voltaire is the one he has erected himself. His work will endure when the Basilisk of St. Peter, the Louvre, and all the buildings which human vanity supposes eternal, have perished.'

Voltaire was delighted at Frederick's subscription (which of course was not limited to words), not only because that great name would look nobly, but for a more characteristic reason. 'It would save money to too generous literary men, who have none.'

Among the 'too generous literary men' were four old enemies—Rousseau, Fréron, Palissot, and La Beaumelle. Their money was returned—except that of Rousseau. And peacemaking d'Alembert had very hard work to get *vif* Voltaire to accept Jean Jacques' gift as a 'reparation.'

Another foe more unforgiving—or more honest—declined to give at all. 'I will not give a sou to the *sub*scription,' says Piron, 'but I will undertake the *in*scription.'

About June 16, Pigalle, sculptor to the King and

Chancellor of the Academy of Painting, arrived at
Ferney, on work intent.   But the model was so agreeable a host !   True, in spite of the parties and distractions, he gave the sculptor a sitting every day.   But as
he never kept still a moment and was dictating letters,
with much vivid French gesticulation, to Wagnière the
whole time, it was not wonderful that on the seventh
day of a visit which was to last eight, M. Pigalle discovered that he had done nothing at all.   Fortunately,
on that seventh day—June 23, 1770—the conversation
turned upon the Golden Calf of the Children of Israel.
Voltaire was so childishly delighted when Pigalle declared that such a thing would take at least six months
to make—as disproving the Mosaic testimony that it was
made in twenty-four hours—that during the rest of the
sitting the model was as quiet and obedient as possible.
The results were so satisfactory that Pigalle resolved
not to attempt another interview, and the next morning
left Ferney quietly and without seeing anyone.

The Golden Calf incident so pleased Voltaire that
he at once wrote it down and dated it.   He repeated it,
with much chuckling, to all his correspondents ; wrote
an article on Casting for his dear ' Philosophical Dictionary,' where he introduced it again, most amusingly ;
and in 1776 wrote a pamphlet—' A Christian against
Six Jews '—in which he put Pigalle's professional
testimony in opposition to that of the sacred writers.

Another account of the episode declares that Pigalle
kept his sitter quiet by talking of his dear ' Pucelle.'

There seems no reason why both stories should not
be true.

Pigalle's statue disappointed his own generation,
and is only a curiosity to ours.

The best statue of Voltaire is usually considered to be

the one by Houdon, of a very old, sitting, draped figure, with a face far from unamiable or unkindly, excessively able and shrewd, with the most steady, penetrating old eyes, and mocking lips closed over the toothless mouth.

Pigalle represented his subject entirely unclad—for the best of all reasons, said Grimm, he could not do drapery.   Good Madame Necker, mindful of her Calvinistic education, objected to the nakedness.   But not old Voltaire.   ' It is all one to me,' he said airily ; and added sensibly, ' M. Pigalle must be left absolute master of his statue. . . . It is a crime . . . to put fetters on genius.'

The want of clothing, however, gave rise to many doubtful jokes in eighteenth-century Paris, and his enemies made very spiteful epigrams on the meagreness of the figure.   ' Posterity will not want to count M. de Voltaire's ribs,' says Fréron sarcastically.   And though Voltaire pretended to laugh at such gibes—and laughed himself at all his bodily defects—he was still morally thin-skinned.   ' A statue is no consolation,' he wrote dismally to d'Argental, ' when so many enemies conspire to cover it with mud.'

But there were more friends to cover it with adulation.   In 1772 Mademoiselle Clairon surprised the *habitués* of her rooms one evening by drawing back a curtain and showing them the bust of Voltaire on an altar.   She put a laurel crown on the head, and in her ' noble and beautiful voice ' recited an ode of Marmontel's which, particularly in its Apostrophe to Envy, produced a great effect.

When Voltaire heard of the incident, he got out his old lyre and thanked Mademoiselle in verse of extraordinary freshness—' very pretty for a young man of only seventy-nine,' says Grimm.

While his statue was the topic of Paris, the original
was entertaining at least three celebrated visitors at
Ferney : Dr. Burney, d'Alembert, and Condorcet.

Dr. Burney, the father of Johnson's dear *protégée*,
Fanny, came to Geneva in the course of his Musical
Tour through France and Italy.

Hearing that Voltaire relentlessly snubbed the
curious idle who only came ' to look at the wild beast,'
the good pompous Doctor was a little nervous of the
reception he might meet.   But all went well.

A servant, presumably Wagnière, introduced Burney to his master's sanctum, and to the library, where
Burney saw a portrait of young Dupuits whom he
supposed to be Voltaire's brother, though Wagnière
told him Voltaire was seventy-eight (he was really
seventy-six), and the difference in age between the
' brothers ' must have been forty years at the least.

Then Dr. Burney was introduced to the great man
himself, who still worked, said Wagnière, ten hours a
day and wrote constantly without spectacles.   The conversation turned on English literature, and Voltaire observed how England had now no one ' who lords it over
the rest like Dryden, Pope, and Swift ; ' and remarked,
when critics are silent it proves not so much that the
age is correct, as that it is dull.   Burney was shown the
model village—' the most innocent and the most useful
of all my works '—and tactfully departed before he
should have taken more than his share of the great
man's time.

D'Alembert arrived at Ferney in the September of
1770.   He was supposed to be *en route* to see Rome and
die.   Frederick the Great had sent him six thousand
francs for the tour.   But either, as d'Alembert told the
King, the prospect of the fatigue and the bad inns

daunted him, or, as Duvernet says, Voltaire's society was too seductive. D'Alembert returned the King half of his money, and in two months was back in Paris.

The Marquis de Condorcet, who then was celebrated as a philosophic and free-thinking noble who had wholly broken with the religion and the traditions of his caste, and now is celebrated as the philosopher and *littérateur* who wrote a brief and scholarly Life of Voltaire and who poisoned himself to escape the guillotine, was a fellow-guest with d'Alembert.

Is it difficult to fancy the conversation between these three men over the Ferney supper table at the magic hour when Voltaire was always at his best, ' at once light and learned,' brilliant and subtle? The tranquil cheerfulness of that true philosopher, d'Alembert—' his just mind and inexhaustible imagination '—soothed the vexations with which he found his irritable host overwhelmed.

Condorcet, whom Voltaire spoke of as having ' the same hatred for oppression and fanaticism, and the same zeal for humanity ' as he had himself, was as exempt from what it was then modish to call 'prejudices,' as the gentle d'Alembert.

Of that brilliant little party there was but one man who still clung to some tenets of the old faith; and that man was Voltaire. Du Pan records how he heard him give an ' energetic lesson ' at his supper table to his two guests, by sending all the servants out of the room in the middle of their conversation. ' Now, gentlemen, continue your attack on God. But as I do not want to be strangled or robbed to-night by my servants they had better not hear you.'

' *Si Dieu n'existait pas   il faudrait   l'inventer*,'

Voltaire had said in one of the most famous lines in the world.

Baron Gleichen, who was at Délices in 1757, records how a young author sought to recommend himself to the great man's favour by saying 'I am an atheist apprentice at your service.' 'But I,' replied Voltaire, 'am a master Deist.'

But the pupils he had taught had gone far beyond his teaching. Diderot spoke of him as '*cagot*'; and the story runs that some fine lady of Paris dismissed him scornfully in the words, 'He is a Deist, he is a bigot.'

He had no further bigotries, it is certain. A thousand stories are told to illustrate his indignation against what he took to be a debasing fanaticism.

A Genevan lady brought to see him her little girl, who was as intelligent as she was pretty and could learn everything but her Catechism, and that she could not understand. 'Ah!' says Voltaire. 'How reasonable! A child always speaks the truth. You do not understand your Catechism? Do you see these fine peaches? Eat as many as you like.'

It is recorded, too, that Voltaire had always a special grudge against Habakkuk: and when someone showed him that he had misrepresented facts in that prophet's history, 'It is no matter,' he replied; 'Habakkuk was capable of anything.'

There are many other such stories told of him. All profane jests are fathered on Voltaire. Some of them have lost their point with the circumstances and surroundings among which they were uttered. Some grow clumsy in translation. Some are without authenticity. That a searching wit like Voltaire, quite unhampered by reverence, must have found abundant subject for

2 s

witticism in the degraded state of the established religion of his country in his time, is palpable enough.

D'Alembert left. It was his last visit to Ferney.

On December 24, 1770, the powerful Choiseul was disgraced and exiled by the far more powerful Dubarry. ' The coachman of Europe,' as Frederick called him, had been infinitely clever and infinitely unlucky. If he had made the army and remade the fleet, expelled the Jesuits, and promoted trade, art, and literature, he had involved his country in wars, for which she had wept tears of blood. He fell : and great was the fall of him.

The tidings were received at Ferney with the utmost consternation. For Voltaire personally Choiseul had done much. He had helped in the affairs of Calas and of Chaumont, in that of the Corneille Commentary, and of the blockade of Ferney. And, more than all, he had protected, with the absolutely necessary protection none but a powerful minister could afford, the colony of watchmakers and weavers.

His disgrace ruined Versoix : and Ferney rocked on her foundations.

The steady resolution, and perhaps the fighting renown, of her old master tided his children over the crisis. But there was famine as well as disturbance abroad in the land, and for a while things looked black indeed.

On January 23 of the new year 1771, Louis XV., d'Aiguillon, the successor of Choiseul, and Maupeou, the Chancellor, suppressed the Parliament of Paris, to the general disgust. Voltaire did not share it. That Parliament, if it had been forced at last to reinstate the Calas, had condemned La Barre, d'Étallonde, and General Lally : it 'was defiled with the blood of the weak and the innocent ; ' had burnt the works of the

Encyclopædists ; and been so fiercely Jansenist that wise men regretted the Jesuits it had ruined.   In its place were to be established six Superior Councils or Local Parliaments, which were to give justice gratuitously and to be the final courts of appeal, thereby saving the nation the enormous expense of conveying accused persons to the capital.   To be sure, the jury system as practised in ideal England was better still.   But in an imperfect world one must be satisfied with imperfect progress.

Voltaire believed the six sovereign Councils to be ' the salvation of France '—' one of the best ideas since the foundation of monarchy.'   As far back as 1769 he had attacked the old Parliament, under a very transparent anonymity, in his 'History of the Parliament of Paris.'

All things considered, there was no wonder that a shrewd Maupeou, knowing how bitterly public opinion was against him, should call to his aid the man ' who had led it and fashioned it to his taste.'   Voltaire put himself at the disposition of Maupeou, and for many a month deafened the enemy with blast upon blast from his famous old trumpet.

If he was quite disinterested—and he was—in working under Maupeou for what he felt convinced was 'the liberty, salvation, and well-being of whole populations,' it was not at all unnatural that Choiseul should find it hard to forgive this active devotion to the policy of his supplanters.

The Duchess, with whom Voltaire had coquetted so charmingly over that pair of silk stockings, was as much offended as her husband.   Madame du Deffand, her dearest friend, was offended too.   And Voltaire spared himself neither pains nor time to restore confidence, to assure the dear exiles of Chanteloup in immense letters of his sincere and unaltering devotion to them: of his gratitude for the powerful protection of the one, and the gracious kindness of the other. Of course such letters had no effect. The haughty little Duchess begged that the correspondence might end. And the most obstinate of men went on writing to her exactly the same.

There was division in his own house on the subject of the Parliament too. His nephew, Mignot, that shortsighted, goodnatured, roundabout abbé, the son of Catherine, and the brother of Mesdames Denis and Florian, was, like his uncle, on the side of the reforms, and on May 20, 1771, was made senior clerk of the new Parliament.

D'Hornoy, on the other hand, Voltaire's great-nephew, had been a councillor of the old Parliament and was exiled with it.

However, politics apart, Voltaire liked both nephews, thought them honest souls, and made them, as has been noted, handsome allowances.

Brochures against the old Parliament and for the new occupied the Hermit of Ferney very actively during the whole of the year 1771, but they did not prevent him carrying on a correspondence with four sovereigns—Catherine, Frederick, Stanislas Augustus Poniatowski, and Gustavus III. of Sweden.

On December 18 he began a new tragedy, 'The Laws of Minos.' It was that dismal thing, a play with a purpose—' to make superstition execrable, and prove that when a law is unequal there is nothing for it but to abolish it.' It was written in honour of Maupeou. The Chancellor's enemies did Voltaire a good turn by preventing it from being played.

Death was busy just now among both friends and foes of Voltaire. He was fast reaching the age when he was naturally the last leaf on the tree. In the December of 1771 died Helvétius, philosopher and farmer-general; in the spring of 1772, Duclos, who had replaced Voltaire as Historiographer of France, and preceded d'Alembert as Secretary to the Academy. Then fell a leaf from the Arouet branch itself. Madame de Florian, always delicate, went the way of all flesh; and by February 1, 1772, her widowed husband had arrived at Ferney in that loud desolation which is the herald of speedy consolation.

He met at Ferney a very pretty, vivacious little Protestant who had been divorced from her first husband for incompatibility of temper. The pair were gaily married before April 1, 1772—to the disgust of Madame Denis, who rightly thought her sister was forgotten too soon, but to the delight of that old matchmaker, Voltaire.

Besides the bride and bridegroom, there was also at hospitable Ferney, Florian's nephew, whom Voltaire called Florianet, an observant youth who lived to write 'The Youth of Florian, or Memoirs of a Young Spaniard,' and who had stayed here before when he was a boy of ten or eleven. He had acted then as a sort of page to Voltaire, and Father Adam had furthered his education by setting him Latin exercises. Voltaire used to help the child out of those intricacies concerning Hostages and the Gate of a City, play games with him, and try to wake in him liveliness and wit. 'Seem witty, and the wit will come' was the advice of the wittiest man of his century.

Florianet was seventeen now, and amused himself, during a visit of two months, with balls, hunting, a

quarrel with his new aunt, and games with Marie
Dupuits' little girl. She was eight years old and very
intelligent, and Voltaire was fond of her with that fond-
ness for all young creatures which is surely an amiable
trait in a busy man.

He was hardly less fond of Wagnière's children (the
Genevan boy was a married man by this time, rearing
a family at Ferney), who used to play about the room
while the Patriarch dictated to their father.

In this spring of 1772 Voltaire was occupied in
building a pretty little house in the neighbourhood for
the Florian husband and wife. The poor bride was not
destined to enjoy it long. She died two years later of a
disease which was called by many extraordinary names
and received the most extraordinary treatment, but
which appears to have been consumption. The Marquis
immediately fell violently in love with someone else.

The only significance of his third Marquise lies in
the fact that she was the bearer of a conciliatory letter
and a copy of his 'Natural History' from the famous
Buffon to Voltaire—the two having previously been on
bad terms.

More visitors flocked to Ferney in the autumn of
1772. Lekain paid a third visit, and, the Genevan
theatre having been burnt, 'bewitched Geneva' at
Châtelaine instead.

Châtelaine was a playhouse which Voltaire had built
on French soil, but only a few yards from the territory
of the republic, to the great umbrage of 'Tronchins and
syndics.'

They did not hate it less in this September,
when Lekain's seductive genius drew their young
people within its walls by half-past eleven A.M. for a
performance which was to take place at four, and the

women wept and fainted at his pathos. Old Voltaire
had a box reserved for him, cried like a schoolgirl at
one moment, and the next applauded as if he were
possessed, by thumping his stick violently on the floor
and crying aloud, 'It's splendid! It couldn't be
better!'

A cool-headed English visitor, Dr. John Moore, who
was here during one of Lekain's visits, described the
performances as only 'moderately good.'

Traveller, physician, and writer, the author of a
popular novel, 'Zeluco,' and the father of the hero of
Coruña, Moore had frequent opportunities of conver-
sing with the famous old skeleton who had so 'much
more spirit and vivacity than is generally produced
by flesh and blood.' He understood Voltaire far
better than most of the English visitors. To be sure,
he could not forgive him his adverse criticisms on
Shakespeare—the king who can do no wrong. But
Dr. Moore, himself a sincere Christian, was one of
the very few who admitted that Voltaire was as sincere
an unbeliever; that his Deism was not an offensive
affectation to shock the devout, but a profound conviction; and that 'as soon as he is convinced of the truths
of Christianity he will openly avow his opinion, in
health as in sickness, uniformly to his last moment.'

Dr. Moore also perceived that here was the man
who was not afraid of dying—only of dying before he
had said all he had to say. He records Voltaire's
famous comparison of the British nation to a hogs-
head of its own beer—'the top of which is froth, the
bottom dregs, the middle excellent.' Moore's 'Society
and Manners in France' contains one of the best,
if not the best, accounts of Voltaire written from
personal observation by an Englishman.

In the midst of the theatrical gaieties news reached
Voltaire of the death of Theriot, on November 23,
1772. Old age, that merciful narcotic, helped to deaden
the blow for Theriot's old friend. Also, Theriot had
long been proven worthless, and he had a great many
of Voltaire's letters in his possession, which roused
Voltaire from grief to anxiety lest they should appear
incontinently in print.

On December 8 he was writing to d'Alembert to
recommend ' brother La Harpe ' (who had so grievously
failed him) for the post, left vacant by Theriot's death,
of Parisian correspondent to Frederick the Great.

At the end of 1772 the jealousy of foolish Denis
made another little *fracas* at Ferney.   A girl of
seventeen, Mademoiselle de Saussure, the daughter of
a famous doctor, and ' a very wideawake little person,'
said Grimm, had the good fortune to amuse, and often
visit, a Voltaire of seventy-eight.   Madame Denis,
who disliked Mademoiselle, not only for herself, but as
being a relative of her sister's supplanter, the second
Madame Florian, made a scandal of the affair.

If ever that homely proverb, ' Give a dog a bad
name and hang him,' was true of anybody, it was certainly true of Voltaire.

It was wonderful that that sensitive niece did not
find a cause of jealousy when, in the June of 1773, an
old friend, La Borde, came back to Ferney, bearing with
him as a present for Voltaire the portrait of Madame
Dubarry, on which that charming and disreputable lady
had imprinted two kisses. Her favour was worth having.
Only twenty-seven years old, and but recently picked up
from the gutter, she was the real ruler of France.   She
had dismissed Choiseul ; she had made Terrai, that
dissolute Controller-General of Finances, whose ' edicts

fell in showers; ' and she used the public treasury as if it were her private purse.

Voltaire knew King and Court too well to neglect such a power. Somehow, in Geneva the winters had been getting longer and more snowy than ever; and always, in his mind, was that old, old idea of seeing Paris once again before he died. And there was no chance of a return if the Omnipotent Woman was unfavourable.

So Voltaire replied with that happy mixture of grace and effrontery for which his youth had been so famous, and in September 1773, as has been noted, he sent Madame the sweetest little watch set in diamonds.

She repaid him for his compliments—on the spot. She helped him to vindicate General Lally.

It must not be thought that statues and visitors, old age in the present, and death in a near future, made Voltaire forget to fight *l'infâme*, or the iniquitous legal system which was often *l'infâme's* strongest support. He never forgot anything; and his mind had room for a thousand interests that never jostled or hurt each other.

In 1772 it had been greatly occupied by the case of the Bombelles.

Madame de Bombelles, a Protestant, had the misfortune to be the wife of a French officer who grew tired of her, and in order that he might marry someone else, discarded his wife on the excuse that they had been married by Protestant rites. The unhappy woman pleaded her case at law. It was decided against her; her marriage declared null and void; ordained that she should pay the costs of the suit; that her child should be educated as a Catholic, at its father's expense. Voltaire pleaded long and loud against a decision so

shameful, and pleaded, as usual, as if the interest in
hand were the only one he had in the world.

But though *l'infâme* was responsible for much, the
cruelly unjust justice of the day had upon its guilty
soul crimes with which *l'infâme* had nothing to do.

There had been the case of Martin—condemned to
the wheel 'on an equivocal meaning.' The wretched
man, arraigned on a wholly unfounded suspicion of
murder, when one of the witnesses said that he did not
recognise him as the person he had seen escaping from
the scene of action, cried out, 'Thank God! There is
one who has not recognised me!' Which the judge
took to mean, 'Thank God! I committed the murder
but have not been recognised by the witness.'

The real murderer confessed before long, but not
before Martin had been tortured and broken on the
wheel, his little fortune confiscated, and his innocent
family dispersed abroad, so that they never even knew
perhaps that their father was proved innocent—too
late.

Voltaire wrote an account of the case to d'Alembert.
'Fine phrases! Fine phrases!' he said once to an admirer complimenting him on his style. 'I never made
one in my life!' He never did. He wrote to make
men act, as he had always written; and the substance
of his tale was ever so great and so moving that the
simpler the form of it, the more effective.

In 1773 he wrote the 'Fragment on the Criminal
Lawsuit of the Montbaillis.'

It is only four pages long. It tells, in language to
be understood of any child, the story of a husband and
wife, snuff-makers of St. Omer, who in July 1770 had
been accused of murdering their drunken old mother.

The inventive French temperament concluded that

they *must* have murdered her, because a drunken mother is a trial, and her loss would be a gain.   A quarrel they had had with her on the last evening of her life (the reconciliation which followed was conveniently forgotten) lent colour to the theory.

The positive facts that the doctor, who was at once called, attributed the old woman's death to apoplexy ; that she not only left no money behind her, but that with her death expired the licence to make snuff, which was her son's only means of livelihood ; that the accused were known to have been patient and affectionate in their filial relationship ; were themselves of quiet and gentle character ; and that there was not a single witness to the crime for which they were arraigned—had no weight with either the populace or the magistrates.

On November 19, 1770, Montbailli was tortured and broken on the wheel ; and his wife, aged only twenty-four, was left in prison in irons, awaiting the birth of her child, and then death by the hand of the executioner.

But that dreadful reprieve gave her relatives time to appeal to the only man in France who could save her.

Voltaire laid the matter before the Chancellor Maupeou.   The case was re-tried.   Both the Montbaillis were declared innocent.   And that fickle and dangerous people who had compassed the death of her husband, and who, but for Voltaire, would have compassed her own, received back the wife with tears of joy.

Voltaire had not spared himself.   If he wrote briefly, he wrote often.   That style, so simple to read, was not nearly so simple to write.   Before things are made clear to the reader they have to be still clearer to the writer, who must know at least twice as much as he tells. Then, too, every fresh case brought Voltaire others. While he was writing pamphlets for the Montbaillis, he was also writing pamphlets on the case of a certain Comte de Morangiés ; he was working hard for young d'Étallonde ; he was appealing for his own poor people of Ferney and Gex ; and he was in the midst of the suit for the vindication of Lally.

General Lally was a hot-headed Irish Jacobite, who had plotted in France for the restoration of the Stuarts, and who, when he was sent to India in the service of France, had declared his policy to be ' No more English in India.'

A clerk called Clive frustrated that little plan. Among a shipload of French prisoners sent to England was General Lally. England released him on parole. He returned to France—a country never noted for her tenderness to the unsuccessful. Besides popular indignation, he had to face that of the disappointed shareholders in the East India Company, and the ill-will of a government who supposed the best way to appease England would be to maltreat Lally.

He ' was accused of all crimes ' of which a man could be capable. He demanded an investigation. ' I bring here my head and my innocence,' he wrote to Choiseul, ' and await your orders.'

He awaited them for fifteen months in the Bastille —untried.

Then a special court was formed of fifteen members of the dying and rotten Parliament of Paris ; and this man, who had ' spent his last rupee in the public service,' was accused of having sold Pondichery to his bitterest foes, the English, and upon not less than one hundred and fifty-nine other counts.

In the teeth of all testimony the unanimous voice of those fifteen judges condemned him to be beheaded. Surly, churlish, and embittered, imprudent speech was proven against him. But no worse offence. ' He is the only man who has had his head cut off for being ungracious.' That coward, the King, shut himself up in Choisy, so that no petition for mercy might reach him.

On May 6, 1766, Lally, General, sixty-four years old, and six times wounded in the service of his adopted country, was taken, gagged and handcuffed, to the Place de Grève and there beheaded. The gag was removed at the foot of the scaffold. But he was wise enough to disappoint the mob, and died without a word.

' It is expedient that one man should die for the people.' That spirit is not extinct in France yet.

But if Lally's innocent blood cried in vain from the ground to King, magistracy, and mob, it reached old ears that to their last hour would never be deaf to the tale of wrong.

' I have the vanity to think that God has made me for an *avocat*,' said Voltaire.

He had closely followed the General's trial. His prosecutor was Pasquier, who had received a royal pension for condemning poor mad Damiens to horrible tortures—Pasquier, ' with the snout of an ox and the heart of a tiger,' and Voltaire's especial detestation.

It may have been that hatred which first made him examine the documents concerning this trial. Also, he had met Lally at Richelieu's, and worked with him at d'Argenson's.

On June 16, 1766, he wrote to d'Alembert, ' I will stake my neck on it he was not a traitor ; ' and a few days later, to d'Argental, ' It is my fate to be dis-

satisfied with the sentences of the Parliament. I dare
to be so with that which has condemned Lally.'

Dissatisfied with wrong? There have been thousands of men good enough for that, who have lived
and died dissatisfied with it, without lifting a finger
to put right in its place.

Months passed, and years. Voltaire inserted in his
'History of Louis XV.' an able exculpation of Lally.
It was something. But it was not enough.

In 1769 he wrote that Lally and his gag, Sirven,
Calas, Martin, the Chevalier de la Barre, came before
him sometimes in dreams. 'People think our century
only ridiculous, but it is horrible.' In 1773 he wrote
that he still had on his heart the blood of Lally and
the Chevalier de la Barre.

Still? For ever, till they were avenged. He had
read English books on Lally's case. The English had
had no reason to love Lally, but they regarded his
sentence as a barbarous injustice.

And then, early in this year 1773, Lally's young
son, whom the father had charged to avenge his
memory, sent his first Memoir on the case to Voltaire
and asked his assistance.

Voltaire had been very ill—really ill, not fancifully
so—with the gout, and he was in his eightieth year.
But this ' avocat of lost causes ' had his old burning
zeal.

He first began by telling the young Chevalier de
Lally-Tollendal, out of his abundant experience, and
in a letter dated April 28, 1773, what to do and what
not to do. 'As for me, I will be your secretary.'
Lally-Tollendal, then two-and-twenty years old, had at
fifteen written a Latin poem on Jean Calas. He thus
already knew his Voltaire. The King had paid for his

education—a confession of, or an *amende* for, the injustice which had killed his father. He was to be one
of the aristocratic democrats of the French Revolution,
a refugee in England, and, in 1815, peer of France.
But now he was nothing and nobody, and alone could
never have fulfilled his father's trust.

For many weeks the labour of ' The Historical
Fragments of the History of India and of General
Lally ' occupied Voltaire ' day and night.' It cost
him, he told Madame du Deffand, more than any other
work of his life. It had to be amusing in the history
because the monkeys, who formed one half of the
nation, would not read history unless it was amusing ;
and pathetic enough, as touching General Lally, to
melt the hearts of the tigers who formed the other
half.

Then there were pamphlets to be written, and
Madame Dubarry to be won over. Through her, Lally-
Tollendal got his commission in the army. Through
Voltaire, on May 26, 1778, Louis XVI. in council
publicly vindicated General Lally.

In a room in the Hôtel Villette, at the corner of
the Rue de Beaune in Paris, a dying old Voltaire
received that news. The splendid intellect which had
served him for more than eighty years, as never mind
served man before, was waning too. But for a moment
its strength came back. To Lally-Tollendal Voltaire
dictated his last letter.

' The dead returns to life on learning this great
news ; he tenderly embraces M. Lally ; he sees that
the King is the Defender of Justice ; and will die,
content.'

With a last flash of his old spirit, he made someone
write in a large hand, on a sheet of paper which he

had pinned to the bed hangings where everyone could see it, the following words :

'On May 26 the judicial murder committed by Pasquier (Councillor to the Parliament) upon the person of Lally was avenged by the Council of the King.'

If ever man carried into the other life the hatred of that oppression and injustice which have made the wretchedness of this to more than half the human race, surely that man was Voltaire.

CHAPTER XLII

LATTER DAYS

VOLTAIRE'S old age was naturally something less eventful than the 'crowded hour' of his youth and manhood. But if ever his private life afforded him a chance of quiet, public events always stepped in to disturb it.

On May 10, 1774, Louis XV. died of the smallpox, to the good and blessing of the world. His old courtier at Ferney no sooner heard the news than he put pen to paper and wrote his Majesty's *Éloge*, 'to be pronounced before an Academy on May 25.'

Of course a eulogy had to be eulogistic. The old hand had not lost its cunning. To flatter the dear departed, to speak of him as a good father, a good husband and master, and 'as much a friend as a king can be;' to offer for his little failings that courtly excuse, 'One cannot be always a king : one would be too much to be pitied,' and to imply that the man was a fool so that the insult sounded like a compliment, why, Voltaire was the one writer in the world who could do it. And he did it.

He turned the occasion to practical use, by preaching against the neglect of inoculation ; and then looked to the future.

What wonder that, for the moment, even this prophet should forget to prophesy Revolution ; should think that he saw already the beginning of the Golden Age—Millennium—all things made new ?

To be sure, he told the government plainly that there were still Frenchmen who were ' in the same legal condition as the beasts of that land they watered with their tears.' And the young King answered by repealing the Tax of the Joyful Accession ; by disgracing Terrai, for whom old Ferney was keeping his last tooth ; by appointing first as Minister of Finance, then as Controller-General, and then as Secretary of State, the great reforming Turgot, one of the most enlightened men in France and already the personal friend of Voltaire. ' If any man can re-establish the finances,' wrote Ferney on September 7, ' he is the man.' And a few days later, when Turgot obtained free trade in grain, the enthusiastic old invalid thanked Nature for having made him live long enough to see that day. Free trade in grain had a very personal application to this master of a town, this founder of a colony. He had d'Étallonde staying with him now ; and next to his arduous and passionate work for the restitution of that young officer's civil rights (' he is calm about his fate, and I—I die of it '), his four hundred children had the largest share of his mind. That they returned his affection and repaid him as they could, was proved when, on Madame Denis's recovery from a dangerous chest complaint in the spring of 1775, they fêted that ' niece of her uncle ' ' with companies of infantry and cavalry, cockades and kettledrums '—all the mummery and millinery which they loved, and their master had loved all his life.

Madame Denis was, it must be remembered, already the legal owner of Ferney. She was to be its practical owner. And it was her old uncle's too sanguine hope

that she would maintain the manufactory after him.
She was certainly pleased at the colonists' rejoicings,
and the colonists were pleased themselves, and Voltaire was highly delighted ; and a quite cool observer,
Hennin, the Resident, noted that it was a grand thing
to see a cavalcade of nearly a hundred men, mounted
and in uniform, from a village where twelve years
before there were twenty families of wretched peasants.

So that, although the year 1775, which was to usher
into Ferney such a succession of visitors as might make
the most sociable heart quail, began with sickness, it
began with rejoicing too.

D'Étallonde was still staying there. Nephew
d'Hornoy was helping Voltaire to work his case. The
Marquis and Marquise de Luchet came to join the
party in the spring, and were here two months—the
Marquis, who was to be one of Voltaire's biographers,
always engaged in mad schemes for making money out
of gold mines ; and the Marquise turning her goodnatured and laughter-loving self into a hospital nurse
and nursing the Ferney invalids unremittingly.

Then came the Florians ; and the Marquis's third
wife brought with her another lively visitor, her young
sister, whom Voltaire called ' Quinze Ans,' ' who
laughed at everything and laughed always.'

They were followed by ecstatic little Madame Suard,
who worshipped Voltaire with the tiresome adoration of
a schoolgirl ; kissed his hands and clasped her own ;
flattered, adored, and coquetted with him ; and went so
far as to declare, in the long and rapturous accounts
she wrote of him, that his every wrinkle was a charm.

With her came her brother, Panckoucke, who wanted
to edit Voltaire's works, but did not yet obtain that
favour. She also found with Voltaire, Audibert, that

merchant of Marseilles, the earliest friend of the Calas ;
and Poissonnier, Catherine the Great's doctor.

In July, Chabanon and Abbé Morellet were both
staying at Ferney. Also in July, an audacious and
wholly unsnubbable person called Denon had forced his
way there too ; asked for his host's bust ; was refused ;
and revenged himself by sending the poor old Patriarch
a most hideous sketch of his lean features which he,
Denon, had made himself. It was very far from being
the only offensive likeness of the great man. Still extant
is a caricature called ' Déjeuner at Ferney,' which
Voltaire used to think was by Huber, and which contains grotesque portraits of Voltaire and Father Adam,
and represents poor Madame Denis, who *was* inclined
to *embonpoint*, enormously fat. But, after all, it was
in the January of this 1775 that Frederick had sent
Voltaire, Voltaire's bust in porcelain with *Immortali*
written beneath it. Here was compensation for many
caricatures.

Little Madame Saint-Julien, who had made Ferney
lace the mode, and was a fashionable philanthropist
when philanthropy was not the fashion, paid another
long visit to Ferney in the autumn, and went back to
Paris to intercede with her influential relatives for
Voltaire's children. She and their father were so
successful that the day soon came when, ' in spite of
the obstinate resistance of the farmers-general,' they
obtained for the colonists that ' moderate and fixed
tariff which freed the country from the despotism of a
pitiless tax,' extorting from the poverty-stricken province of Gex alone the exorbitant sum of not less than
forty thousand livres annually.

The grateful colonists had fireworks and illumina-
tions on that good Butterfly's birthday ; and in December

VOLTAIRE.

From the Etching by Denon.

they fêted old Voltaire himself, filled his carriage with
flowers, and decorated the horses with laurels.

The visitors did not cease with the new year 1776.
Nay, one came who came to stay. Mademoiselle Reine-
Philiberte de Varicourt was the niece of those six
poor gentlemen whose estates Voltaire had reclaimed
in 1761 from the Jesuits of Ornex. Bright, honest, and
good, well deserving that charming name of Belle-et-
Bonne with which old Voltaire immediately christened
her, the unfortunate girl had no *dot* and was destined
to a convent.

But Madame Denis took one of her goodnatured
likings to her. She was girlishly kind to old Voltaire,
while he on his part soon worshipped her pretty face,
virgin heart, and bright intelligence. No 'narrowing
nunnery walls' for her ! Marie Dupuits had husband
and child to think of now, and Marie had never had
Reine-Philiberte's dignified good sense.

Belle-et-Bonne fell into place at once. She became
a regular, and not the least delightful, member of the
heterogeneous Ferney household.

Another Englishman, Martin Sherlock, visited it in
April 1776, and wrote his experiences, in his 'Letters
of an English Traveller,' in French, which has been
retranslated into his native tongue.

Voltaire, who was accompanied by d'Hornoy, met
his guest in the hall, showed him his gardens, spoke a
few words to him in English, told an anecdote of Swift,
talked of Pope, of Chesterfield, of Hervey, and with his
old passionate admiration of Newton. Stopping before
his bust, he exclaimed, ' This is the greatest genius that
ever existed ! ' There was no dimming of the old mind, no
lacklustre, no weariness. The England he had not seen
for nearly fifty years was still a vivid and a present reality.

On one of his visits—Sherlock paid two—Voltaire
showed his guest his shelves filled with English books—
Robertson, ' who is your Livy ; ' Hume, ' who wrote
history to be applauded ; ' Bolingbroke, ' many leaves
and little fruit ; ' Milton, Congreve, Rochester.

He criticised the English language—' energetic,
precise, and barbarous.'   He explained to Madame
Denis the scene in Shakespeare's ' Henry V.' where the
King makes love to Katharine in bad French.   He
spoke ' with the warmth of a man of thirty.'

Quaintly dressed in white shoes and stockings, red
breeches, embroidered waistcoat and bedgown, and a
gold and silver nightcap over his grey peruke, old
Voltaire apologised for this singular appearance to his
guest by saying in English that at Ferney they were
for Liberty and Property.   ' So that I wear my nightcap and Father Adam his hat.'   Later, he added gravely,
' You are happy, you can do anything. . . .   We cannot even die as we will.'

During the conversation he had uttered what his
visitor called ' horrors ' about Moses and Shakespeare.

Nothing proves better the young vigour of this marvellous old mind than the strength of its animosities.
The ' let-it-alone ' spirit of old age was never this
man's while there was breath left in his body.   ·At the
end of 1773 he had attacked another literary foe—an
ungrateful *protégé*, ' the inclement Clement '—in the
' Cabals,' a satire in which ring out clearly the notes
a younger hand had struck in ' Akakia ' or in ' Vanity.'

Then on March 10, 1776, Fréron died of mortification
at the suppression of his ' Literary Year,' and up gets
Voltaire and says he has received an anonymous letter
asking him, if you please, to endow Frélon-Fréron's
daughter !   This is too much.   Voltaire suggests that

Madame Fréron wrote that letter. And the Frélons say
Voltaire invented it himself. And Voltaire is as spry
and alert and angry as when he first hated Fréron,
thirty years ago.

But these enemies he knew, or had known, in the
flesh.

To admire or to despise Shakespeare was but a
literary question. Old Eighty-two in this July of 1776
took it as a burning personal one. He had not precisely adored Shakespeare in the ' English Letters.' A
barbarian, a monster—but of very great genius. For
the sake of that genius he had permitted the polished
French people to condone that ' heavy grossness ' and
the shocking lack of taste ; and in his famous criticism
on ' Hamlet,' written in 1748, though he *had* called its
author ' a drunken savage,' he had found in the
play, not the less, ' sublime touches worthy of the
loftiest genius.' To Sherlock, but three months ago,
though he had uttered ' horrors ' in his criticism, he
had admitted that ' amazing genius ' again.

And now one Letourneur publishes a new translation of the great William, and takes upon himself to
call him the ' god of the theatre,' the only model for
true tragedy ; and ignores Corneille and Racine (to say
nothing of the author of ' Zaire ') *in toto.*

Then Voltaire beat his breast and tore his hair to
think that it was I—I—-who showed to the French the
pearls in this English dunghill ; that I suffered persecution for telling them that though the god had feet of
clay, the head and heart were gold.

So in a rage M. de Voltaire sat down and wrote a
letter to the Academy—' his factotum against Shakespeare ; ' gave himself the lie ; literally translated many
passages, knowing, as he had said himself, that in a

translation the letter killeth and the spirit giveth life ; presented, as he meant to do, a gross and coarse Shakespeare, an indecent buffoon who had ' ruined the taste of England for two hundred years.' Various persons rushed into the fray on either side.

On August 25, Voltaire's letter was read at a public meeting at the Academy, and a goodnatured Marquis de Villevieille galloped off post-haste to Ferney to tell of its success. But there had been dissentient voices. Anglomania was already a power in the land. The young Queen had her Crawfords and Dillons, her English garden, her English jockeys, her English ' biliard.' D'Alembert was too cool, too cool ! The untrammelled nature of the great Diderot was formed to appreciate the broad and daring genius of the great Englishman. And Madame Necker, with the sure instincts of a clever woman, criticised Voltaire's letter in a letter to Garrick. Voltaire had but shown Shakespeare's dead body—' But I—I have seen the soul animating it, and know it is something more even than a majestic ghost which Garrick, the enchanter, summons from the grave.'

The letter to the Academy was the last utterance on the great Englishman of the man who—whether he hotly regretted it, as he did now and in the famous Preface to ' Semiramis,' or was, or said he was, proud of it, as when he wrote to Walpole—first revealed Shakespeare to the people of France.

August saw the arrival of a visitor who was hereafter herself to be a celebrity, Madame de Genlis. Now only thirty years old, she was not yet famous for her literary works or that grave and religious turn of mind which did not prevent her occupying the very equivocal position of *gouvernante* to the children of the

Duke of Orleans. As Madame Suard came to Ferney
prepared to go into raptures, so Madame Genlis came
prepared to disapprove.

The serious lady carried out her intention as
thoroughly as the frivolous one. Her account of her
visit contains much more about herself than about
Voltaire, but states, no doubt very truly, that the impiety of his conversation was shocking, and, certainly
untruly, that his manners lacked tact and urbanity.
For this too particular lady the very trees in the
Ferney garden grew too low and upset her temper and
her hair; while the wild enthusiasm for their host of
her companion, a painter, M. Ott, quite distressed a
person who had so firmly resolved not to make a fool
of herself in that direction.

As her point of view was unfavourable, her testimony as to her host's 'ingenuous goodness' to his
colonists, to the perfect modesty and simplicity with
which he regarded his great work for them, is the
more valuable. She confirmed the opinion of many
others as to the piercing brilliancy of the old eyes—
'which have in them an inexpressible sweetness.'
Madame Saint-Julien was there at the same time—
little and gay and kind—and presently Marie Dupuits'
little girl ran into the room and put her arms round
Grandpapa Voltaire's neck.

During this August, Voltaire, rather proud of the
transaction, 'borrowed Lekain,' who was acting at Court,
from Marie Antoinette. The Hermit of Ferney was too
toothless to act himself, but his earliest passion was also
his latest. There was the most charming little theatre
in the village of Ferney now. Lekain acted in that and
at Châtelaine. The young Queen's graciousness in
lending her player made artful old Voltaire long to

have 'Olympie' acted before her; to have her for his
protectress; to see with his own eyes ' her whose least
charm,' as he said, ' was loveliness.'

Picture the delight of the whilom author of ' The
Princess of Navarre' when he was commissioned to
write a *divertissement* for her benefit. He wrote, or
rather reproduced a sketch of a *fête* given at Vienna
by the Austrian Court sixty years before, and called it
' The Host and Hostess.' The thing was meritless,
but not objectless, though it failed in its object—the
rapprochement of Ferney and Versailles.

Then M. de Voltaire must needs write an allegory,
' Sésostris,' to flatter the *beaux yeux* of the Queen,
and to show what a King might do for the good of his
people.

To the year 1776, besides the Battle of Shakespeare,
belong two more fights—the last of Voltaire's life.
Beauregard, Rohan, Jore—how far they were away!
But the spirit of their old antagonist had not waxed
faint.

The first fight was only a skirmish, it is true.
Father Adam had been spoilt, of course. From being
an inoffensive, lazy person—' the only idler in a house-
ful of busy people '—he had become assertive, worrying,
and quarrelsome. He had fallen out with Bigex, the
copyist, in 1769; and as a result Bigex had had to
leave. And now the Father must go himself. It was
characteristic of the man who had allowed Jore a pension for life, that he should send after this ungrateful
priest, who owed him thirteen years' hospitality, presents of money.

In the second fight, the very last of his life, occur-
ring in the December of 1776, Voltaire matched steel
with a worthier foe. It was in answer to an attack

made upon him by an Abbé Guénée that he wrote the bold and brilliant, if neither deep nor sound, 'Christian against Six Jews,' which advanced Pigalle's evidence on the subject of the Golden Calf, and might have better confuted Guénée if that reasoner had not been on his own ground and most cool and subtle in argument.

But if his foes did not spare this old Voltaire, neither did his friends. In the early days of 1777 Moultou introduced at Ferney a wearisome play-wright called Berthe, who would persist in reading aloud his tedious play to their host. 'Here the Chevalier laughs,' read Berthe, as a stage direction. 'Happy man!' murmured Voltaire. When the listener could bear it no longer, he feigned the most violent colic that ever man had suffered. The next day Berthe came again, and so did the colic. 'If God had not come to my aid,' said Voltaire to Grimm, 'I should have been lost.'

It was in 1777 that Voltaire amused himself by competing, under a pseudonym, for a prize offered by the French Academy for the best translation of the sixth book of the 'Iliad.' It did not gain a prize. It was not even good. But that such a man at such an age should have been 'sleeplessly active' enough to enter into such a competition, makes the thing worth recording.

But worse than unsuccessful translations and dull plays, worse than being beaten in a verbal quibble with a priest, was a mortification this vain old heart received in the June of 1777.

Joseph II., the young Emperor of Austria, brother of Marie Antoinette, and himself something of a philo-sopher, had been the lion of the spring in Paris. It was confidently expected by d'Alembert, Frederick the Great—everyone, including Voltaire himself—that on his return home the celebrity would do what all celebrities did—visit the King of their kind at Ferney.

On June 27 Voltaire wrote airily to say that he did not expect his Majesty. What in the world was there for him to see in this manufactory of watches and verses? But all the same, when the day came, Ferney rose up very early in the morning and from eight o'clock was ready in its best clothes, with its master in his great peruke, waiting. A splendid dinner had been prepared. The condition of the road from Ferney to Versoix had been improved by its owner. All was in readiness.

Presently the sound of the rumbling of the travelling carriage is heard in the distance. If his Majesty had not meant to call at the château, why choose this route? There were others. ' This is Ferney! ' says the coachman. ' Whip up the horses! ' cries the Emperor. And the imperial *cortège* dashes through Ferney, and past the windows of the expectant château itself, at a gallop. When it is added that his Majesty alighted at Versoix and examined that infant colony, and that when he reached Berne he paid a special visit to Voltaire's great rival, Haller, it will be seen that he meant to offend.

It is to the credit of a plucky old heart that Voltaire quite refused to acknowledge himself snubbed, pointed out that he had always said his Majesty would not come, and that ' my age and maladies prevented me from finding myself on his route.' But if he swallowed it with a smile, the pill was a bitter one not the less. ' This disgrace ' the poor old man called it, writing in confidence to his Angel. But the ' disgrace,' if any,

was not Voltaire's, but the man's who, privately con-
fessing himself a philosopher, was afraid to visit
Voltaire lest he should be openly accounted one, and
offend an austere mother.

The Emperor's neglected visit was the last mortification of the man who had had many, and had felt all
with an extraordinary sensitiveness.

But, after all, ' the end of all ambition is to be happy
at home,' and Voltaire had many consolations.

The good, fat, Swiss servant, Barbara, was one.
Voltaire was at last learning a little how to grow old,
and now went to bed at ten and slept till five, when Baba
would bring him his coffee.　One day he took it into his
head to mix some rosewater with it, as an experiment.
The result was an acute indigestion.　He rang the bell
violently.　Enter Baba.　' I am in the agonies of death.
I put some rosewater in my coffee and am dying of it.'
' Sir,' says the indignant Baba, ' with all your cleverness
you are sillier than your own turkeys.'

But nearer and dearer than a Baba could be was
Belle-et-Bonne.　By this time she had become like the
old man's daughter.　With rare tact she had succeeded in endearing herself to him without offending
Madame Denis.　She would arrange his papers for him,
and keep the desk which hung over his bed, and ' which
he could lower or raise at pleasure,' in that order and
neatness his soul loved.

' Good morning, *belle nature*,' he would say when
she greeted him in the morning ; and when she kissed
his old parchment face would declare it was Life kiss-
ing Death.　It was Belle-et-Bonne who could soothe
his irritability or impatience—' You put me on good
terms with life.'

And it was Voltaire of eighty-three who taught

Mademoiselle Reine-Philiberte de Varicourt how to dance.

In the summer of this 1777 there arrived unexpectedly one day at Ferney a worn-out *roué* of a Marquis de Villette, who had passed two or three months here in 1765, and with whom Voltaire had since corresponded.   Rich, gallant, well born, a society verse-maker, this ' ne'er-do-weel of good company ' was the sort of person who sounds attractive on paper, and in real life is wholly objectionable.   Voltaire— Voltaire !—had tendered him moral advice and urged him to reform.   He had known the young man's mother—herself a woman of irregular morals—and from these two facts arose an entirely unfounded scandal, that Voltaire was Villette's father.

He was soon to be a sort of father-in-law.   Villette, now some forty years old, and having run away from an intrigue and a duel in Paris, met Belle-et-Bonne at Ferney ; saw her walking in the procession of the *fête* of St. Francis (always kept enthusiastically by the colony of François Marie Arouet), with flowers at her breast, a basket with doves in it in her hand, and her face bright, beautiful, and blushing.

What was there to do but to fall in love with her ? Wagnière, who hated Villette, said that he played fast and loose with Mademoiselle for three months.   However that may have been, Voltaire approved of his suit. To be sure, Belle-et-Bonne was too good for him.   But she had no *dot*—if a pretty face, an innocent heart, youth, dignity, and intelligence count for nothing—so she would have no choice.   And any husband is better than none—when none means a convent.   *Enfin,* where to find a French marquis of stainless reputation in the eighteenth century ?   It was said that Voltaire had

offered Villette a *dot* with his wife, and the disinterested
Villette had refused it.　And if that is not a sign of
reformation—what is ?

So in November 1777 Mademoiselle de Varicourt
was married in the Ferney chapel at midnight, with
her six uncles preceding her up the aisle, and Papa
Voltaire, in Catherine's sable pelisse, to give her away.

The young couple spent the honeymoon at Ferney,
and through it Voltaire was working at his two last
plays, ' Irène ' and ' Agathocle.'

It is marvellous, not so much that a man of eighty-
three should write bad plays, as that he should write
any.

No wonder that the new tragedy, ' Irène,' went ill at
first.　And not so very wonderful that the old playwright
should follow his immemorial habit and rewrite till
it satisfied him.　He lost three months over it.　And, as
he remarked most truly, ' Time is precious at my age.'

So when ' Irène ' was impossible he turned to
' Agathocle.'

Madame Denis's easy tears and laughter over the
two pieces were no sound criticism.　Villette and
Villevieille, then staying at Ferney, admired politely as
visitors.　The playwright, whose vanity has been ex-
cellently defined as ' a gay and eager asking of assurance from others that his work gave them pleasure,'
was delighted with the compliments.　But he accepted
correction in that spirit which showed that his vanity
' never stood in the way of self-knowledge.'

' If I had committed a fault at a hundred,' he said,
' I should want to correct it at a hundred-and-one.'　So
when Condorcet, more honest than the visitors, paid
him the finer compliment of assuring him that such
work as he had produced in ' Irène ' was not worthy

of his genius, he took that assurance in excellent
part ; and though by January 2, 1778, ' Irène ' had
been read and welcomed by the Comédie Française,
he went on correcting and altering it to the end of the
month.

He was spurred to do his best by the fact that
Lekain declined to play the *rôle* written for him. No
letters could have been kinder, wiser, or more conciliatory than those his old host and friend wrote to
the great player.

The part should be rewritten for him !

He was also spurred to do his best by the fact that
' Irène ' was to be the means, the excuse, the reason to
take him to Paris.

Paris !   The idea had been simmering long.   Paris !
It was twenty-eight years since he had left it, for a few
months at the most.   To be sure, he had been far
happier at Ferney than in the riot and fever of that
over-rated capital.   In answer to those who talked
about the stagnation of the country, and talked of it as
if it were some narcotic trance which numbed brain
and use, Voltaire could point to the best work of his
life.   Near him, bound to his heart by many cords,
was the smiling cosmos of the industrial Ferney which
he had drawn from the chaos of a barren and starving
province.   Here were his gardens and farms ; the house
he had built, and loved as one can only love the work
of one's own brain ; the books and pictures he had col-
lected ; the thousand household gods from which the
young part easily, but which the old regard with a
personal affection.

Then, Ferney was safe.   And in Paris—' Do you
not know there are forty thousand fanatics who would
bring forty thousand fagots to burn me ?   That would

be my bed of honour.'　If Louis XV. was dead, so was
a friendly Pompadour.　Choiseul and Madame Dubarry
were banished.

Good Louis XVI. hated this infidel of a Voltaire, and
was just shrewd enough in his dullness to fear him.　It
was Louis, still a king, who, asked what play should
be performed at the theatre, replied, ' Anything, so long
as it is not Voltaire.'　It was Louis Capet in the Temple
who is reported to have said, pointing to the works of
Rousseau and Voltaire in the library of the tower,
' Those two men have lost France.'

The brilliant Queen, who had permitted M. de
Voltaire to write her a *divertissement* and to steal
Lekain, was something more favourable.　But the
Queen—extravagant and childless—was the most un-
popular woman in France.　In 1776 she had compassed
the fall of Turgot, Voltaire's friend, the hope of his
country.　In Paris, now, there was but one minister
who was even tepidly favourable to the great recluse of
Ferney, and that was Maurepas.

Altogether, the time seemed hardly ripe.　But ' if
I want to commit a folly,' Voltaire had written to
Chabanon in 1775, ' nothing will prevent me.'

If a king had once been too strong for Voltaire, he
may well have known now that he was stronger than
any king.　Besides, he had never been formally banished.
' I do not wish Voltaire to return to France ' was not
an edict after all.　Had he ever forgotten he was still
Gentleman-in-Ordinary?　And as for the danger to his
person—seriously, what could be done to an old man
of nearly eighty-four ?　Then, too, he needed a change.
His health, though he was fond of repeating that he
had as many mortal diseases as he had years, was quite
good enough to permit him to take one.

Then there was ' Irène,' which he could see put into rehearsal himself ; and then—then—then—there was the domestic influence of all Ferney urging him to take the step, to make up his mind, to go back to glory, to honour, to life.

Madame Denis, of course, longed for Paris. Her sixty-eight years and a chest complaint had not cooled her zest for pleasure and admirers. And if you do not go, Uncle Voltaire, whether you are banished or no, three parts of Europe will think you are ! She had long ago inspired Marie Dupuits with her own love of amusement. The Marquis de Villette was constitutionally even less able to endure the country than Mama Denis. He had the finest house in the capital, which had once been the Bernières' house, where Voltaire had stayed as a young man, which stood at the corner of the Rue de Beaune on what is now the Quai Voltaire, opposite the Tuileries, and which is entirely at Papa Voltaire's service ! Put all these persuadings and persuaders together before a man already more than half inclined to go, and the result is easily foreseen.

On the evening of February 3, 1778, Madame Denis and the *ménage* Villette left Ferney to prepare the Hôtel Villette in Paris against the arrival of M. de Voltaire.

On February 5 Voltaire himself, accompanied only by Wagnière and a cook, set out in their travelling carriage. There was a painful farewell from the colonists. The poor people felt that their protector was leaving them for ever. It was in vain he promised them that he would be back in six weeks at the latest. That he really intended thus to return is partially proved by the fact that he did not even arrange his manuscripts and papers before leaving.

LOUIS XVI.

From the Portrait by Callet in the Petit Trianon.

The first night was spent at Nantua.

At Bourg, where the horses were changed, Voltaire was recognised and had to escape from the crowd who surrounded him by locking himself up in a room in the posthouse. Of course the innkeeper produced his best horses, and called out in his enthusiasm, 'Drive fast ! Kill the horses—I don't care about them ! You are carrying M. de Voltaire ! '

The *incognito* Voltaire had resolved to maintain was already a thing of the past. He had begun to taste what are called the delights or the drawbacks of fame, according to the temperament of the speaker.

The second night was passed at Sanecey. On the third, at Dijon, some of his adorers insisted on dressing up as waiters and waiting upon him at supper in order to get a good view of him. Others serenaded the poor man outside his bedroom window. In Dijon he made an appointment with a lawyer, and transacted some business.

The next stop was at Joigny. A spring of the carriage broke when they were near Moret, but Villette arrived to rescue them from that very common dilemma, and met them with *his* carriage, in which they pursued the journey.

The nearer they approached to the capital, the higher rose Voltaire's spirits. He told stories with inimitable gaiety. ' He seemed twenty.'

At half-past three on the afternoon of February 10 they reached Paris. When the custom-house officer inquired if they had anything against regulations, Voltaire replied that there was nothing contraband except himself. He grew more and more lively every moment. They had no sooner arrived at the Hôtel Villette than this gay young traveller must step round

to the Quai d'Orsay to see the Comte d'Argental.
Friends for sixty years, their friendship had been strong
enough to bridge a gulf of separation which had lasted
more than half their long lives. Madame d'Argental
had died in the December of 1774. There was but one
Angel now. He had taken wing too, for the moment,
Voltaire found when he reached the house. But the
old man was no sooner back in the Hôtel Villette than
d'Argental arrived and the two fell on each other's
necks. 'I have left off dying to come and see you,'
says Voltaire. But there was a shadow on their
happiness. D'Argental brought bad news. Two days
earlier, on February 8, Lekain, whose first part had
been Titus in Voltaire's 'Brutus,' played his last part
in 'Adélaïde du Guesclin.' He died, in spite of all the
skill of Tronchin. Voltaire 'uttered a great cry.'
Lekain had been his friend. Lekain was to have
played in 'Irène.'

Belle-et-Bonne tells how the two old men sat up
late into the night discussing the additions Voltaire
had made in that play.

But for it, but for the thousand distractions of this
new world, the loud acclamations, the surging stream
of visitors the moment brought, Voltaire might have
mourned Lekain longer.

But he was back in Paris. When he left it, he was
a power, a danger, a fear. He had returned to it a king,
and awaited his crowning.

CHAPTER XLIII

THE LAST VISIT

MORLEY speaks of Voltaire's last visit as ' one of the historic events of the century,' ' the last great commotion in Paris under the old *régime*.' ' A ghost, a prophet, an apostle,' says Grimm, ' could not have excited a more fervent interest.'

The Salons worshipped the man who for sixty years had been the first wit of the wittiest age in history—the author of that dear, daring, ribald, wicked ' Pucelle.'

The Philosophers kissed the hem of the garment of the author of ' The Philosophical Dictionary.'

The Academy fell at the feet of him who had attempted every kind of literature and failed in none.

The Drama welcomed not only the most famous playwright since Corneille and Racine, but the man who for sixty years had not ceased to try to improve the civil status of actors.

The thrifty *bourgeois* left their shops and stood in crowds outside the Hôtel Villette, waiting to see him who was himself of their order and had fought for its rights and rent earth and heaven with cries against its wrongs.

The Protestant came to worship him who had preached Tolerance, defended the Calas, and flung all the weight of his scorn and passion against a law which proclaimed the heretic's wife his mistress, and their children bastards.

The submerged, the *canaille*, fierce and hungry-eyed, were among the street crowds to see him who had pleaded against a criminal code which punished petty theft, blasphemy, and desertion in time of peace, by death; meted to the hapless imbeciles, called sorcerers, the vengeance of superstition and fear; and robbed the children of the condemned by confiscating their goods to the King.

Court and Church paid him the higher compliment of fearing him.

The preachers denounced the apostate from their pulpits. Here is he who has not only, having examined the evidences of Christianity, boldly declared that he finds them absurd and inadequate, but has also dared to attack the evil lives of the believers, tyranny, oppression, persecution, calling them the inevitable consequence of the Faith, and so the most powerful of all arguments against it.

Anti-Christ! Anti-Christ!

King and ministers turned and looked at each other in consternation. Surely there was somewhere an edict of banishment against this person? But where? If it had been found, no one would have dared to put it into execution.

The Paris which had once imprisoned him for teaching it how to become free, and persecuted him for opposing persecution, was at last the Paris of Voltaire, and not the antechamber of the Kings of France.

On the day after his arrival, Wednesday, February 1., 1778, he received three hundred visitors. In an outer room were Madame Denis and Villette. And within, his crown an old nightcap and his royal robes a

ancient bedgown, sat the King of intellectual France.
The courtier bred in Courts knew well how to play his
Majesty. Easy and gracious in manner, no visitor went
away without a *mot*, an anecdote, a happy quotation
he could repeat to his friends—'I heard it from the
great Voltaire.' One of the guests was the perfidious
La Harpe, who had not seen his old friend since they
parted in anger at Ferney ten years ago, and who
found, he said, the wit undimmed, the memory unim-
paired.

In intervals between the departure of one guest and
the admission of the next—if there could have been
any such intervals—the old playwright dictated a new
line or a correction for ' Irène ' to Wagnière, and then
went on receiving half Paris. ' All Parnassus was
there, from the mire to the summit,' said Madame du
Deffand. In that crowded day, her old friend found
time to write her a little note and tell her how he had
arrived, dead, but was risen again to throw himself at
the feet of his Marquise.

Thursday, February 12, brought a congratulatory
deputation from the Academy, which was represented
by three personal friends of Voltaire—Saint-Lambert,
Marmontel, and the Prince de Beauvau. His Majesty
received them with ' a lively recognition,' and sent a
cheerful message to the Academy that he hoped to
visit it in person.

Gluck, the great musician, and Piccini the lesser,
came to do homage, one after the other, on February 13. ' Ah ! that's as it should be ! ' says old Voltaire. ' Piccini comes after Gluck.'

The Comédie Française sent a congratulatory deputation on Saturday the 14th, and much laboured flattery in an address delivered by Bellecour and Madame

Vestris. Voltaire responded in the same manner—
exaggerated. 'We all played comedy beautifully!'
he said, with a twinkle, afterwards.

For the rest of that day his talk to his guests was
graver than usual. He discussed politics with them—
and the French politics of 1778 were enough to sober
Folly itself. A weak King, a ruined Treasury, a corrupt Church—and, as Voltaire himself wrote to Florian
a week or two later, in the social state 'a revolting
luxury and a fearful misery.'

He showed his guests a letter he had just received
from another King who was neither fool nor feeble,
and who ruled a kingdom which beside starving France
was Utopia, El Dorado, Paradise.

By Sunday, February 15, Voltaire was ill. But
then Tronchin was in Paris! Voltaire had not written
to that old friend for a matter of ten years—except
'a *billet-doux* on arriving' in the capital. But
though Tronchin disapproved of almost everything
Voltaire did and thought, the good Doctor loved the
man as a woman loves an engaging and ill-trained
child.

He forgave the ten years' silence and the Châtelaine
theatre, even old Voltaire's truculent unbelief—came
to him, looked at him with those serene, wise eyes,
forbade all going out, and commanded absolute rest.

Voltaire had been going to the theatre to-morrow.
Well, he could give that up. But rest? Madame
Necker called to see him this very day—Sunday. And
how, pray, could he decline to receive the wife of her
husband, the woman who had done so much for him
in the matter of the Pigalle statue, and who, distantly
related to Belle-et-Bonne, had sternly disapproved of
her innocence being used to reform a wickedness like

Villette's and had only brought herself with difficulty to enter that scoundrel's house ?   Voltaire received her with the most delightful *empressement*.

And then, waiting to see him was the 'wise and illustrious' Franklin, philosopher and politician, who until Voltaire's arrival had himself been the lion of Paris.   How to refuse *him* ?   He came into the presence chamber, bringing with him his grandson. Voltaire spoke in English until Madame Denis told him that Franklin perfectly understood French.   There were twenty persons or so in the room.   The two great men talked of the government and constitution of the United States.   ' If I were forty,' says Voltaire, ' I should go and settle in your happy country.'

Then Dr. Franklin presented his grandson, a lad about seventeen.   Voltaire raised his hands above the boy's head and blessed him, 'uttering only these words,' and in English—' God and Liberty.'

He told the story himself to several of his correspondents.   It moved his old heart.   And the persons who saw the scene—to be sure, they were French and ready to be affected at anything—shed tears.

The Franklins had not been gone an hour before Voltaire was receiving Lord Stormont, the English ambassador, and Belbâtre, a famous performer on the harpsichord.   Rest ?   Dr. Tronchin already knew the temper and disposition of his invalid, and something, though not yet all, of the selfish and pleasure-loving character of his Denis and his Villette.   Voltaire was sent to bed.   And prudent Tronchin inserted a notice in the 'Journal de Paris' stating that M. de Voltaire had lived since he came to Paris on the capital of his strength instead of only on the income, as all his friends must wish ; that that capital would very soon

be exhausted, ' and we shall be the witnesses, if we are
not the accomplices, of his death.'

The notice did not appear until February 20, and
by the 19th this marvellous old man was at least well
enough to be assigning the parts in ' Irène.'   Richelieu,
himself eighty-two, came to help him in this delicate
task.   The magnificent marshal, in spite of the care
and splendour of his dress, did not look nearly so
young and vigorous as the attenuated figure in bedgown and nightcap, with his sunken eyes afire and all
his old keenness and spirit.   Besides settling parts,
he was now rewriting the play itself so enthusiastically,
that wretched Wagnière did not even have time to
dress himself.

The next day, February 20, that poor, shameful,
tawdry favourite, Madame Dubarry, came out of her
social banishment to see this new king, Arouet.   Le
Brun, poet, and once benefactor of Marie Corneille, who
had written an inflammatory ode in praise of the
monarch and wanted to see if it had been appreciated,
closely followed the Dubarry.   He tells how Voltaire
contrasted the fresh, fair innocence of Belle-et-Bonne
with the stale and painted charms of the last avowed
mistress of a King of France.

Le Brun himself was characteristically received
with ' You see, Sir, a poor old man of eighty-four, who
has committed eighty-four follies.'   The story runs
that Voltaire had said the same to Sophie Arnould, and
that that sprightly person had replied, ' Why, that's
nothing !   I am only forty and I have committed a
thousand.'

It was on this same day, February 20, that Voltaire
received a letter from Abbé Gaultier, who had been a
Jesuit for seventeen years and a curé for twenty, and

now had a post at the Hospital of the Incurables.
Gaultier was anxious for the salvation of Voltaire's
soul, and that he should have the saving of it. Voltaire responded favourably ; and the next day, the 21st,
received the priest. Gaultier and Wagnière both give
accounts of the interview. Both may have lied. One
must have. The truth seems to be that Gaultier was
ushered into a salon full of people, whom Voltaire soon
dismissed. He took the priest into his private room,
where—to make a long matter short—Gaultier offered
himself as Voltaire's confessor. The Patriarch asked
if anyone had suggested to him to make that offer—
the Archbishop of Paris, for instance, or the Curé of
Saint-Sulpice, in whose parish Villette's house was
situated. Gaultier replied, No ; and Voltaire said he was
glad of the assurance. A long conversation ensued.
Voltaire declared that he loved God ; and Gaultier
answered that he must give proofs of it. They were
three times interrupted—by the Marquis de Villevieille,
nephew Mignot, and Wagnière. Madame Denis came
in to beg that her uncle might not be tired and worried.
When Gaultier was dismissed, it was with the promise
that he should be received again.

When Wagnière asked Voltaire what he thought of
Gaultier, Voltaire replied that he was 'a good fool.'
He appears to have thought that he would be more
easily satisfied than shrewder men, and that if it came
to the dreadful necessity of a confession as an insurance
of decent and honourable burial, Gaultier would be the
best confessor.

A few days later a certain Abbé Martin thrust
himself in and imperatively insisted that the sceptic
should make confession then and there to him. ' I
have come for that. I shall not move an inch.'

'From whom do you come, M. l'Abbé?'

'From God Himself.'

'Well, well, Sir—your credentials?'

The Abbé was dumb. The inconsistent old Patriarch, feeling that he had been severe, went out of his
way to be more than usually kind and agreeable during
the rest of the visit.

But such incidents made one ponder. To avoid the
sickness which would make confession a necessity was
the obvious thing to do. But to keep well meant to
rest. And every hour that struck, every turn of the
wheel, brought fresh excitements, fresh work, fresh
visitors.

On the very day of Gaultier's visit, February 21,
came Madame du Deffand, whose long friendship and
'herculean weakness' had enabled her to brave the
crowds that surrounded Voltaire, and visit him first
about a week earlier, on February 14. Her account of
that occasion has been lost. But the most ennuied and
world-weary worldling of any time confessed that it had
been delightful.

On this February 21 the event had lost the one
great antidote to boredom—novelty. Denis was '*gaupe*,'
and Villette 'a *plat* person of comedy,' and Belle-et-
Bonne damned with faint praise as 'said to be
amiable.'

But in the presence of Voltaire, her correspondent
since her youth, her warmest sympathiser when blindness fell upon her, even Madame du Deffand forgot
again for a while what a bitter and empty world that
is where Pleasure is the only god and to be amused
the be-all and end-all of existence. Old Voltaire
entertained her with a lively account of Gaultier's
visit.

But, all the same, he had not forgotten that that incident had a very serious side.

Four days later, on February 25, about midday, he was dictating in bed, when suddenly, in a violent fit of coughing, he broke a blood-vessel. Wagnière, terrified, rang the bell loudly. Madame Denis ran into the room, and Tronchin was summoned immediately. It had been so easy to laugh at Gaultier with a blind old *mondaine* when one felt lively and well! But now—call him at once! Turning to the persons in his room, the old man bade them all remember that he had fulfilled 'what they call here one's duties.' Tronchin came, bled the patient, and, what was likely to be far more useful, sent him a very excellent and strong-minded young nurse who was to refuse admission to all visitors, and a surgeon who was to stay in the house all night.

Meanwhile, Protestant Wagnière, who regarded his master's dealings with the priests as disgraceful to his honour in this world and very unlikely to save his soul for the next, had not summoned Gaultier.

The next day, February 26, Voltaire wrote the priest a little note: 'You promised, Sir, to come and hear me. Come as soon as you can.' Madame Denis added her entreaties in a postscript. But, it being nine o'clock at night when Gaultier received the letter, he did not come to the Hôtel Villette till the next day, when his penitent could not, or would not, see him.

By Sunday, March 1, he was well enough to listen to La Harpe reading a canto of 'La Pharsale'—so loudly that he could be heard in the street.

On the Monday morning d'Alembert came to see the sick man. Voltaire told him that he had 'taken the leap,' and sent for Gaultier. There had been other priests, said d'Alembert, writing to Frederick the Great, who had thrust themselves into his room, preaching at him like fanatics, ' whom the old Patriarch, from goodness of heart, had not ordered to be thrown out of the window.' Gaultier was more moderate and reasonable than his brethren ; and, thinks d'Alembert, if Voltaire has the natural weakness to feel that it is of consequence what becomes of the remains of poor humanity after death, he is right to do as he proposes to do—as all the world does, the good Protestant as well as the godless pagan. This is d'Alembert's attitude to the matter throughout.

Later on that same day, Gaultier reappeared. He was ushered into the sick room. Voltaire sent the servants out of it. Wagnière listened at the door, which was luckily only a sort of paper screen. He was very much agitated by those fears for his master's honour. When Voltaire called him and bade him bring writing materials, the servant was too moved to answer the question as to what ailed him. Voltaire took the pen, wrote his statement or profession of faith, which declared that he had confessed to Gaultier, that he died in the Catholic religion in which he was born, and that if he had scandalised the Church he asked pardon of God and of it. D'Alembert—the truthful d'Alembert—says that Voltaire told him he added the last phrase at the request of the priest, ' and to have peace.'

But to that ' zeal in concessions,' which had always made him as vigorously thorough in his lies as he was thorough in his good deeds, the addenda may in part be attributed.

The Marquis de Villevieille and Abbé Mignot readily signed what Gaultier lightly called ' a little declaration which does not signify much.' Wagnière hotly declined.

Before leaving, Gaultier proposed to give the sick man the Communion. Voltaire excused himself. He coughed too much, he said. He gave Gaultier, according to the custom, twenty-five louis for the poor of the parish, and the priest left.

There was one man about Voltaire, but only one, who wished him to declare, not what it was expedient to think, but what he really thought : what were the convictions of his soul, and the creed of his heart.

A few days earlier, on February 28, at the earnest request of Wagnière and at a moment when he solemnly believed that his last hour had come, Voltaire had written down, clearly and firmly, his real faith.

'I die adoring God, loving my friends, not hating my enemies, and detesting superstition. February 28, 1778. Voltaire.'

So far as a few weak words can express any man's attitude towards the Supreme Being and his own fellow-sinners, this confession expresses Voltaire's.

It is still preserved in the National Library at Paris.

On the following day, March 3, Gaultier returned. He wanted, or rather his superiors, the Archbishop of Paris and de Tersac, the Curé of Saint-Sulpice, to whom he had shown the confession, said that *they* wanted, one more detailed and less equivocal. The truth was Saint-Sulpice would have liked the credit of such a conversion himself. This 'man of little understanding and a bigoted fanatic,' as d'Alembert called him, was not a person to be offended. He had, as parish priest, the disposal of the bodies of those who died in his parish.

Voltaire would not see Gaultier. But from that stormy sick bed, on March 4, he wrote the most graceful of conciliatory letters to offended de Tersac; and laconically announced to poor Gaultier, in a note, that Villette had given orders that until M. de Voltaire was better, no priest, except the Curé of Saint-Sulpice, should be admitted to the house.

Persistent Gaultier returned in a week and was again refused admission. Deathbed conversions were his speciality, and he was not going to be cheated of this one without a struggle. Meanwhile Voltaire upset all his plans by recovering rapidly. Paris, who had heard much more than the truth concerning this illness and confession, avenged herself for her anxiety by epigrams. It was right that the Curé of the Incurables should attempt such a conversion! The patient himself (whose every utterance was reported) declared that if he had lived on the banks of the Ganges he would have died with a cow's tail in his mouth. To die with a lie in it did not shock Paris in the least.

To find excuses for Voltaire's act, it is as necessary, as it is now impossible, to realise fully the conditions of life and death under a government which permitted no liberty of conscience, and in which men were either orthodox or anathema.

There were other troubles besides religious ones to harry this old patient of eighty-four out of a sick bed to the grave before his time.

Tronchin wanted Voltaire's real good, and Voltaire's real good meant Ferney and repose; while Villette was all for himself, pleasure, and Paris. One day the doctor turned the Marquis by force out of the sick room. Villette called in a rival practitioner, Lorry—famous and free-thinking—and no doubt was disappointed

VOLTAIRE'S DECLARATION OF FAITH.

From the Original in the Bibliothèque Nationale, Paris.

when Tronchin worked amicably side by side with his
confrère.

A College of Physicians could not have kept Voltaire,
when he began to recover a little, from doing as he
liked. He was soon sitting up in bed, working on
'Irène' and dictating to Wagnière as usual. Visitors
thrust themselves in again. Poets came to read their
complimentary odes. One writer announced to Voltaire
in a most wearisome prepared speech, that to-day he
had come to visit Homer, to-morrow he would visit
Euripides, the next Sophocles, the next Tacitus, the
next——' Sir, I am very old,' says the voice from the
bed ; ' if you *could* pay all these calls in one——'

Another flatterer said that, having surpassed his
brethren in everything, Voltaire would surpass Fontenelle himself in length of days.

'Ah! no, Sir. Fontenelle was a Norman : he
cheated even Nature.'

By March 10 the invalid was not unnaturally worse
again, and Tronchin kept him in bed, although, or
perhaps because, there was a rehearsal of 'Irène'
actually going on in the house at the moment.

The next day, Madame Vestris, who was to play in
'Irène,' was allowed to see him about her part. The
maddening placidity with which she delivered lines
intended to be passionately pathetic did not help to
soothe the invalid's irritable and nervous condition.
He told her how fifty years ago he had seen Mademoiselle Duclos reduce the whole house to tears by a
single line; and talking to Mademoiselle Clairon afterwards, he hit the imperturbable Vestris hard in a *mot*
well understood of all Paris.

He had himself recited with extraordinary feeling a few lines out of his last play. 'Ah!' said Clairon,

' where will you find an actress to render them like
that ?   Such an effort might kill her.'

' So much the better,' answers the poor old playwright viciously. ' I should be only too glad to render
the public such a service.'

The mediocrity of the other actors also grievously
afflicted the overwrought mind and body of the sick
man.   There came, indeed, times when he sank into a
sort of stupor : when nothing seemed to matter ; when
he was indifferent or unconscious that Madame Denis
was conducting rehearsals and giving away the first-
night tickets on her own responsibility, and that d'Argental and La Harpe were making such alterations
in ' Irène ' as they deemed fit.   He must have been really
ill.   In four days, it is said, he had aged four years.
The trumpet blasts of adulation in prose or verse,
always appearing in the newspapers, had no power to
rouse him ; and as for the abuse—' I received such
abominations every week at Ferney,' he said, ' and had
to pay the postage ; here I get them every day, but
they cost me nothing—so I am the gainer.'

On March 14 Madame Denis presided over the
last rehearsal of ' Irène,' and on March 16 was the
first performance.

The playwright, who had written and rewritten
it, laboured at it, as he said himself, as if he had
been twenty, was in bed in the Hôtel Villette, not too
ill to be interested in its success, but past any great
anxiety concerning it

The house was crowded.   Marie Antoinette was
there—Marie Antoinette, who had been brilliantly imprudent enough to inquire why, if Madame Geoffrin,
' the nurse of the philosophers,' had been received at
Court, Voltaire should not be ?   She had a notebook

in her hand, and put down therein all the pious and
edifying passages to prove to her absent lord that
M. de Voltaire's conversion was real! Her brother-
in-law, d'Artois, was there; the Duke and Duchess of
Bourbon : all Versailles, but the King.

The play, or more correctly the playwright, was received with tumultuous applause. 'Irène' was feeble
and tired, like the old hand that had written it. But
here and there, where the bright flame of a dying genius
flickered up for a moment, the house applauded madly,
and to parts wholly meritless listened in respectful
silence. After each act, messengers were despatched
to tell Voltaire all was well. At the end of the last,
Dupuits rushed to announce a general success, and the
sick room quickly filled with congratulating friends.
'What you say consoles but does not cure me,'
said the poor old invalid. But he roused himself
enough to inquire which verses were the most applauded, and to chuckle joyfully when he heard of the
delighted reception of those which smote the clergy
hip and thigh.

On March 19 the 'Journal de Paris' published a
very sanguine account of Voltaire's health. 'His
recent indisposition has left no after-effects.' It was
certainly true that he was better again. He received a
deputation from the Academy congratulating him on
'Irène,' and by March 21 was well enough to go out in
a carriage. He was recognised and surrounded by the
people in the streets, and when he regained the Hôtel
Villette there was a deputation of Freemasons waiting
to see him. There was no peace for him, in fact, at
home or abroad. His whole visit to Paris was like the
progress of a popular sovereign who has no officials to
ensure his comfort and privacy.

Being better, the most natural thing to do was to go over ' Irène.' He sent for an acting copy. Directly he saw how it had been tampered with, he fell into the greatest rage in which Wagnière, after twenty-four years' service and a much richer experience of his master's *vifness* than Collini, had ever seen him. He forced Madame Denis to confess. He pushed her away so that she fell into an armchair, or rather, says Wagnière spitefully, into the arms of Duvivier, that dull young man she afterwards married. Then the indignant uncle sent the niece out (it was raining too) to d'Argental's house to fetch the manuscripts and plays with which he had intrusted that old friend. His rage lasted for twelve hours. He roundly abused both d'Argental and La Harpe. And then, for he was the same Voltaire, he apologised to both with a most generous humility.

On March 28 he went to see Turgot—' Sully-Turgot '—the man who had ' saved the century from decadence,' and whose disgrace in 1776 Voltaire had felt as a keen personal grief and an irreparable public disaster. The meeting was very French and effusive. But it was not, for that, insincere. ' Let me kiss the hands of him,' cries old Voltaire, ' who has signed the salvation of the people.'

The day of this King's coronation had been fixed for March 30. The nominal King sat aloof and sulky at Versailles. But what did that matter ? The Queen, keener-eyed, saw in Voltaire a rival force not to be disregarded. And when Artois heard of Voltaire's death—' There has died a great rogue and a great man,' said he. From an Artois it was no bad testimony.

At four o'clock in the afternoon of this March 30

a gorgeous, blue, star-spangled coach waited at the door of the Hôtel Villette.

And presently there gets into it, amid the shouts and acclamations of his subjects, a very, very lean old figure, in that grey peruke whose fashion he had not altered for forty years, a square cap on the top of it, a red coat lined with ermine, Ferney white silk stockings on the shrunken legs, large silver buckles on the shoes, a little cane in the hand with a crow's beak for a head, and over all this extraordinary fancy dress (it was only rather less remarkable in Paris in 1778 than it would be in Paris to-day) Catherine's sable pelisse.

Thus dressed, he was driven through tumultuous crowds to the Louvre, where two thousand persons received him with shouts of ' Long live Voltaire ! '

The Academy met him in their outer hall—an honour never accorded to anyone, even to princes. Twenty Academicians were present. The absentees were all churchmen. The King was conducted to the Presidential Chamber, and there unanimously elected to the next three months' Presidency. Then the Perpetual Secretary, friend d'Alembert, rose and read a so-called Eulogy of Boileau, which was really a Eulogy of Voltaire. The serene dignity of the Secretary contrasted not a little with old Voltaire's painful efforts after self-command. It was twenty-eight years since he had been among them. It was thirty-five since, as a body, they had refused him admission. And now—— !

He paid a brief visit to d'Alembert's office, and then got into his carriage again. The crowds had increased. All sorts and conditions of men were here to welcome him who had pointed the way to freedom —who, unlike all other kings, was of the people, and so,

for them. Frenzied, as in another frenzy they had
hooted the Calas to judgment through the streets of
Toulouse, and as but a very few years later they might
have hooted Voltaire himself to the Place de la Guillotine, they applauded and worshipped him now. The
Villettes and Madame Denis met him at the Comédie
Française. Their protection was necessary. The
people clambered on the carriage itself to see him, to
touch him. One man seized Belle-et-Bonne's little
hand instead of the Patriarch's. 'Ma foi!' he said.
'This is a plump hand for eighty-four!'

She and Madame Denis preceded him to the box
set aside for the Gentlemen-in-Ordinary. Then, with
the women pressing on him and plucking the fur from
his pelisse to keep as souvenirs, Voltaire made his way
through the house to the passionate acclamations of
the crowded audience. He would fain have concealed
himself behind Belle-et-Bonne and his portly niece.
'To the front!' cried the gods. And to the front
he came. Opposite him was the royal box, in which
was Artois who had been with the Queen at the opera,
but had slipped away to do homage to a greater
royalty.

Then another cry shook the house. 'The crown!'

Brizard, the actor, came forward and put a laurel
crown on the old poet's head. 'Ah, God! You will
kill me with glory!' he said. He took it off and put
it on Belle-et-Bonne's. And the house bade her give
it back to him. He resisted. And then Prince de
Beauvau came forward and crowned him again. By
this time the whole auditorium was on its feet. The
passages were full to suffocation. The actors, dressed
for their parts, came before the curtain to join in the
enthusiasm. The delirium lasted for twenty minutes.

The air of the theatre was black with the dust caused by the movement of so great a multitude, struggling to see.

At last the play began. It was ' Irène,' of course— ' Irène,' now at its sixth representation.

The audience had read their own meaning into its lines. They applauded wildly throughout. At the end the curtain was raised again. On the stage was a pedestal, and on the pedestal the bust of Voltaire which had been brought from the hall of the Comédie where it had recently been placed. Actors and actresses were grouped round it, holding garlands of flowers. Some of the audience, despite the new regulations, had crowded on to the stage for a better view.

Then Brizard, dressed for his part of monk in ' Irène,' placed his laurel garland on the head, and the whole company followed his example. From the house burst a roar which sounded as if it was from one throat as it was from one heart. For the first time in France, said Grimm, there was no dissentient voice. ' Envy and hatred, fanaticism and intolerance, dared not murmur.' Perhaps even at that delirious moment the old Patriarch recognised the triumph, not as his, but as philosophy's: and rejoiced the more. ' It is then true, Sire,' he wrote on April 1, in his last letter to Frederick the Great, ' that in the end men *will* be enlightened, and those who believe that it pays to blind them will not always be victorious.'

March 30, 1778, is a great day in the history of France as celebrating, not the honour of Voltaire, but of that ' happy revolution he had effected in the mind and the conduct of his century.'

Villette drew him forward to the front of the box, and while he stood there for a moment the applause redoubled.

Then Madame Vestris, who had played 'Irène,' came forward and recited an ode by the Marquis de Saint-Marc. Voltaire, writing to Saint-Marc the next day, thanked him for having made him immortal in the prettiest verses in the world. The ode was not bad ; but if it had been it would have been applauded and encored just the same. Copies were circulated through the house.

On the stage one woman came forward and impulsively kissed the bust, and other enthusiasts followed her example.

A stranger, entering at the moment, supposed himself to be in a madhouse.

The curtain fell again ; and again rose, this time on 'Nanine.' Once more, it was not the play that counted, but the playwright. When the curtain fell for the last time, he made his royal way to his carriage between lines of women sobbing with emotion. Some persons seized his hands and kissed them with tears. Others fell upon the horses to stop them and cried for torches. Thus lighting him, crowds accompanied his carriage home, shouting, dancing, and weeping. When at last he reached the Hôtel Villette, worn out with the glory and the high-pitched emotions of the day, the poor old Patriarch himself wept like a child. 'If I had known the people would commit such follies I would never have gone to the Comédie.'

But it was the next morning which, like all next mornings, was the real time for reflection. Here was the man who, more than any other Frenchman who ever lived, understood the national temperament. 'Capable of all excesses,' ' the Parisians pass their time in hissing and clapping—in putting up statues and pulling them down again.' 'You do not know the French, he said to Genevan Wagnière ; 'they would have done as much for Jean Jacques.' ·'They want to stifle me under roses.'

The reflections showed a just judgment. But, coming at such a time, they showed, too, a man old, tired, and at the end of his tether. Tronchin had long said that to survive such a life as he had been living the last few weeks, his body must be made of steel.

Long and bitterly discussed, but this ' next morning ' become a pressing and imminent question, was the return to Ferney. To go—or to stay ? On the one side were Villette, and Madame Denis. They were not the rose, but it was delightful to live near the rose. The one, despite the good and pretty wife, had already been drawn back again into the vile dissipations of the capital. The other was not only out at entertainments all day, but at sixty-eight was coyly coquetting with her Duvivier.

In the second camp was Wagnière, who, besides having left home, wife, and children at Ferney, was sincerely devoted to his master's real good ; the judicious, clear-seeing d'Alembert, young Dupuits, and above all, Dr. Tronchin. Fearless and upright, the great Doctor made one last passionate appeal to his patient to go while there was time. ' I would give a hundred louis to see you back at Ferney. Go in a week.'

' Am I fit to travel ? ' says the poor old Patriarch.

' I will stake my head on it,' says Tronchin.

The thin trembling hand grasped the strong one.

' You have given me back my life.'

Voltaire was so much moved that the serene Tronchin, nay, the very cook who happened to be in the room at the same moment, was moved too.

Tronchin wrote off immediately to Ferney for

Voltaire's coachman and carriage. Madame Denis's vociferous indignation was wasted on him. Little Madame Suard, the sprightly visitor of Ferney, must have been as delighted as all others who put Voltaire's life above their own pleasure. She came to see her old host. ' We shall kill him,' she said, ' if he stays here.'

But Madame Denis was not going back to the dismal solitude and the ice and snow of Ferney without a fight. Is it the Villette house you do not like ? She hurried out, and nearly took one in the Faubourg Saint-Honoré, with a beautiful garden where Uncle Voltaire could fancy himself in the country. The negotiations for it fell through. But there is what might be made a very fine house in the Rue Richelieu, and which has the enormous advantage of being quite close to the home of your butterfly philosopher, Madame Saint-Julien ! Voltaire at eighty-four, and with, as he pointed out to his every correspondent, at least two mortal complaints, actually consented to buy this unfinished house. He would live there eight months of the year, and the other four at Ferney. Still, those other four were to be taken at once. He would go now—soon ! If he *could* go, that is. But had he not just been elected to three months' Presidency of the Academy? His vacillations were the despair of Tronchin—ay, and the despair of himself. He longed to go, but he could not go. Madame Denis, with the most limitless capacity for nagging ever vouchsafed to mortal woman, volubly assured him that influential friends had told her that if he did go, he would never be allowed to return.

True, on April 2 ' Irène ' had been performed at Court. That did not look like a new edict of banishment. But then the author had not been asked to see

his play. Perhaps that *did*? Then it was said the
Queen herself had had an idea of slipping into the
theatre on that great 30th of March to see the crowning
of the people's King—only—only—the other King had
peremptorily forbidden her. A dog Voltaire had been
fond of at Ferney came to Paris with one of the Ferney
servants and bounded in to lick his master's hand with
the touching, dumb joy of animal affection. 'You see
I am still beloved at Ferney,' says the old man.
Villette and Madame Denis took very good care that
that dog should never enter the house again. They
tried to get rid of Wagnière—his influence was so bad
and so powerful. They failed in this. But, after all,
they succeeded in their main object.

When a man's foes are those of his own household,
resistance is peculiarly difficult.

'I have seen a great many fools,' Tronchin wrote on
April 6, 'but never such an old fool as he is.'

The exhaustion consequent on his crowning had
passed away. With it passed away, too, the idea of an
immediate return to Ferney.

By that day, April 6, the 'old fool' was well enough
to go on foot, in spite of adoring crowds, to the
Academy.

A seller of books on the way naïvely begged him ' to
write me some and my fortune will be made.' ' You
have made so many other people rich ! Write me some
books ! I am a poor woman.' Among the people he
heard himself often called by that name which was a
sweeter flattery to his soul than all odes and plaudits—
' the man of Calas.'

The next day he was made a Freemason, and in the
evening went to see the unacknowledged actress-wife of
the Duke of Orleans.

On April 11 he returned Madame du Deffand's visit.
She forgave him for not coming before ; but the Convent
of St. Joseph, in which she lived, found it hard to forgive him for coming at all and profaning their holy
place with his presence. He paid other visits. One
old friend, the Comtesse de Ségur, was dying when he
saw her. For a little, the charm of his reminiscences
brought back to her their youth. When he visited her
again, remembering only that he, like herself, stood on
the brink of eternity, she passionately conjured him to
cease his ' war against religion.' He turned upon her
fiercely, forgetting her womanhood and her dying.
That stern, terse creed he had hammered and forged
for himself was as dear to him as was to her the fuller
faith she had accepted without trouble or thought.
The room was full of people. The guests paused to
listen. Voltaire remembered himself : offered sympathy,
suggested remedies, and left, greatly moved.

Another visit was yet more pathetic. He went to see
Egérie de Livri, once the vivacious poor companion of the
Duchesse de Sully and would-be actress, and now the
Marquise de Gouvernet. In this withered old woman
of eighty-three what traces were there of the brilliant
girl to whom a Voltaire of five-and-twenty had taught
declamation and love, who had gaily forgotten him for
de Génonville, and graciously remembered him when
he had immortalised her in ' Les Vous et Les Tu ' ?
Above him, on the wall, smiled the picture he had given
her—his dead self, by Largillière. A ghost ! A ghost !
He left her, profoundly saddened. She sent the portrait
to him at the Hôtel Villette, and he gave it to Belle-et-
Bonne.

Another friend came to see him one morning—
Longchamp—from whom he had parted eight-and-

twenty years ago, and with whom were connected
many memories, of the Court and of Paris, of Cirey
and Madame du Châtelet.

If the man had cheated his master, he had loved
him too. The things are not incompatible.

These meetings made the old heart yearn again
for quiet and Ferney. But there was still so much
to do !

Besides his plays to be corrected and personally
supervised in rehearsal, a new grand scheme had been
filling his mind, quickening his last energies, bringing
back the resolute passion of his youth.

On April 27 he attended a *séance* at the Academy.
Abbé Délille read a translation of Pope's 'Epistle to
Arbuthnot.' Well, one Academician had known the
thing in the original and the author in the flesh. He
sat and listened attentively. Then he got up. An admirable translation, gentlemen. But our language is,
after all, poor—poorer than it need be in poetic expression. Why, for instance, should we not call an actor
who plays tragedy, a tragedian ? And why—why should
this Academy not undertake the reconstruction of the
French Dictionary ? The one we have is unworthy of
us—dull, inadequate, impossible. The Academy is
called the lawgiver of language to the people of France.
Let it worthily prove itself so ! The work shall not
only be useful, but patriotic. Each member shall take
a letter. As for me, gentlemen, I am willing to consecrate to such a task the brief remainder of my days.
The old man spoke with the fire and the vigour of
youth. Some of his auditors were incompetent for
the task he proposed to them ; many were lazy and
apathetic.

But the octogenarian who had suggested it went

home with his soul on fire, drew paper and pen towards him, and began, through domestic disturbance and the ceaseless round of visits, to elaborate his scheme.

Two days later he received an ovation from the Academy of Sciences. D'Alembert read a Eulogy, written by Condorcet, of Trudain, Councillor of State, who had helped Voltaire with his colony at Ferney. To eulogise Voltaire himself followed in natural sequence. Franklin was there too. Old Voltaire spoke to him. 'Embrace in the French fashion!' cried a voice : and they did.

At the end of April it was decided that Wagnière should leave for Ferney, to get there papers and books of which Voltaire had need. It was a bitter parting. The servant had done his best to make his master go with him. But Tronchin was not always at his side, and Denis and Villette were. Then there were his plays still needing correction. And now that Dictionary scheme, so hotly resolved upon—how to abandon *that*? Then, too, the Abbé Beauregard had preached in glowing vituperation at Versailles against all the philosophers, and one philosopher in particular. The kingly party, as well as the ecclesiastical, was mad to hound this Voltaire out of Paris.

There had been many times in his life when he had perforce to turn his back on the enemy and fly. But those had gone by for ever.

On April 27 he signed the contract of purchase for the new house in the Rue Richelieu.

On the 29th, Wagnière left. Both knew the parting was their last. But neither could face the fact.

Life went on with a madder rush when the secretary had gone. Visits succeeded to visits. One ovation brought another. All the *mots* the Patriarch uttered

(and numbers he did not) were recorded in the newspapers. His every action was noted—his very motives
guessed. Through all he was working feverishly—
without the invaluable help of Wagnière and with his
strength kept up by drugs—on that scheme for the
Dictionary.

It was ready by May 7. He went to the Academy.
Upon some of the brethren at least—they were almost
all young enough to be his grandsons—had fallen that
fatal mental inertia, that deadly sleep which paralysed
the brains of half aristocratic France just before the
Revolution. Nothing matters! Nothing is worth
while! With eyes and heart aglow, this old Voltaire
read aloud his brief and masterly plan. It remains
that upon which all great dictionaries in Europe and
America have been modelled to this day.

He recommended it with a zeal of which he alone
was capable. Tronchin speaks of it as his 'last
dominant idea, his last passion.' If he had been a
boy of twenty, with name and fortune to make by this
Dictionary alone, he could not have been more eager.
In the end he obtained a unanimous consent to his
scheme. But it was cool—cool! He insisted on the
immediate division of the letters among the members.
He himself took A. It meant the most work. That he
also wrote a part of T is certain.

One old member reminded him of his age, and he
turned upon him in reply with 'something more than
vivacity.' The *séance* ended.

'Gentlemen,' says old Voltaire, 'I thank you in
the name of the alphabet.'

'And we,' replied Chastellux, 'thank you in the
name of letters.'

That evening Voltaire was present *incognito* at

the performance of 'Alzire.' Of course he was recognised. For three-quarters of an hour the howls of
applause never ceased. Then he himself begged silence
from the house. As he left it, the people, pressing on
him, thrust odes of inflammatory flattery into his hand.
This mob was enthusiastic enough. But those
Academicians, his brothers, with all the world to con-
quer—their apathy lay heavily on his soul. If death
came to him, the only young man of them all, would
they go on with' his scheme? He doubted them.
'They are sluggards,' he said passionately to Tronchin,
'who wallow in idleness; but I will make them march.'
He must write them a Discourse to sting them and
shame them. No man in the world had so much and
so ably used the fine, pliant, delicate machinery of the
French language, as he had. In the most perfect
French in the world he had alike coquetted with
women in drawing-rooms and spoken his great message
to the race. He loved the tool with which he had
carved immortal work. The day was not long enough
to say what he had to say upon the language he had
adorned. Far on into the night—brain and nerve
stimulated by strong coffee—he wrote on the subject
that possessed his soul. The sleep he had banished
deserted him now when he called it. He wrote on.
There was so little time! There was so much to do!
Not afraid of death, but of dying before he had finished
his work—that description was true to the finest shade
of meaning. The coffee aggravated the internal disease
from which he suffered. But he wrote on. On May 11
he could not go to a meeting of the Academy. But
he could still write. The strong sun of that long life
was fast sinking below the horizon, and the night

coming when no man can work. The old brain nerved itself to one last effort. The old hand wrote on.

' Whoso fears God, fears to sit at ease.'

Doubtful in morals, and a most trenchant unbeliever, the scoffer Voltaire yet sets a splendid example to all inert Christians who, comfortably cultivating the selfish virtues, care nothing for the race and recognise no mission but to save their own miserable souls.

Who has done more good for the world—the stainless anchorite, be his cloister a religious one or his own easy home ; or this sinner, of whom it was said at his death, with literal truth, that the history of what had been accomplished in Europe in favour of reason and humanity was the history of his writings and of his deeds ?

CHAPTER XLIV

THE END

THE accounts of the dying of Voltaire would fill a volume. Round this great deathbed were gathered persons who each had a different end to serve by differently describing it.

Villette wanted to prove himself the wise and unselfish friend; and Madame Denis must appear the tenderly devoted niece.

The Abbé Depery published an awful description of these last moments, which he declares he heard from Belle-et-Bonne. She was dead when he made the statement; and 'it is easy to make the dead speak.' But if that fearful story had been true, this girl, who passionately loved her more than father and dedicated the remainder of her days to his memory, would hardly have repeated it. Lady Morgan, who saw her in Paris forty years later, declares that she spoke of the dying man's peace, tranquillity, and resignation.

D'Alembert, Grimm, and Condorcet naturally wished to see a death, firm, consistent, and philosophic : and they saw it.

Dr. Tronchin, the sincere Christian, would fain have beheld a repentant sinner. Failing that, what could he see but the 'frightful torment' of the wicked to whom Death is the King of Terrors, 'the furies of Orestes,' the *sæva indignatio* of Swift?

Gaultier naturally did not wish to own that he had missed so illustrious a conversion. He did not own it: he said the convert's mind was wandering.

But, after all, it matters not how one dies, but how one has lived. Deathbed utterances, even if truly reported, are to be attributed less to the illumined soul than to the diseased body. If at last the horrors of the Great Change and the awful prospect of the unknown Eternity overwhelmed this unbeliever, as at such an hour they have overwhelmed many sincere Christians, that fact is no confession that Voltaire gave the lie to the convictions of his life.

For more than sixty years they had been those not of a man in the careless vigour of health, or of a thoughtless profligate, or of an indifferent, but of one who had always known his tenure of life to be frail; who had realised the consolations of the religion he could not believe, and yearned for that faith he could never have.

If, at the last, his priestly counsellors did succeed in terrifying the old dying mind, enfeebled by the dying body, by their threats of Judgment and Eternity, what use to his soul, or the cause of their Christianity?

It is the eighty-four years of vigorous life and passionate utterance that count before God and man, and not the dying minutes.

Out of lies innumerable, then— some witnesses took their testimony of the deathbed of Voltaire from the cook of the Hôtel Villette—the following account has been sifted.

On some day, which was either May 12 or shortly after it, the old man met Madame Denis and Madame Saint-Julien when he was out walking.

He said he was ill and going to bed. Two hours later his good Butterfly came to see him. She found

him very feverish, and begged that Tronchin might be
sent for.

Madame Denis, remembering the Doctor's counsels,
declined to summon him.

The patient grew worse. Villette sent for a local
apothecary, who came with medicine which the sick
man was at first too wise to take. But he was ill and
old, and Madame Denis was naggingly persistent.
He took, not enough said Madame Denis; too much
said Madame Saint-Julien, who tasted it. Anyhow, he
grew worse. That evening old Richelieu came to see
him and recommended a remedy—laudanum—which
he had himself been in the habit of taking for the gout.

With the night the patient's sufferings increased.
He sent for the laudanum.

Madame Saint-Julien and a relative (most likely
d'Hornoy), who were there when it came, implored
caution. The audacious ignorance of Madame Denis
had no fears.

Wagnière, who of course was not present, declares
that his master characteristically seized the remedy and
took too much, too often. D'Alembert—the notoriously
truthful—says that he never took any: the bottle was
broken. However that may be, he grew alarmingly
worse.

At last Dr. Tronchin was called. But the patient
was already past human aid. Suffering agonies from
his internal disease, a fearful and most exhausting
nausea, all the torments of ruined nerves and exhausted
brain, and unable to eat or sleep, the old man could still
turn to the good physician and apologise to him for the
liberty he had taken with his dying body. Tronchin
had been right ! He should have gone back to Ferney.

Often and often he called for Wagnière. By his

side, always one may hope, was the good and gentle
woman he had married to Villette.   Constantly in and
out of the sick room were a motley crowd—Madame
Denis, Abbé Mignot, d'Hornoy, Lorry, Villette himself,
besides Tronchin and a servant, Morand.

On May 16 the poor old man revived a little.   To
this day belong the last verses of the easiest and most
limpid verse-writer of all time.   They were written in
reply to some lines of the Abbé Attaignant, and appeared in the 'Journal de Paris.'   To them the dying
writer added a few piteous words in prose.   'I can
do no more, Monsieur. . . .   The mind is too much
affected by the torments of the body.'

On May 25 d'Hornoy wrote to Wagnière urging his
instant return.   The patient was kept alive only by
spoonfuls of jelly; and his exhaustion and feebleness
were terrible.

By the next day the watchers had abandoned all
hope.   He revived, indeed, to hear the news of the
vindication of Lally.   That would have roused him
from the dead.   He dictated his last letter.   For the
moment, joy made mind triumph over matter, as it had
done with this man all his life long.   But his doctors
could not be deceived.   He was dying.

One of them was watching anxiously now for the
signs of that repentance he longed for.   'Religious
toleration, the most difficult conquest to wring from
the prejudices and passions of men,' Voltaire had not
been able to wring from one of the best friends he
ever had.   Tronchin wrote bitterly of this deathbed.   In his zeal for some proof, some confession of
the fallacy of that stern creed of negation, since called
Voltairism, the great Doctor almost forgot his compassion and his friendship.

D'Alembert records that on May 28 Mignot went to fetch de Tersac.

De Tersac replied to the effect that it was no use visiting a man whose reason was already dimmed, but that unless he made a far fuller and more orthodox profession of faith than he had yet made, he would not accord him Christian burial.

Mignot, himself a personage, a member of the Grand Council and the head of an abbey, threatened to apply to the Parliament for justice. De Tersac replied that he could do as he pleased.

For two days more, Voltaire lingered—sometimes quite unconscious, but sometimes wholly sensible. On the morning of Saturday, May 30, Gaultier again wrote to him offering his services.

At six o'clock in the evening of that day, Mignot fetched Gaultier and de Tersac.

D'Alembert told Frederick the Great that de Tersac approached Voltaire, saying loudly 'Jesus Christ!' and that Voltaire, rousing a little from his stupor, made a motion with his hand—'Let me die in peace.'

Grimm and La Harpe tell the same story with unimportant variations. It may be true. 'Spare me three things,' said Madame du Deffand on her deathbed—perhaps remembering Voltaire's—'Let me have no questions, no arguments, and no sermons.'

Saint-Sulpice thought, or said that he thought, Voltaire too ill to make a confession. The persons about the bed took no pains to contradict him.

At nine o'clock in the evening the priests left. For three hours Voltaire was dying—calmly and peacefully, say some; in 'all the terrors of the damned,' say others. But the truth, none knows.

Ten minutes before he died he took Morand's hand. 'Farewell, my dear Morand. I am dying.' He never spoke again.

At a quarter-past eleven on the evening of Saturday, May 30, 1778, in the eighty-fourth year of his age, died François Marie Arouet de Voltaire.

His relatives had concealed the dangerous nature of his illness from the world. Madame Denis had written, even to Wagnière, and as late as May 26, a letter of pretended hopefulness. King, priests, and prejudice were strong. Mignot and d'Hornoy knew well that it would be necessary to act cautiously, and to act at once. They had been professionally advised not to contest at law the question of burial.

From de Tersac they obtained a formal consent in writing that the body of Voltaire might be removed without ceremony. 'I relinquish to that end all parochial rights.'

Gaultier declared, also in writing, that he had been to Voltaire at his request, and found him 'not in a state to be heard in confession.'

On the night of May 30 the body was embalmed. The heart was taken out and given by Madame Denis to Villette.

Early in the morning of Sunday, May 31, Mignot, taking with him the two priests' declarations and Voltaire's confession of faith made a few weeks before, left Paris in a post-chaise for his Abbey of Scellières, at Romilly-on-Seine, in Champagne, one hundred and ten miles from Paris.

On the same evening, when the capital was dark and the streets deserted, two other carriages left the Hôtel Villette. In one was the body of the dead man, dressed, and lying on the seat like a sleeping traveller.

A servant was also in the carriage. In the next came d'Hornoy and two distant cousins of Voltaire, who, after Mignot, were his nearest male relatives. This dreadful *cortège* ' stopped at no inn, alighted at no post-house.'

At midday on June 1 it reached Scellières. The Abbé Mignot had obtained, on the strength of the clerical certificates and Voltaire's written profession of faith, the consent of his prior that the great man should be buried there.

At three o'clock in the afternoon the body was laid in the choir, and vespers for the dead were sung over it. It remained there all night, surrounded by torches.

Early the next morning, June 2, before many of the assembled clergy of the district whom the prior had summoned, Voltaire was buried with full rites and the honourable and decent burial he had desired.

Only a small stone marked his resting place, with the bald inscription ' Here lies Voltaire.'

After all, he needed no epitaphs. He had avenged the oppressed and enlightened the ignorant.

On June 3, the bishop of the diocese sent a mandate forbidding the burial. It was too late. On that day Mignot and the other relatives returned to Paris.

The city had heard of Voltaire's death by now : the devout with exultation, the philosophers with profound grief. The authorities had, indeed, forbidden the newspapers to publish any obituary notice of Voltaire or even to mention his decease. At the theatre no piece written by him was to be played for twenty-one days. The Academy was forbidden to hold the service at the Cordeliers customary on the death of a member.

But these restrictions of a petty tyranny had the effect of all such restrictions—the exact opposite to what was intended.

The heart of Paris would have throbbed the quicker for a Voltaire's death in any case. But for those prohibitions it throbbed with indignation too.

'You are right, Saint-Sulpice,' said one of many bitter epigrams the occasion produced. 'Why bury him? . . . Refuse a tomb, but not an altar.'

In this June following his death, his will, made at Ferney in September 1776, was proved. Terse, lucid, and able, it is characteristic of the man who wrote it. Voltaire appointed Madame Denis his residuary legatee. To Mignot and d'Hornoy he left one hundred thousand francs each; to Wagnière, eight thousand livres; to Madame Wagnière and Bonne-Baba, his clothes, and to Bonne-Baba eight hundred livres as well. Each servant was to have a year's wages. To Rieu, that ex-American officer, were left such English books from the library as he might choose: to the poor of the parish of Ferney—'if there are any poor'—three hundred livres; and to the curé a diamond, five hundred livres in value. Voltaire also appointed fifteen hundred francs to be given to the lawyer who was to help Madame Denis in the execution of his will.

It will be observed that the legacies to the servants, and particularly to faithful Wagnière, were very small. Hoping against the knowledge he had of her character, Voltaire had supposed that Madame Denis would continue his generosity towards them. Wagnière, true to his master's person and honour in life, was true to his memory after death. He uttered not a word of complaint.

In the August of 1778 d'Alembert chose Voltaire as

the subject for the prize poem of the Academy; and until his own death, five years later, never ceased to work for the posthumous glory of the man he had loved.

The once false La Harpe also eulogised Voltaire, and wrote a play in his honour ; and the scholarly Condorcet wrote his Life.

But it was not Paris alone which did homage to this greatness. If ever man had been a citizen of the world, Voltaire had been.

On November 26, 1778, Frederick the Great, now President of his own Academy, read to it Voltaire's Eulogium. It is a most generous testimony to the character of that brilliant, irritable, and delightful child of genius whom the great King had so hotly loved and loathed. As an appreciation of his works, it is worthless. Frederick the Great was no literary critic. But it poured burning contempt on the ' imbecile priests ' of Paris who had refused such a man the last offices of the dead, and not all the authorities in the world could keep it out of their capital.

In the May of the following year, to shame those ' imbecile priests ' the deeper, although he had, as he put it, no idea of the immortality of the soul himself, Frederick had a mass for Voltaire's said in the Roman church at Berlin. A little later the faithful and persevering d'Alembert proposed that that King should erect a statue to his friend in that same church. Frederick did not see his way to this. He had in his own possession a finer monument to Voltaire's greatness—a part of that correspondence which is one of Arouet's ' surest titles to immortality ' and contains at once 'the history of Voltaire *intime* and of the eighteenth century.'

No one had mourned Voltaire more passionately than the other great sovereign, Catherine. ' Since he is dead, wit has lost its honour : he was the divinity of gaiety.' To her, he had been much more than that. He had ' formed her mind and her head.'

He had left his library, except its English books, with his other effects, to Madame Denis. In the December of 1778 Catherine completed the purchase of those 6,210 volumes with their copious marginal notes, with manuscripts, original letters, and papers concerning the trials in which Voltaire had been engaged. Some months later she sent for Wagnière to arrange them. When he had finished his work, she came to look at it. Bowing before Voltaire's statue she said, ' There is the man to whom I owe all I know and all I am.' Hearing that Wagnière was poorly provided for, she magnificently gave him a pension for life. He visited Frederick, and returned to live and die at Ferney. One of Voltaire's editors, passing through that village in 1825, found the secretary's son still living there— a Justice of the Peace.

To get rid of her uncle's library was for Madame Denis but to free herself of one useless encumbrance. There was another. What was the use of Ferney to such a woman ? Ice and snow, weavers and watchmakers, country, retirement, solitude—she hated them all. Her uncle's poor people had never been anything to her—except when they fêted and made much of her on a birthday. Return to them ? Never. She sold Ferney to Villette. To the indignation of her relations and of the whole Academy—particularly d'Alembert, who was as jealous for dead Voltaire's honour as a mother for her daughter's good name— she insisted on marrying her Duvivier. It is a little satisfactory to learn that that dull person (in society he was popularly known as the Extinguisher) avenged Voltaire by bullying the woman who had bullied him.

Madame Denis never had any interest but as the niece of her uncle. With his death she fades into the commonplace obscurity for which she was made.

The Villettes retired to Ferney. In her old home, when her husband had once more forgotten the fatal attractions of the capital, he and Belle-et-Bonne lived not unhappily. But the weaving and watch-making industry declined. The pilot was no longer at the helm. The strong hand and all-directing brain which had turned starving idleness to affluent industry, and established trade on a sound business basis, were no longer there to hold and supervise. Ferney fell back into the nothingness from which a master-mind had drawn it.

Presently Villette became heavily inculpated in the famous Guéménée bankruptcy for thirty-three millions. He sold Ferney, where he had retained Voltaire's rooms as they had been at the time of his death, and where, a cherished possession, he had kept the dead man's heart enclosed in a silver vase. Husband and wife came up to Paris and lived in the Hôtel Villette, where Belle-et-Bonne continued the tender charities which were the solace of her life, and surrounded herself with relics and mementoes of her dead Voltaire.

In March 1779 M. Ducis was installed in Voltaire's vacant chair in the French Academy. According to custom, he read the Eulogy of his predecessor. The time for official prohibitions was past. No government had been able to prevent the Hermit of Ferney being known to the whole world as ' the great Voltaire ' for many years before his death. He was the great

Voltaire still. Grimm declares that no meeting of the
Academy ever attracted such crowds. When some
clerical member dared to suggest that all expressions
contrary to religion and morals should be erased by
some friendly hand from Voltaire's works, he was hissed
and groaned into silence.

On the first anniversary of his death, ' Agathocle,'
his last tragedy, still incomplete, was performed in
Paris, with a prologue by d'Alembert.

A complete edition of Voltaire's works appeared
in 1780.

In 1784 there were secretly circulating in Paris the
' Memoirs for the Life of Voltaire,' written by himself
in 1759 and revenging himself on Frederick for Freytag
and Frankfort with the most cool and deadly spite.
The man who wrote them, in that perfectly easy and
limpid French of which he was always master even
when he was by no means master of himself, had never
intended them to be published. He burnt the original
manuscript ; but he had two copies made. It will not be
forgotten that La Harpe and Madame Denis were dismissed from Ferney for having stolen one of them. One
became the property of Catherine the Great. The other,
Madame Denis, remembering that ' wearisome niece ' and
the ' Golden Lion,' sent in 1783 to Beaumarchais, then
editing Voltaire's works. He did not dare to include the
' Memoirs ' therein, in Frederick's lifetime. But they
were passed from hand to hand in Paris, and it was
doubtless well for Voltaire's fame that Frederick had
already eulogised him and said masses for the peace of
his soul. The ' Memoirs ' are now always included in
Voltaire's works. It is not, all things considered,
wholly his fault that many people, ignorant of the
circumstances under which it was drawn, have assumed

the malicious caricature of Frederick therein contained
to be a faithful portrait.

For thirteen years the body of him ' who against
monks had never rested, among monks rested peacefully '
enough.   The Revolution he foresaw had come, though
not as he had foreseen it.

His ideal of government had been a purified and
constitutional monarchy, but always a monarchy.   ' My
muscles are not very flexible : I do not mind making
one bow, but a hundred on end would fatigue me.'
By 1790 Louis XVI. was a king only in name.   In
that year the Abbey of Scellières, with all other religious houses, became the property of the nation.
Villette had not merely fallen in with the views of the
Revolution.   They had been his when such convictions
were dangerous and awkward, and he never forgot that
Prophet of Revolution, Voltaire.   It was through
Villette that the Quai de Théatins, on which the Hôtel
Villette stood, was renamed the Quai Voltaire.

In November 1790, after a performance of ' Brutus,'
Charles Villette, ex-Marquis, harangued the audience
and passionately pleaded, ' in the name of the country,'
that the remains of Voltaire might be brought to Paris
and honourably buried.   ' This translation will be the
dying sigh of fanaticism.'   The idea pleased a people
agog for excitement and drunk with the first deep
draughts of a liberty which for centuries they had not
been allowed even to taste.

On June 1, 1791, the National Assembly made
Louis XVI. sign the decree which ordained that the
ashes of his great enemy should be transferred from the
church of Romilly to that of Sainte-Geneviève in Paris
—Sainte-Geneviève, which was henceforth to be called
the Pantheon of France.

On July 6 a funeral car, decked with laurels and oak leaves, drawn by four horses and escorted by a detachment of the National Guard, left Romilly-on-Seine and began its solemn triumphal progress to Paris. On the front of the car was written ' To the Memory of Voltaire.' On one side, ' If man is born free, he ought to govern himself ; ' on the other, ' If man has tyrants, he ought to dethrone them.'

As it passed through the villages, the villagers came out to greet it with wreaths of flowers and laurels in their hands. Mothers held up their babies that they too might say that they had seen this great day ; old men pressed forward to touch and be healed. At night the villages through which the procession passed were illuminated ; by day could be seen triumphal arches, girls dressed in white, and garlands of flowers. Out of their ignorance and wretchedness, this *canaille* recognised him who had wept and clamoured for the rights of all men and made freedom a possibility even for them.

At nightfall on July 10 the *cortège* reached Paris. The sarcophagus was placed on an altar on the ruins of that tower of the Bastille in which Voltaire had been twice a prisoner.

On the altar was the inscription, ' On this spot, where despotism chained thee, receive the homage of a free people.'

All Sunday night the sarcophagus remained there. At three o'clock on the sunny afternoon of Monday, July 11, it was placed on a car designed by David, and drawn through Paris, escorted by an enormous company, organised, orderly, and representing every rank and condition. Here were the men who had demolished the Bastille, carrying its flag, and in their midst that terrible virago who had led them in the fray.

Here were citizens with pikes, Swiss, Jacobins, actors, and bodies of soldiers. Some carried banners with devices from the dead man's writings. Some, dressed in Greek costume, carried a gilt model of the famous statue by Houdon. Among the self-constituted guard were many who, not a month before, had brought back that other King to his capital—from Varennes—with howls, insults, and imprecations.

Singers and music preceded the car itself. Supported on four great wheels of bronze, it looked like a magnificent altar. On the summit was the sarcophagus, and on that a full-length figure of Voltaire reclining in an attitude of sleep and with a winged Immortality placing a crown of stars on his head. On the sarcophagus was written, in words of noble simplicity, 'He avenged Calas, La Barre, Sirven, and Montbailli. Poet, philosopher, historian, he gave a great impetus to the human mind : he prepared us to become free.' The whole structure, forty feet high, was drawn by twelve white horses, two of which, it is said, had been furnished by Marie Antoinette. On the car were such inscriptions as—' He defended Calas.'   ' He inspired toleration.' ' He claimed the rights of men.'

Behind it walked Belle-et-Bonne and her husband, with their little girl in her nurse's arms. Then came deputations from the National Assembly and the Courts of Justice, and then another detachment of military.

The procession itself consisted of a hundred thousand persons. Six hundred thousand more witnessed it.

It first stopped at the Opera House. The operatic company came forward and sang that song in Voltaire's ' Samson ' which became, with the ' Marseillaise,' *the* song of the Revolution—

Wake, ye people ! Break your chains !

'TRIOMPHE DE VOLTAIRE.'

From a Contemporary Print.

After the Opera House, the Tuileries was passed. Every window was filled with spectators, save one. Behind that, closed and barred, sat the most unhappy of monarchs, Louis and Marie Antoinette, awaiting doom.

The next stop was in front of the Hôtel Villette. Upon a platform outside it were fifty young girls dressed in white, and before them the two daughters of Calas in deep mourning. They kissed the sarcophagus of ' the man of Calas ; ' and Belle-et-Bonne lifted up her child as if ' to consecrate her to reason, to philosophy, and to liberty.'

The next stop was at the old Comédie Française— the scene of Voltaire's earliest dramatic triumphs, and where now was his bust with the inscription, ' He wrote " Œdipe " at seventeen.'

At the Théâtre Français, become the Theatre of the Nation, were garlands and music and the inscription, ' He wrote " Irène " at eighty-four.' And once more a chorus sang the spirited song out of ' Samson.'

At last, at ten o'clock at night and in a drizzling rain, the Pantheon was reached.

The sarcophagus was lifted into the place designed for it—near the tombs of Descartes and Mirabeau.

The history of Voltaire after death could be elaborated into a volume. But, after all, it throws no light on his life and character, only on those of the friends who loved him, the enemies who hated him, and the mob who went mad over him.

When it is considered that to the excesses of that mob he would have been passionately opposed, and that the only Revolution he desired was gradual, temperate, and unbloody, it may well be doubted if, had he lived till 1791, his last journey would not have been, like that of many other patriots, to a very different accompaniment and a very different destination.

For a while he was allowed to rest in that quiet and honoured grave.

But 1814 saw the restoration of those Bourbons whose hatred for him was hereditary.

With the connivance of the ministry, the tombs of both Voltaire and Rousseau were violated, their bones removed in a sack at night to a waste place outside the city, and emptied into a pit filled with quicklime. That long-dreaded fate — 'thrown into the gutter like poor Lecouvreur'—was Voltaire's after all.

But those dishonoured ashes and that unhallowed burial keep his memory more vividly alive than the marble tomb of a Pantheon.

The violation was discovered in 1864, when, the Villette family becoming extinct, Voltaire's heart became the property of the nation.

It was decided to place it with his ashes in the Pantheon. But the tomb was empty.

The Marquis de Villette died in 1793, thereby escaping the guillotine, to which he had been condemned for refusing to vote for the death of the King. Belle-et-Bonne, a widow at thirty-six, consecrated her life to Voltaire's memory.

In 1878 his centenary was celebrated with the warmest enthusiasm by the most fickle capital in the world.

Victor Hugo eulogised Voltaire with much emotion and applause, and fervent words which mean nothing in particular. But the fact that the Fighter had been dead a century did not prevent him from being still a cause of strife. Dupanloup, Bishop of Orleans, hotly attacked the infidel and demanded an injunction against a new edition of his works, which was refused.

This was the last famous assault on the Great Assaulter. France, perhaps even Catholic France, recognises in some sort the debt she owes to Voltaire. Is not the enemy who shows a nation her weak points, forces her to look to her ships and her armaments, to remedy abuses in her organisation, and feebleness, viciousness, and incompetency in her servants, something very like a friend in disguise?

It may be truly said that Voltaire did good to Roman Catholicism by attacking much that degraded it; by hooting out of it the superstition and tyranny which have made some of the noblest souls on earth decline it; and by forcing its children to give a reason for the faith that was in them.

Then, too, if the Church of Rome could withstand that deadly, breathless, and brilliant onslaught called Voltairism, she may well point triumphantly to the fulfilment of that ancient prophecy and consolation, 'The gates of hell shall not prevail against it.'

To the Church in France it may be acknowledged that Voltaire was not wholly an evil, while to her country he was a great glory.

In England there is still against him a prejudice, which, said Buckle, nothing but ignorance can excuse. To the ordinary Briton Voltaire is only a very profane scoffer who made some rather amusing and very doubtful jokes.

Yet this was he who, as Frederick the Great said, was extraordinary in everything. Here was the man who was poet, playwright, novelist, letter-writer, historian, critic, philosopher, theologian, socialist, philanthropist, agriculturist, humorist, reformer, wit, and man of the world.

England has no counterpart for him. But then neither has France, nor any other country. Think of the great names of earthly fame. Of which can it be said—with even approximate truth—'Here is another Voltaire'?

As a poet, he was the king of those society verses which he modestly said himself 'are good for nothing but society and only for the moment for which they are written.'

But such as they are—madrigal, epigram, epitaph, the gracefullest flattery in four lines, and the daintiest malice in a couplet—if Voltaire had written nothing else, his supremacy in these alone would have given him a perpetual place in the literature of his country.

His longer and graver poems are immortal for what he said, not for how he said it.

As a playwright, his tragedies were the most famous of his age. Ours applies to them those fatal adjectives —fluent, elegant, correct. Without any of the indomitable life and swing which characterise almost all his other works, they were perfectly suited to that exceedingly bad public taste which preferred smoothness before vigour, and a careful consideration of the unities to the genius of a Shakespeare.

Voltaire's comedies are only sprightly and fluent.

As a historian, whether in prose or verse, he is celebrated for his broad and comprehensive views, his enormous general knowledge (for his time), 'the vehemence and sincerity of his abhorrence of the military spirit,' his savage hatred of the religious *culte*, and his inimitably interesting and vivacious style. Until his day the learned rarely had wit and the witty rarely had learning. Voltaire set an example which has been singularly little followed : he made facts more amusing than fiction.

His fiction indeed is, with the multitude, one of his chief titles to fame. But all his fiction, rhyming or prose, was to teach facts ; though his art was so perfect that the facts never spoilt the fancy. He was the pioneer in France of the short story, the *conte*. There may be traced, in a slight degree, the influence of Swift. But Voltaire's satire is gayer, brighter, and cleaner than the great Dean's.

Voltaire is the first letter-writer in the world. He was himself interested in everything, and so interesting to everybody.

His letters contain not only his own best biography, and not only the literary history of the eighteenth century. They touch on all contemporary history— social, religious, scientific, political. They are at once the wittiest and the most natural extant. He wrote with that liquid ease with which a bird shakes out his song. His French is at one and the same time the most perfect French for the Frenchman and the stylist, and the simplest for the foreigner to understand.

Beside his letters, with their easy grace and wealth of world-wide knowledge, Horace Walpole's are but the gossip of a clique ; Madame de Sévigné's the chit-chat of a boudoir ; Lady Wortley Montagu's coarse and clumsy ; and Pope's stilted and artificial. They are also comparatively free from the indecency which mars many other of Voltaire's writings and almost all the correspondence of his age. His letters remain (as early as 1872 there were seven thousand of them in print, and Beuchot thought at least as many more undiscovered) an almost inexhaustible gold mine of literary delight, and a most liberal education.

As a blasphemous mocker at some of the most sacred convictions of their souls, Voltaire has been naturally, when he touches on religion, anathema not only to Roman Catholics, but to all Christians. The liberal-minded will be ready to own that to attack a system he not only believed to be false but actively harmful, was well within his rights. It is his method which inspires just indignation. A profoundly serious subject has a right to profoundly serious treatment. But, after all, Voltaire's gibes and laugh turn against himself. Who believes a scoffer? If he had not jeered at the creed of Christendom, he would have made more converts to the creed of Voltaire.

What was his creed? It had only one article. 'I believe in God.' In that belief 'one finds difficulties; in the belief that there is no God, absurdities.' 'The wise man attributes to God no human affections. He recognises a power necessary, eternal, which animates all nature; and is resigned.'

As for the immortality of the soul, it seems, contrary to the opinion of many of his biographers, that Voltaire rather longed to believe in it, than that he did so. 'But your soul, Sir—your soul? What idea have you of it? From whence does it come? Where is it? What is it? What does it do? How does it act? Where does it go? I know nothing about it and I have never seen it.' 'For sixty years I have tried to discover what the soul is, and I still know nothing.'

His practical scheme of religion he expressed himself. 'To worship God; to leave each man the liberty to serve Him in his own fashion; to love one's neighbours; enlighten them if one can, pity them when they

are in error; to attach no importance to trivial
questions which would never have given trouble if no
seriousness had been imputed to them. That is my
religion, which is worth all your systems and all your
symbols.'

The stumbling-blocks he found in the road to
Christianity—that is to Roman Catholicism, the only
form of Christianity to which he addressed himself
—were twofold. The mental stumbling-block was
miracle; and the moral, the lives of the believers.
He considered the second to be the natural fruit of
the first : that the Christian belief must be destroyed to
destroy the wickedness, darkness, cruelty, and tyranny
he found in Christian lives; that men ' will not cease
to be persecutors till they have ceased to be absurd.'

It should be remembered—it is not often remembered
—that, in the words of Morley, 'there is no case of
Voltaire mocking at any set of men who lived good
lives,' and that ' the Christianity he assailed was not
that of the Sermon on the Mount.'

Regarding the problems of the future life, of
future awards, punishments, and compensations, and
the manifold mysteries of this world, he was, broadly
speaking, an Agnostic.

' Behold, I know not anything.'

But Voltaire's real claim to eternal remembrance
is far less how he thought or what he wrote, than what
his writings *did*.

Some of them are obsolete to-day because they so
perfectly accomplished their aim. Who wants to read
now passionate arguments against torture, and scathing
satires on a jurisdiction which openly accepted hearsay
as evidence ?

In his own day those writings produced many

practical reforms, and paved the way to many more. Through them, he was himself enabled to be a philanthropist in an age when the prosperous elder brothers of the world looked up to God from stricken Abel with that scornful question, ' Am I my brother's keeper? ' Through them, he saved innocent lives and restored stolen honour.

But his Ferney, his Lally, Calas, Sirven, La Barre, were only types of his work for all the race.

He found the earth overspread with hideous undergrowths of oppression and privilege, intolerance and cruelty ; and he destroyed them.

He found the good land covered with abuses in Church and State and every social order ; abuses political, personal ; of the rights of the living, and the decent respect owed to the dead—and he uprooted them. With a laugh and blasphemy on his lips, but with eyes and soul afire and the nervous, tireless hands trembling with eagerness, the most dauntless, passionate, dogged little worker in all human history hewed and hacked at the monstrous tyrannies of centuries, and flung them, dead, from the fair and beautiful soil they had usurped.

At last, after sixty years of superhuman effort, he had cleared the place and made it ready for the planting of the Tree of Liberty.

Whoso sits under that tree to-day in any country, free to worship his God as he will, to think, to learn, and to do all that does not intrench on the freedom of his fellow-men—free to progress to heights of light and knowledge as yet unseen and undreamt—should in gratitude remember Voltaire.

FINIS

INDEX

DATE DUE

DATE DUE			
FEB 1 8 2000			
FEB 2 1 2001			
30 505 JOSTEN'S			